CHRIST & THE BIBLE

Bob Whittet
- Feb. 1979 -

JOHN W. WENHAM

InterVarsity Press
Downers Grove
Illinois 60515

Third American printing,
September 1977

© *1972 by The Tyndale*
Press, Leicester, England.
First American printing,
April 1973, by InterVarsity
Press, Downers Grove, Illinois
with permission from Inter-Varsity
Fellowship, London.
All rights reserved.
No part of this book may be
reproduced in any form without
written permission from InterVarsity
Press, Downers Grove, Illinois.

InterVarsity Press is the book
publishing division of Inter-Varsity
Christian Fellowship, a student
movement active on campus at
hundreds of universities, colleges
and schools of nursing. For
information about local and regional
activities, write IVCF, 233 Langdon
St., Madison, WI 53703.

ISBN 0-87784-760-6
Library of Congress Catalog
Card Number: 72-97950

Biblical quotations are from the
Revised Standard Version of
the Bible, copyright 1946 and
1952, unless otherwise stated.

Printed in the United
States of America

CONTENTS

INTRODUCTION

The Christian community has a divided mind about its text-book. Throughout this century those holding a conservative doctrine of the Bible have looked mainly to the writings of B. B. Warfield for its scholarly exposition. Between the years 1882 and 1915 his minute and massive scholarship produced a series of first-class articles on this theme, selections of which were later published under the titles *Revelation and Inspiration* (1927) and *The Inspiration and Authority of the Bible* (1959). These articles gave a positive exposition of the biblical basis of the doctrine which may well never be surpassed, but they were miscellaneous in character, with much overlapping of material, and they were never intended to be a systematic treatment of the subject. Nor did they attempt to deal with the mass of critical objections which are persistently urged against the doctrine of infallibility.

Many years ago the author set out to write a book on the nature, interpretation and application of holy Scripture. It soon became clear that the nature of Scripture provided more than enough material for one book and that any systematic treatment of interpretation and application must be left behind. But the attempt to expound the nature of Scripture and defend it against the main attacks of criticism, in spite of every effort at conciseness, grew into a work of nearly a quarter of a million words. It seemed desirable that this should be broken up into four separate but mutually dependent books, in the hope (but not with the promise!) that they might be finished and published successively. The thesis of the whole tetralogy is that Christ's view of Scripture can and should still be the Christian's view of Scripture.

It is thus an attempted re-statement of the traditional
Christian attitude to the Bible. The title suggested for the whole
work was 'The Christian View of the Bible'. This was adopted
to highlight the fact that Christ had a particular and ascertain-
able view of Scripture. Working with this title in mind does not
of course imply that the author thinks himself to have the right
answers to all the critical problems. As far as these are concerned, it is *a* Christian's (often very tentative) view of the Bible.
Furthermore, the books deal primarily with problems of criticism, which are the problems which first obtrude themselves
upon those who study the Bible in the context of modern
thought. The deeper problems of theology and philosophy (as
of interpretation and application) which have eventually to be
faced are only touched on incidentally.

This first book tries to show what Christ's view of Scripture
was, why we should regard his view as authoritative, and what
books and texts should be regarded as Scripture. The second looks
at the moral difficulties of the Bible. The third proposed book
would deal with the main problems arising from Old Testament criticism. The fourth proposed book is concerned with the
problem of harmonizing the Gospels.

During the past two hundred years, since the age of the
Enlightenment, a vast literature has poured forth arguing the
impossibility of this traditional Christian attitude. Any attempt
to deal with this flood of literature is almost ludicrously am-
bitious. The field covered is the province of a whole range of
specialists, whose output has been enormous. The need is to sort
out the *significant* elements of this technical material and to
bring them together in a non-technical way. No-one could be
more conscious than the author of the impossibility of doing
justice to such a task. Owing, however, to the remarkable
stability both of the presuppositions and of the methods of
reasoning which have been adopted for more than a hundred
years, the task is somewhat less fantastic than might appear. At
any rate I have tried to identify these significant elements and
the literature which bears directly and helpfully upon them and
to eliminate everything else. I have therefore whittled down
references to current literature in order to leave only those
which seem either necessary or markedly useful. The book is not

for specialists and I have attempted as far as possible to omit things which the non-specialist does not want and the specialist does not need. Some matters which can be easily verified elsewhere I have touched on lightly, while others I have thought it necessary to justify and document in some detail. At the risk of being called simplistic, I have tried at every point to write as simply as the material will allow.

The work is addressed to Christians – to those who believe that Jesus was God Incarnate, the supreme revelation of God. It is addressed furthermore to Christians who believe that at least in a general sense the Gospels give a substantially true account of the Jesus of history.[1] The argument is, I believe, to some extent new. Hitherto Christians who have been unsure about the status of the Bible have been caught in a vicious circle : any satisfactory doctrine of the Bible must be based on the teaching of the Bible, but the teaching of the Bible is itself suspect. The way out of this dilemma is to recognize that *belief in the Bible comes from faith in Christ, and not vice versa*. The argument is as follows : if the Gospels are substantially true, we are justified in regarding as historical those features in them which are often repeated and which are found in a variety of Gospel strata. Three such features are Jesus' attitude to the Old Testament, his attitude to his own teaching and his attitude to the continuing witness of his disciples after his death. He regarded the teaching of the Old Testament, his own teaching and the teaching of his apostles as the teaching of God, and therefore as wholly true and trustworthy. Thus belief in Christ as the supreme revelation of God leads to belief in scriptural inspiration – of the Old Testament by the direct testimony of Jesus and of the New Testament by inference from his testimony. The argument here is inductive. At no important point is a conclusion based upon a single passage, but on the concurrent witness of a large number of passages.

The new argument has necessitated a new methodology. It starts by accepting as valid the characteristic Christian experience of conversion. A convert from a non-Christian religion

[1] It is quite outside the scope of this book to argue the substantial truth of the Gospels, but an Additional Note on Radical Criticism of the Gospels (with suggestions for reading on the subject) is on p. 38.

or from modern secular society seldom arrives at the decisive moment of faith with a view of biblical inspiration already formulated in his mind. His quest is a wrestling with the Christ portrayed in the New Testament and witnessed to by Christians. As he progresses in his search the Gospels seem to him more and more to have the ring of truth. At last he comes to the moment when he says, 'Lord, I believe.' He has arrived at faith with a conviction about the basic truth of the New Testament witness to Christ, but without necessarily any clear beliefs about the truth or falsity of many of the details or about the status of the Bible as a whole. God has become real to him in Christ through the external witness of the gospel and the internal witness of the Holy Spirit. In conversion he has made the discovery that God, made known in Jesus Christ, is the centre and starting-point of all true knowledge.

Growth in the knowledge of the things of God (which includes progress in theological understanding) comes by holding fast to the centre and by working outwards from there. There is a progression : God; God revealing himself; God revealing himself supremely in Christ; Christ teaching the truth of Scripture; finally, with Scripture as guide, the Christian exploring the apparently limitless jungle which makes up the world of phenomena. To start with phenomena and attempt to build up anything more than a superficial understanding of the world without revelation is foredoomed to failure. Both in the case of the Bible and in the case of the world of nature, the parts must be understood from the whole, not the whole from the parts. A God-created theology demands a God-centred methodology.

We believe, therefore, that it is methodologically sound to start with Christ as he is portrayed in the Bible. We must get a grasp on what is recorded of his teaching as a whole before indulging in criticism of the parts. By this means it is possible with entire integrity to progress from faith in Christ to a carefully thought-out view of Scripture without getting bogged down in criticism. In genuinely Christian thinking faith in Christ must remain master and criticism remain servant at every point. If this faith in Christ can once again take possession of Christian thinking, we believe that the Christian community will regain a common mind about its textbook.

JESUS' VIEW
OF THE
OLD TESTAMENT

1

We shall extract evidence for Jesus' view of the Old Testament from all the Gospels without discrimination. This is *not* (we re-emphasize) to prejudge the question as to whether everything in the Gospels is accurate; we recognize that, for some, certain parts of the Gospels have less value as historical evidence than others. Provided that we avoid an almost total scepticism with regard to the Gospels, we can at this stage of the argument allow a great variety of critical conclusions. What one critic will allow and another refuse is usually heavily influenced either by subjective considerations or by the exigencies of some hypothesis for which there is no demonstrative evidence. To embark upon a critical discussion of each passage would be likely to prove as inconclusive as it was laborious. All we ask is that the reader should accept the truth of the Gospel picture in general outline.

If it turns out that this approach produces a consistent view of Christ, that in itself will tend to confirm the belief that the Gospels are presenting a figure of history, and that the Jesus they depict is not (as radical critics maintain) the creation of diverse minds from a diverse and scattered community. But the reader can, if he wishes, make his own subtractions according to the best of his critical judgment as he goes along; but we think that, using fair methods, such subtractions will not affect the final result until the Gospel picture of Christ has been reduced to that of a ghost. Even then the result will not be contrary to our conclusions; it will merely be uncertain through lack of evidence.

When we turn to the teaching of Jesus as recorded in the Gospels, we have a wealth of relevant material coming from all four Gospels and from all the four major strata of the Synoptic

Gospels : Mark, the material peculiar to Matthew, the material peculiar to Luke, and the material common to Matthew and Luke (usually called 'Q'). We are not confined simply to two or three key statements, but we have a host of quotations and allusions thrown up spontaneously from a great variety of situations, and these are often the more telling for revealing his basic assumptions rather than his specific teachings. We can hear Christ preaching to the multitude and instructing disciples, refuting opponents and answering enquirers; we can hear him in his private conflict with the tempter at the beginning of the ministry and in his final instructions prior to the ascension. As we proceed it will become clear that, throughout the whole range of the material, his attitude is unchanging. We shall examine in turn his attitude to the truth of the history, to the authority of the teaching and to the inspiration of the writing. As the evidence is assembled, it will lead us to a firm and objective historical conclusion. We shall see that to Christ the Old Testament was true, authoritative, inspired. To him the God of the Old Testament was the living God and the teaching of the Old Testament was the teaching of the living God. To him[1] what Scripture said, God said.

THE TRUTH OF OLD TESTAMENT HISTORY

He consistently treats the historical narratives as straightforward records of fact. We have references to : Abel (Lk. 11:51), Noah (Mt. 24:37–39; Lk. 17:26, 27), Abraham (Jn. 8:56), the institution of circumcision (Jn. 7:22; cf. Gn. 17:10–12; Lv. 12:3), Sodom and Gomorrah (Mt. 10:15; 11:23, 24; Lk. 10:12), Lot (Lk. 17:28–32), Isaac and Jacob (Mt. 8:11; Lk. 13:28), the manna (Jn. 6:31, 49, 58), the wilderness serpent (Jn. 3:14), David eating the shewbread (Mt. 12:3, 4; Mk. 2:25, 26; Lk. 6:3, 4) and as a psalm-writer (Mt. 22:43; Mk. 12:36; Lk. 20:42), Solomon (Mt. 6:29; 12:42; Lk. 11:31; 12:27), Elijah (Lk. 4:25, 26), Elisha (Lk. 4:27), Jonah (Mt. 12:39–41; Lk. 11:29, 30, 32), Zechariah (Lk. 11:51). This last passage brings out his sense of the unity of history and his grasp of its wide sweep. His eye

---

[1] This echoes a sentence of B. B. Warfield, *Biblical Foundations* (London, 1958), p. 58, which echoes an earlier sentence of Augustine, *Confessions*, xiii.29.

surveys the whole course of history from 'the foundation of the world' to 'this generation'. There are repeated references to Moses as the giver of the law (Mt. 8:4; 19:8; Mk. 1:44; 7:10; 10:5; 12:26; Lk. 5:14; 20:37; Jn. 5:46; 7:19); the sufferings of the prophets are also mentioned frequently (Mt. 5:12; 13:57; 21:34–36; 23:29–37; Mk. 6:4 (cf. Lk. 4:24; Jn. 4:44); 12:2–5; Lk. 6:23; 11:47–51; 13:34; 20:10–12); and there is a reference to the popularity of the false prophets (Lk. 6:26). He sets the stamp of his approval on passages in Genesis 1 and 2 (Mt. 19:4, 5; Mk. 10:6–8).

Although these quotations are taken by our Lord more or less at random from different parts of the Old Testament and some periods of the history are covered more fully than others, it is evident that he was familiar with most of our Old Testament and that he treated it all equally as history. Curiously enough, the narratives that are least acceptable to the so-called 'modern mind' are the very ones that he seemed most fond of choosing for his illustrations.

The possibility of non-literal interpretation

It is of course arguable that our Lord's use of the Old Testament stories does not of necessity imply that he regarded them all as unimpeachable history. It is perfectly possible to use avowed legends and allegories to illustrate spiritual truth. The stories of Ulysses and the Sirens or Christian and Doubting Castle may quite properly be used as illustrations of spiritual truth without implying a belief in their historicity. None the less, despite this theoretical possibility, a review of the way in which our Lord in practice used these narratives seems decisively to forbid such a conclusion. In some of the passages quoted, while there is no evidence to suggest that our Lord understood them in any but a literal way, a literal meaning is not essential to the force of the passage. The references to the ordinance of monogamy 'from the beginning of creation', for instance, do not seem to necessitate a literal interpretation of chapters 1 and 2 of Genesis for their validity (Mk. 10:2ff.; cf. Mt. 19:3ff.). Seldom can a non-literal meaning be applied without some loss of vividness and effectiveness, but there would be no essential loss in meaning if the injunction 'offer . . . what Moses commanded'

(Mk. 1:44; *cf.* Mt. 8:4; Lk. 5:14) were to be read 'offer the things which the law of Moses commands'; or if for 'Moses said, Honour your father . . .' (Mk. 7:10) we were to read 'The law of Moses says, Honour your father . . .'. The reference to 'Solomon in all his glory' would be as graphic of a legendary figure as of a historical one.

There are a dozen other passages where an Old Testament story might arguably be taken in a non-literal sense,[2] but as the matter is pursued the impression gains in strength that our Lord understood the Bible stories in a natural way and that his teaching should be taken quite straightforwardly. The impression is strongly reinforced when we come to a further collection of passages where the historical truth of the saying seems to be essential to its validity.

While hesitating to place great weight upon a single passage, it is difficult to deny that the words of T. T. Perowne on Matthew 12:41 are applicable to a number of passages made use of in the Gospels. Jesus says, 'The men of Nineveh will arise at the judgment with this generation and condemn it; for they repented at the preaching of Jonah, and behold, something greater than Jonah is here.' Perowne comments : 'Is it possible to understand a reference like this on the non-historic theory of the book of Jonah?' The future Judge is speaking words of solemn warning to those who shall hereafter stand convicted at his bar. Intensely real he would make the scene in anticipation to them, as it was real, as if then present, to himself. And yet we are to suppose him to say that imaginary persons who at the imaginary preaching of an imaginary prophet repented in imagination, shall rise up in that day and condemn the actual impenitence of those his actual hearers.'[3]

There is of course a non-literal element here, as in all portrayals of the world to come. This rising up on the day of judgment is not presumably to be pictured literally as individuals standing up to make accusation at the Great Assize. The rising up is the resurrection itself. The resurrection to life of the peni-

---

[2] These are discussed in the author's *Our Lord's View of the Old Testament* (London, 1964), pp. 11–14.

[3] T. T. Perowne, *Obadiah and Jonah* (Cambridge, 1894), p. 51. The book of Jonah is further discussed on pp. 74f.

tent Ninevites is itself the witness against our Lord's impenitent
hearers. It might not be impossible to take this as an illustration
from a current folk tale, yet it is difficult to avoid the conclusion
that this and several other passages are deprived of their force if
their historical basis is removed, and in all honesty there seems
no hint that our Lord intended anything of the sort. This conclusion is reinforced by the immediate juxtaposition in this
passage (Mt. 12:42) of the visit of the Queen of the South as a
strictly parallel illustration. To regard the book of Jonah as
intentional parable, or allegory, or historical fiction may be
plausible enough; but not the book of Kings.

'As were the days of Noah, so will be the coming of the Son of
man' (Mt. 24:37) is very similar. The context is most solemn.
Our Lord has introduced his statement with the tremendous
assertion, 'Heaven and earth will pass away, but my words will
not pass away.' Then, drawing a vivid picture of the everyday
life of those who lived in the days before the flood, he says : 'so
will be the coming of the Son of man.' It is quite true that a
popular preacher may play upon the emotions of his hearers by
painting a graphic and moving picture of scenes which are
avowedly fictitious, and, if he should round off such an account
with a dramatic 'And the same will happen to you!', it might be
very powerful. But it is in fact an oratorical device to arouse the
imagination which adds nothing to the argument. Here our
Lord is building up a solemn warning by appealing to the dread-
ful acts of God recorded in Holy Scripture, which both he and
his hearers know to be of divine authority. To Capernaum he
uttered a warning based on another terrible act of judgment.
'For if the mighty works done in you had been done in Sodom,
it would have remained until this day. But I tell you that it shall
be more tolerable on the day of judgment for the land of Sodom
than for you' (Mt. 11:23, 24). Since Noah's flood and the
destruction of Sodom are taken as historical in these passages,
the same must apply to Luke 17:26–32, which ends with 'Remember Lot's wife'. Again, with encouragements and warnings
about more immediate coming events, historical happenings of
the past are used as a foundation for future expectations. Looking over the whole sweep of biblical history from the first book
of the Hebrew Canon to the last, he says, 'that the blood of all

the prophets, shed from the foundation of the world, may be required of this generation, from the blood of Abel to the blood of Zechariah, who perished between the altar and the sanctuary. Yes, I tell you, it shall be required of this generation' (Lk. 11:50ff.). The issue of Old Testament history was to find its fearful consummation in the events of AD 70. And it was the divine aid given to the persecuted prophets in earlier times that was to be the stay of persecuted disciples. 'Rejoice and be glad, for your reward is great in heaven, for so men persecuted the prophets who were before you' (Mt. 5:12).

When our Lord said, 'Your father Abraham rejoiced that he was to see my day . . . Before Abraham was, I am' (Jn. 8:56ff.), they took up stones to cast at him. But if Abraham and the Messianic promise were not historical, these sayings were in fact meaningless. At Nazareth 'they . . . were filled with wrath . . . and led him to the brow of the hill on which their city was built, that they might throw him down headlong' (Lk. 4:28, 29). But his offending remarks about the commission of Elijah to Sidon and of Elisha to Syria (Lk. 4:25–27) had no validity unless these things really happened.

THE AUTHORITY OF OLD TESTAMENT TEACHING

Pharisees and Sadducees

Our Lord uses the Old Testament as the court of appeal in matters of controversy. Alike with Pharisee and Sadducee he does not call in question their appeal to Scripture; rather he rebukes them for their failure to study it sufficiently profoundly. Even the seemingly wasteful expenditure of time and effort by the Pharisees on detailed legal formulation that resulted from their study of the Torah he commends rather than condemns. 'These you ought to have done,' he says. Their mistake was not that they applied the law too rigorously, but that they have left undone the weightier matters of the law (Mt. 23:23). Matthew gives two most remarkable instances of this teaching – so remarkable that it is unlikely that the sayings were invented, particularly after Gentiles had gained full recognition in the church. The first is the passage which precedes the 'It was said to the men of old . . . but I say to you . . .' section of the Sermon on the Mount: 'Think not that I have come to abolish the law and the prophets; I have come not to abolish them but to fulfil them. For truly, I say to you, till heaven and earth pass away, not an iota, not a dot, will pass from the law until all is accomplished. Whoever then relaxes one of the least of these commandments and teaches men so, shall be called least in the kingdom of heaven; but he who does them and teaches them shall be called great in the kingdom of heaven. For I tell you, unless your righteousness exceeds that of the scribes and Pharisees, you will never enter the kingdom of heaven' (Mt. 5:17-20). Jesus taught his disciples the need for obedience to the law, first and foremost in spirit, but also in letter.

The second passage is even more remarkable: 'The scribes and the Pharisees sit on Moses' seat; so practise and observe whatever they tell you, but not what they do; for they preach, but do not practise' (Mt. 23:2, 3). To Jesus, scribal lore was valuable if linked with spiritual understanding: 'every scribe who has been trained for the kingdom of heaven is like a householder who brings out of his treasure what is new and what is old' (Mt. 13:52). There is no hint of a belittling of Old Testament teaching. Rightly understood that teaching was the 'Word' and 'Commandment' of God. Wilful spiritual obtuseness and the displacement of Scripture by 'tradition' (mere 'precepts of men') were the twin evils which made that Word of none effect (Mt. 15:1-9; Mk. 7:1-13). Compare John 5:39-47, where the Jews who did not believe, who would not come to Jesus for life, who had not the love of God in them, are shown to have searched the Scriptures in vain. They had set their hope on Moses, but Moses himself proved to be their accuser. They did not really in their hearts believe him – hence their unbelief towards Jesus. 'For', he said, 'he wrote of me. But if you do not believe his writings, how will you believe my words?' (verses 46, 47). Faith, love and a right attitude of will are the key to an understanding of Moses and of Christ.

The Sadducees escape no more lightly. Their supposed rationality is met by the fierce and scathing denunciation, 'You are wrong, because you know neither the scriptures, nor the power of God' (Mt. 22:29; cf. Mk. 12:24). Jesus had not been content with the knowledge of the letter of Scripture shown by the Pharisees and had been concerned that there should be

genuine spiritual understanding. But in speaking to the Sadducees he makes it plain that such understanding does not come
by a study of Scripture enlightened only by a human reason; it
comes through a knowledge of the Scriptures which has been
illuminated by the power of God. He concludes his answer to
the problem of the future state of the much married lady by a
further appeal to the Bible: 'Have you not read what was said
to you by God, I am the God of Abraham . . . ?' (Mt. 22:31, 32;
cf. Mk. 12:26; Lk. 20:37).

The right use of reason

Jesus condemns neither minuteness of study nor the exercise of
reason. His condemnation comes when the wickedness of men
so perverts their reason or their methods of study that they become blind to the inner principles of the divine revelation. He
himself knew how to stimulate the exercise of reason and repeatedly he encouraged his hearers to go beneath the externals
of Scripture language and think out its underlying principles.
This comes out clearly in his exposition of 'You shall not kill'
and 'You shall not commit adultery'. It is also most powerfully
displayed in his two quotations of Hosea's 'I desire steadfast
love and not sacrifice' (Ho. 6:6; Mt. 9:13; 12:7). In two quite
different contexts, neither of which has any direct reference to
sacrifice (one relating to his practice of consorting with tax-
collectors and the other to sabbath-observance), he rebukes the
Pharisees for failure to grasp the implication of Hosea's words.
He demands more thought, not less; but it must be thought
conducted in a humble and teachable spirit directed by God
himself. This need for divine instruction is brought out in John
6:45, where he refers to the Old Testament itself as already
looking forward to such a God-given spiritual illumination.
He quotes Isaiah 54:13, which says, 'All your sons shall be
taught by the Lord.' He requires that study and thought be
applied to the records objectively given, but this study must be
conducted under the subjective influence of him who gave them.

A guide to ethics

We see the same conclusion arising out of his use of the Old
Testament as a guide in matters of ethics. The Old Testament

provides objective moral standards which demand the obedience of our inmost hearts. The answer to the young man who enquired how to gain eternal life is given in the form of a series of quotations from the Ten Commandments, together with the injunction from Leviticus, 'You shall love your neighbour as yourself' (Mt. 19:18, 19; *cf.* Mk. 10:19; Lk. 18:20).

When the lawyer asked the question, 'Which is the great commandment in the law?' Jesus replied with two quotations from the Pentateuch : 'You shall love the Lord your God with all your heart, and with all your soul, and with all your mind. This is the great and first commandment. And a second is like it, You shall love your neighbour as yourself.' To him these two quotations sum up the teaching of the Old Testament. 'On these two commandments', he says, 'depend all the law and the prophets' (Mt. 22:37–40; *cf.* Mk. 12:29–31).

Note carefully that to our Lord these two commandments sum up, not the New Testament, but the Old. Many people think that these two commandments are the heart of the New Testament, forgetting that they stand in the law of Moses, dating back centuries before the time of Christ. According to our Lord they are the heart of the Old Testament. Or, to be more precise, they are the heart of the Old Testament law. There is no higher law than the Old Testament law as here expressed, and never can be. The New Testament does not reveal a higher *law*: it reveals the gospel. The demands of God's law had proved far beyond the reach of sinful men and it had brought only condemnation. The gospel was good news of salvation to the helpless and the condemned. It is extraordinary what a hold this utterly unbiblical notion of the contrariety of the two Testaments has obtained. We have had so much erroneous teaching for so many years that even intelligent people often really believe that the two Testaments represent two irreconcilably opposed points of view; the Old Testament God being a God of wrath and the New Testament God a God of love. Such a view would have been repudiated by our Lord and by every New Testament writer with horror. To them the God of the Old Testament and the God of the New Testament are the same; in both he is a God of wrath and of love. The great difference between the Old and New Testament is that in the former the gospel (though by no means invisible) is veiled, whereas in the latter it is clearly revealed.

Thus, 'On these two (Old Testament) commandments', he says, 'depend all the law and the prophets.'

In passing, it is perhaps worth while to point out that here – as also in the Golden Rule ('Whatever you wish that men would do to you, do so to them': Mt. 7:12), of which he says, 'this is the law and the prophets' – he sets his seal upon the sacred writings considered as a unitary whole.[4] Also the summary itself brings home forcibly the fact that within the Old Testament all its elements are not equally fundamental. Laws are a necessity of social life, but cases often arise where the law gives no specific ruling. He makes it clear that in such cases guidance is to be found, not in a multiplication of casuistical rules, but by appealing from the less fundamental principle to the more fundamental. In other words, he is simply saying once again that the mind of God is to be found by a spiritually-minded approach to the Scriptures. The Scriptures are the court of appeal, but their study must be prompted by a love for God and man.

G. Vos describes Jesus' treatment of the law like this: 'He once more made the voice of the law the voice of the living God, who is present in every commandment, so absolute in his demands, so personally interested in man's conduct, so all-observant, that the thought of yielding to him less than the whole inner life, the heart, the soul, the mind, the strength, can no longer be tolerated. Thus quickened by the spirit of God's personality, the law becomes in our Lord's hands a living organism, in which soul and body, spirit and letter, the greater and smaller commandments are to be distinguished, and which admits of being reduced to great comprehensive principles in whose light the weight and purport of all single precepts are to be intelligently appreciated.'[5]

[4] 'The law' or 'the law and the prophets' often seems to be shorthand for 'the Law, the Prophets and the Writings', the three sections of the OT Scriptures. The Psalms, which occupy a great place in the thoughts of Jesus, belong to the Writings. In quoting Ps. 82:6 he says: 'Is it not written in your *law*?' (Jn. 10:34). 'The Writings' did not become the universally accepted title of the third section of the OT Canon till much later. See further, p. 158 n. 3.
[5] G. Vos, *The Teaching of Jesus concerning the Kingdom of God and the Church* (Grand Rapids, 1951), pp. 61ff.

Accommodation to the beliefs of his hearers

The use of Scripture as a court of appeal in controversy is undoubted, but it again suggests the possibility that Jesus is simply
taking his contemporaries on their own ground without com-
mitting himself to the correctness of their premises. In other
words, that again we have *ad hominem* arguments, aimed more
at discrediting his opponents than laying foundations on which
to build eternal truth. Indeed may we not go even further, and
suggest that (since his aim was the positive one of leading his
contemporaries forward from their valuable, though imperfect,
Old Testament conceptions of the character of God) he deliberately refrained from unsettling them by questioning their conception of the inspiration of their Scriptures, allowing the
gentler processes of passing time gradually to bring home to
them the imperfect character of what they had hitherto
revered?

Plausible though this is, it seems impossible to accept it as
being Christ's real view. In other respects he does not show himself unduly sensitive about undermining current beliefs. He is
not slow to denounce Pharisaic traditionalism; in the Sermon
on the Mount, for instance, he carefully distinguishes between
the divine law and later false deductions; on another occasion
he honours the scribes and Pharisees who 'sit on Moses' seat'
upholding the law of God, yet rebukes them for binding 'heavy
burdens, hard to bear' (Mt. 23:2-4). He is not slow to repudiate
nationalist conceptions of Messiahship. He is prepared to face
the cross for defying current misconceptions. Surely he would
have been prepared to explain clearly the mingling of divine
truth and human error in the Bible, if he had known such to
exist. The notion that our Lord was fully aware that the view of
Holy Scripture current in his day was erroneous, and that he
deliberately accommodated his teaching to the beliefs of his
hearers, will not square with the facts. His use of the Old Testament seems altogether too insistent and positive and extreme.
What (according to the Gospel records) he actually says is that
the 'scripture cannot be broken' (Jn. 10:35); 'Not an iota, not a
dot, will pass from the law' (Mt. 5:18); 'It is easier for heaven
and earth to pass away, than for one dot of the law to become

void' (Lk. 16:17). There is a tremendous moral earnestness when
he says to the Pharisees, 'Well did Isaiah prophesy of you hypo-
crites, as it is written, "This people honours me with their lips,
but their heart is far from me; in vain do they worship me,
teaching as doctrines the precepts of men". . . . You have a fine
way of rejecting the commandment of God, in order to keep
your tradition! . . . making void the word of God' (Mk. 7:6–13).
It is no mere debating-point that makes him say to the Sadducees, 'You are wrong, because you know neither the scriptures
nor the power of God' (Mt. 22:29). When speaking of the irre-
trievable separation in the after-world, he puts into the mouth
of Abraham these words, 'They have Moses and the prophets;
let them hear them . . . If they do not hear Moses and the
prophets, neither will they be convinced if some one should rise
from the dead' (Lk. 16:29–31). As we have already seen, when
he quotes instances of the fearful judgments of God, he does so
to bring home the seriousness of contemporary issues.

The temptation

The suggestion that his use of the Old Testament is of an *ad
hominem* nature breaks down most obviously in the account of
the temptation. There he introduces each of his three answers
by the decisive formula, 'It is written' (Mt. 4:4ff.; Lk. 4:4ff.).
Are we asked to believe that the *homo* here concerned would be
content to submit to rebuttal by an argument based on a false
premise? Whether the devil is regarded as personal or impersonal, it is equally clear that Jesus understood 'It is written' to
be equivalent to 'God says'. There is a grand and solid objec-
tivity about the perfect tense γέγραπται, 'it stands written':
'here is the permanent, unchangeable witness of the Eternal
God, committed to writing for our instruction'. Such it appears
to have been to Jesus' inmost soul, quite apart from the con-
venience of the standpoint to him in controversy. In the hour of
utmost crisis and at the moment of death words of Scripture
come to his lips: 'My God, my God, why hast thou forsaken
me?' (Ps. 22:1; Mt. 27:46; Mk. 15:34); 'Into thy hands I commit my spirit' (Ps. 31:5; Lk. 23:46).

Post-resurrection teaching

Any lingering doubts that we might have as to the fundamental importance of the Old Testament to Jesus are dispelled by a consideration of his post-resurrection teaching. Between his resurrection and ascension Jesus transcended human limitations very much more obviously than before, and then, if at any time during his earthly ministry, we must believe that he had access to the mind of God. During the post-resurrection period he gave his final instructions to the leaders of the embryo church and emphasized again to their rapidly developing understanding the fundamentals on which the church was to be built. It would appear from Luke's account that the main burden of this teaching was an exposition of the Old Testament. Tracing through 'all the scriptures', 'beginning with Moses and all the prophets', he showed from each of the three collections of sacred writings – the Law, the Prophets and the Psalms – how they were fulfilled in him (Lk. 24:25–47). At first it seems tantalizing that Luke should speak of these expositions only in general terms, when a detailed account of our Lord's teaching would have proved so interesting to us; but is it not probable that Luke has preserved the main ingredients of his teaching – not in the Gospel, but in Acts? In the earliest years of the church its members were almost all Jews and its message was being presented almost entirely to Jews, with the result that their chief preoccupation was to demonstrate that the Old Testament found its true fulfilment in Jesus. The outline of their apologetic would have been derived from what they had learnt from their risen Master.[6] Thus the general apostolic use of Scripture, and particularly the records of the early chapters of Acts, must be regarded as important witnesses to our Lord's own teaching. As we shall see later, the teaching of the New Testament writers underlines that of Christ.

THE INSPIRATION OF THE OLD TESTAMENT WRITINGS

Our Lord not only believed the truth of the Old Testament history, and used the Scriptures as the final authority in matters of faith and conduct, he also regarded the writings themselves as

[6] See C. H. Dodd, *According to the Scriptures* (London, 1952), pp. 109f.

inspired. To him, Moses, the prophets, David and the other Scripture-writers were truly inspired men with a message given by the Spirit of God; but there is no trace of the modern idea that the men were inspired but not the writings. Rather, if anything, might one infer the reverse. The Old Testament makes no attempt to gloss over the sins of its saints. The greatest of them, such as Moses and David, are convicted of grievous sin, and our Lord would have had no desire to whitewash their characters. But their *writings* come in a different category.

Their writings are authoritative. This, however, is not by reason of the authority of the human author, but because God is regarded as the ultimate author. The authors are real authors – there is no idea of a mechanical dictation – yet none the less it was God's Spirit who was speaking through them, and it is the divine authorship which gives them their importance. Our Lord can preface a quotation of Scripture by 'Moses said' (Mk. 7:10), 'Well did Isaiah prophesy' (Mk. 7:6; *cf.* Mt. 13:14), 'David himself, inspired by the Holy Spirit' (Mk. 12:36); he can refer to the abomination of desolation, 'which was spoken of through Daniel the prophet' (Mt. 24:15, RV mg.). But, as is clear from the context, the injunctions 'Honour your father and your mother' and 'He that speaketh evil of father or mother, let him die the death' do not derive their authority from the fact that Moses uttered them, but because they are commandments of God. Without the original 'God spake these words' or 'The Lord said unto Moses', the expression 'Moses said' would have had no force. The words of Isaiah and Daniel likewise gain their authority because they are prophets, the essence of prophecy being that the prophet speaks God's words, or (more vividly) God speaks *through* the prophet. David (who, incidentally, is actually called a 'prophet' in the very first Christian address delivered after the ascension – Acts 2:30) is expressly said by our Lord to have spoken 'in the Holy Spirit'.

Fulfilment of prophecy

Our Lord's references to the necessity for the fulfilment of the prophecies of Scripture are numerous. It is not always easy to discern the principles of interpretation which govern our Lord's understanding of prophecy, prophecies being sometimes inter-

preted literally and sometimes typologically. But these exegeti-
cal problems (to which we shall return later[7]) serve only to throw
into stronger relief the implied God-givenness of the whole body
of prophetic writings which by divine necessity must be fulfilled. The fact that the correspondence between prophecy and
fulfilment is by no means obvious on the surface makes the
conviction that these ancient writings contain the foreshadow-
ing of present events the more remarkable. Our Lord not only
sees the fulfilment of prophecy in events that have already taken
place, but he is possessed of a sense of divine predestination in
the events that lie ahead. These things must assuredly come to
pass in order that the Scriptures may be fulfilled.

Here are the more important references to his teaching about
the fulfilment of prophecy: 'Today this scripture has been fulfilled in your hearing' (Lk. 4:21). 'This is he of whom it is
written, "Behold, I send my messenger before thy face . . ."'
(Mt. 11:10; cf. Lk. 7:27). 'Elijah does come first to restore all
things; and how is it written of the Son of man, that he should
suffer many things and be treated with contempt? But I tell you
that Elijah has come, and they did to him whatever they
pleased, as it is written of him' (Mk. 9:12, 13). 'Behold, we are
going up to Jerusalem, and everything that is written of the Son
of man by the prophets will be accomplished. For he will be
delivered to the Gentiles, . . . they will scourge and kill him, and
on the third day he will rise' (Lk. 18:31–33). 'These are days of
vengeance, to fulfil all that is written' (Lk. 21:22). 'The Son of
man goes as it is written of him, . . .' (Mt. 26:24; Mk. 14:21).
'For I tell you, that this scripture must be fulfilled in me, "And
he was reckoned with transgressors"; for what is written about
me has its fulfilment' (Lk. 22:37). 'You will all fall away because of me this night; for it is written, "I will strike the shepherd . . ."' (Mt. 26:31; cf. Mk. 14:27; Zc. 13:7). 'Do you think
that I cannot appeal to my Father, and he will at once send me
more than twelve legions of angels? But how then should the
scriptures be fulfilled, that it must be so? . . . all this has taken
place, that the scriptures of the prophets might be fulfilled'

---

[7] See pp. 100ff. For a full treatment see R. T. France, *Jesus and the
Old Testament: His Application of Old Testament Passages to Himself
and His Mission* (London, 1971).

(Mt. 26:53–56; *cf.* Mk. 14:49). ' "O foolish men, and slow of heart to believe all that the prophets have spoken! Was it not necessary that Christ should suffer these things and enter into his glory?" And beginning with Moses and all the prophets, he interpreted to them in all the scriptures the things concerning himself' (Lk. 24:25–27). ' "These are my words which I spoke to you, while I was still with you, that everything written about me in the law of Moses and the prophets and the psalms must be fulfilled." Then he opened their minds to understand the scriptures, and said to them, "Thus it is written, that the Christ should suffer and on the third day rise from the dead, and that repentance and forgiveness of sins should be preached in his name to all nations, beginning from Jerusalem" ' (Lk. 24 :44–47). 'The scriptures . . . bear witness to me; . . . If you believed Moses, you would believe me, for he wrote of me. But if you do not believe his writings, how will you believe my words?' (Jn. 5:39–47). 'I am not speaking of you all; I know whom I have chosen; it is that the scripture may be fulfilled, "He who ate my bread has lifted his heel against me" ' (Jn. 13:18; Ps. 41:9). 'It is to fulfil the word that is written in their law, "They hated me without a cause" ' (Jn. 15:25; Ps. 35:19). 'None of them is lost but the son of perdition, that the scripture might be fulfilled' (Jn. 17 :12). Our Lord's acceptance of the divine character of the prophetic Scriptures is clear and full and emphatic.

'Scripture' and verbal inspiration

Though in any balanced statement of the doctrine of biblical inspiration it is most important to remember how our Lord acknowledged the real authorship of the human writers, yet it is also important to note carefully that his references to human authorship are quite secondary. Often he is content to speak simply of 'scripture', God being the implied author. Here are some of the references: 'Today this scripture has been fulfilled in your hearing . . .' (Lk. 4:21). 'Have you never read in the scriptures: "The very stone which the builders rejected . . ."?' (Mt. 21:42; *cf.* Mk. 12:10; Lk. 20:17; Ps. 118:22). 'How then should the scriptures be fulfilled, that it must be so?' (Mt. 26:54). 'The scriptures . . . bear witness to me' (Jn. 5:39). 'He who believes in me, as the scripture has said . . .' (Jn. 7:38).

'The Scriptures' collectively state, and each individual 'scripture' states, the teaching of God. Similarly, for him to say (as he does in so many other places) 'Have you not read . . . ?' is equivalent to 'Do you not know that God has said . . . ?' (*cf.* Mt. 12:3; 19:4; 21:16; 22:31; Mk. 2:25; 12:10, 26; Lk. 6:3). The same force is to be given to the word γέγραπται, 'It is written', already mentioned in connection with the temptations, but used often at other times (Mt. 11:10; 21:13; 26:24, 31; Mk. 9:12, 13; 11:17; 14:21, 27; Lk. 7:27; 19:46). The inspiration implied by these phrases is not applied only to oracular prophetic utterances but to all parts of Scripture without discrimination – to history, to laws, to psalms, to prophecies.

This witness of our Lord to the inspiration of the writings demands specially careful attention, because, wittingly or unwittingly, it is continually being contradicted by Christian writers. It often takes the form of a repudiation of the whole notion of verbal inspiration as obviously outmoded, or even of a denial that in a formal sense there is any difference between the inspiration of the Bible and other great literature. A doctrine of verbal inspiration plainly needs careful statement, but that some sort of verbal inspiration is taught by Christ is clear, seeing that it is to the writings rather than to the writers that he ascribes authority. Writings are made up of words, therefore there must be some form of word-inspiration. Scripture is Scripture to Christ because it has (in a way which other writing has not) God as its primary author.

Interchangeability of 'scripture' and 'God'

One further point of extreme interest gives a final illustration of this notion of the divine character of Scripture. It arises from the remarkable interchangeability of the terms 'God' and 'scripture' in certain New Testament passages. We find cases where 'scripture' is used when one would expect 'God', and 'God' is used when one would expect 'scripture'.[8] Romans 9:17 reads, 'The scripture says to Pharaoh, "I have raised you up for the

[8] This is an example of metonymy, a figure of speech in which 'the writer' may be put for 'the thing written' or 'the thing written' for 'the writer'. (Thus 'Shakespeare says' could be used to mean 'the works of Shakespeare say', or '*Hamlet* says' could be used to mean 'Shakespeare, as he expresses his mind in *Hamlet*, says'.)

very purpose of showing my power in you".' This means simply, 'In the scripture narrative, God says to Pharaoh . . .', but 'scripture' has been personalized and allowed to replace 'God'. Similarly in Galatians 3:8 it says, 'The scripture, foreseeing that God would justify the Gentiles by faith, preached the gospel beforehand to Abraham.' There is one instance of Jesus doing the same thing, though in the reverse direction. In Matthew 19:4, 5 an Old Testament sentence, which in its context is not a statement by God, is referred directly to God as its author. Our Lord says, 'He who made them . . . said, "For this reason a man shall leave his father and mother".' The quotation is from Genesis 2:24, which in the context is not a statement attributed to God but is simply a comment introduced into the course of the narrative by the writer of Genesis. The natural use would be, 'Scripture said, For this reason . . .', but the actual use is, 'He which made them (*i.e.* God) said. . . .' So truly is God regarded as the author of scriptural statements that in certain contexts 'God' and 'scripture' have become interchangeable. Jesus never exalts the Scriptures for their own sake, yet he never allows a wedge to be driven between the Scriptures and the message of Scripture. What Scripture says is the word of God – God is its author. Thus to our Lord the Old Testament is true as to its history, it is of divine authority, and its very writings are inspired by God Himself.

ALLUSIONS TO THE OLD TESTAMENT

We have now covered the ground sufficiently to give a clear idea of our Lord's view of Scripture, but the citation of a number of outstanding references cannot of itself convey the full weight of the evidence, for there must be added the many allusions which slip out in the course of his teaching. The Sermon on the Mount, for instance, has few explicit quotations, but it is so encrusted with Old Testament language and ideas that it is impossible to say which is conscious allusion and which is not. There is a shading off from conscious allusion to the adoption of Old Testament word- and thought-forms, which makes classification impossible, and which shows how the Holy Scriptures had penetrated the warp and woof of Christ's mind. It would take too long to examine the vast number of references in his teachings one by one, and the further evidence is not required to prove a case already adequately established, but it is perhaps worth while just to mention a few of the more interesting allusions.

There are three peculiar to Mark. 'He puts in the sickle, because the harvest has come' (Mk. 4:29) recalls Joel 3:13; 'having eyes do you not see, and having ears do you not hear?' (Mk. 8:18) is from Jeremiah 5:21; and 'their worm does not die, and the fire is not quenched' (Mk. 9:48) is from Isaiah 66:24. In the Sermon on the Mount, the phrase 'the pure in heart' and the sentence 'the meek shall inherit the earth' are not original to Jesus, but come from the Old Testament (Pss. 73:1; 37:11). 'Depart from me, you evil-doers' (Mt. 7:23; cf. Lk. 13:27) is Psalm 6:8. 'Children will rise up against parents ...' (Mt. 10:21, 35; Mk. 13:12; cf. Lk. 12:53) is Micah 7:6. In Matthew 18:15–20 we have one of our Lord's very rare items of ecclesiastical legislation: the sentence 'that every word may be confirmed by the evidence of two or three witnesses' comes from Deuteronomy 19:15. The parable of the wicked husbandmen (Mt. 21:33–41; Mk. 12:1–9; Lk. 20:9–16) recalls Isaiah 5. The Mount of Olives discourse (Mt. 24; Mk. 13; Lk. 21) is full of Old Testament language. Luke 19:44, '(they shall) dash you to the ground, you and your children within you' echoes that fiercest of imprecatory psalms, Psalm 137.

The total impression that these and many other allusions in the Gospels give is that the mind of Christ is saturated with the Old Testament and that, as he speaks, there flows out perfectly naturally a complete range of uses varying from direct verbal quotation to an unconscious utilization of scraps of Old Testament phraseology. There is no trace of an artificial quotation of Scripture as a matter of pious habit, but his mind is so steeped in both the words and principles of Scripture that quotation and allusion spring to his lips naturally and appositely in all sorts of different circumstances.

OBJECTIONS AND CONCLUSION

But is there not another side to this question? Did not our Lord at times qualify or even abrogate some of the Old Testament's teaching? Did he not on various occasions treat the Scriptures in

a much freer way than this summary would suggest – in a way
that revealed a quietly critical element in his approach to them?
J. K. S. Reid, for instance, says : 'There is a class of sayings (or
actions) in which he improves upon what is written in the
Scripture he knew, and another where he endorses what is
there.'[9] B. H. Branscomb says: 'He flatly rejected a portion of it
by appealing to another portion.'[1]

There are four main examples of our Lord's teaching that
have been used to illustrate the thesis that he criticized, and so
by implication repudiated, parts of the Old Testament. To
deal with the three of lesser importance first.

The sabbath

Our Lord said, 'The Son of man is lord even of the sabbath'
(Mk. 2:28; *cf*. Mt. 12:8; Lk. 6:5). This hardly seems to merit
comment, because it so obviously cannot seriously be used to
illustrate a lower view of the Old Testament. The Pharisees had
objected to the rubbing of the ears of corn. Quite the reverse of
appealing away from Scripture, our Lord answers them by
an appeal to Bible history, reminding them of what David did.
He repudiates the petty traditions of the elders in favour of a
sane and spiritually-minded attention to the Old Testament.
The passage is indeed significant, not for its lowered view of
Scripture, but for the height of our Lord's claims implied in it.
It was God who gave the sabbath law, and Jesus claimed to
possess God's authority to define the limitations of that law.

Sacrifice

Our Lord's twofold citation of Hosea 6:6[2]: 'I desire steadfast
love and not sacrifice', has been used as an example of his
critical approach to the Old Testament in setting aside most
important elements of Jewish ceremonial. It is very doubtful
whether Hosea's own words or our Lord's quotation of them
contained or conveyed to those who heard them any idea of a
literal abrogation of sacrifice. Certainly the Gospel contexts
suggest nothing of the kind, and such thoughts do not appear

[9] J. K. S. Reid, *The Authority of Scripture* (London, 1957), pp. 26of.
[1] B. H. Branscomb, *Jesus and the Law of Moses* (London, 1930), p. 155.
[2] See p. 18 above.

to have been seriously entertained by the apostles till some years after the ascension. At least they did not take their Master seriously or literally enough to abandon the sacrificial worship in Jerusalem. The biblical writers are by no means as literal as we normally are, and yet we should not misunderstand an impassioned clergyman who said: 'I want your spiritual devotion, not your money.' We should not necessarily expect to see church collections suddenly disappear! But even if we take it entirely literally, it has still proved nothing at all. No Christian, not even the Seventh Day Adventist, believes that the Mosaic sacrificial system is now binding; yet the whole Christian church for many centuries held the view that the Mosaic injunctions were truly given by God, but that many of them were temporary, until such time as they had been fulfilled in Christ. For the Son of God to abrogate a law of God is by no means to deny that it was first enacted by God.

'Cleansing all foods'

Mark 7:18, 19: 'Do you not see that whatever goes into a man from outside cannot defile him, since it enters, not his heart but his stomach, and so passes on? (Thus he declared all foods clean.)' This has been used similarly as showing our Lord's abrogation of the distinction between clean and unclean animals. But if the apostle Peter, after his vision of the great sheet let down from heaven (Acts 10:9–16), looked back and saw in this saying an implicit, earlier abrogation of the distinction between clean and unclean foods, it involves no denial of the divine origin of the law that is now repealed. Indeed the context points precisely the other way. Mark 7:1–13, which immediately precedes, is a devastating attack on those who leave the commandment of God and hold fast the tradition of men.

'But I say to you ...'

Of primary importance is the famous section of the Sermon on the Mount in which our Lord's sayings are contrasted with what was said to them of old time (Mt. 5:17–48). Christ used the language of loftiest authority, 'It was said ... but I say. ...' This passage is often construed by superficial readers as being a repudiation of the 'barbarous' ethic of the Old Testament and a replacement of it by a contrasted Christian ethic. It is suggested that Christ was declaring the teaching of the Old Testament to be fundamentally wrong and was putting a new and true doctrine in its place. If this were a correct interpretation it would be remarkable enough as a claim to authority as a teacher, but in fact it is quite mistaken. He made, if possible, an even higher claim. He deliberately set the Old Testament on the highest pinnacle of authority and then proceeded to set himself above it. He introduced the passage with the words: 'Think not that I have come to abolish the law and the prophets; I have come not to abolish them, but to fulfil them. For truly, I say to you, till heaven and earth pass away, not an iota, not a dot, will pass from the law until all is accomplished. Whoever then relaxes one of the least of these commandments and teaches men so, shall be called least in the kingdom of heaven; but he who does them and teaches them shall be called great in the kingdom of heaven.'

It has been a common practice to find two sources for the Sermon on the Mount: the first (as quoted above) accepts the strict rabbinical doctrine of Scripture, and the second ('but I say to you') overthrows it. There is an intrinsic absurdity about combining two contradictory sources in this way, but as D. Daube has shown, the sequence of *principle* ('think not that I have come to abolish)' and *cases* ('you have heard') is very common in Rabbinic literature. 'To fulfil' – *qiyyem*, 'to uphold' – the law, is 'to show that the text is in agreement with your teaching'. The test of any teaching is whether you can give full effect to, 'uphold', every word of the law.[3] So it is that, after the opening passage concerning the blessedness of discipleship, the very first truth which our Lord drives home is the authority of the Old Testament and the sermon virtually ends with 'this is the law and the prophets' (Mt. 7:12). It is rounded off with an earnest appeal to beware of false prophets and to build on Jesus' words.

What our Lord did was not to negative any of the Old Testament commands but to show their full scope and to strip off current misinterpretations of them. Our Lord evidently did not himself make it clear to his disciples that he intended the abro-

[3] D. Daube, *New Testament and Rabbinic Judaism* (London, 1956), pp. 6of.

gation of Levitical sacrifices and all the paraphernalia of temple worship. It was left to Paul to bring into clear light the implications of his teaching and (even more important than his teaching) of his death and resurrection. It is certainly not to the Sermon on the Mount that we are to look for an abrogation of the Old Testament. Our Lord did not say, 'The Old Testament says, You shall do no murder. I say, You may commit murder.' What he did teach is that God does not restrict the commandment to the mere letter of the law, but that he disapproves of the hating spirit which leads to murder, and of lustful intentions which in God's sight are equivalent to adultery.

Divorce

As his teaching on divorce (Mt. 5:31, 32; *cf.* 19:3ff.; Mk. 10:2ff.; Lk. 16:18) is often regarded as an instance of our Lord giving to an Old Testament passage something less than divine authority, it may be worth while making a short digression to clear up a common confusion. Deuteronomy 24:1–4 gives strict instructions that a wife, formally divorced and re-married, may on no account return to her former husband: 'When a man takes a wife and marries her, if then she finds no favour in his eyes because he has found some indecency in her, and he writes her a bill of divorce and puts it in her hand and sends her out of his house, and she departs out of his house, and if she goes and becomes another man's wife, and the latter husband dislikes her and writes her a bill of divorce and puts it in her hand and sends her out of his house, or if the latter husband dies, who took her to be his wife, then her former husband, who sent her away, may not take her again to be his wife, after she has been defiled; for that is an abomination before the Lord.'

This is one of the statutes and ordinances which 'the Lord your God commands you to do' (Dt. 26:16), and there is no good ground for thinking that either our Lord himself or his questioner, in referring this injunction to Moses, meant thereby to deny that it came from God. The question was what deductions might be drawn from it. It was currently interpreted as giving divine approval for divorce and was misquoted in the form given in Matthew 5:31 : 'Whoever divorces his wife, let him give her a certificate of divorce.' But it is not a command to divorce; it is not properly a permission to divorce, since the divine pattern of Genesis 2:24, where the man 'cleaves to his wife, and they become one flesh', had never been modified; it is rather a disapproving recognition of the fact of divorce, with regulations to mitigate its worst evils. It is in the form : 'If ... and if ..., then. ...' The law gave civil permission, but not moral permission for divorce.

There are two possible interpretations of our Lord's teaching on this matter, and neither of them denies the divine origin of the Mosaic command. Either, the 'permission' for divorce was a law for the spiritually immature Israel and the revocation was a new law for the spiritually more mature church – that is, there were two different laws for two different sets of circumstances, and both were given by God. Or, the 'permission' for divorce was a *law* – a law of Israel's statute-book, designed to meet the practical needs of a very imperfect people; whereas the teaching concerning the indissolubility of marriage was an *ideal* – an ideal for mankind in general and for Christians in particular. This distinction between laws and ideals is a very simple one, yet it is very fundamental and is often overlooked. No wise law-giver – least of all the all-wise Law-Giver – would frame a law on the principle that hate is equivalent to murder, or lust to adultery. Law can deal only with overt acts, not with secret thoughts. A wise ideal and a wise law, though emanating from the same person, must of necessity be very different. The ideal will in a sense be far higher than the law. It is this confusion between ideal and law or, in other words, between moral law and civil law, which leads the superficial reader to regard the Sermon on the Mount as a repudiation of the Old Testament when, in fact, it is explicitly stated to be a fulfilment of the law and prophets. The same thing is clear in Mark 10:2–12, where Jesus goes back to Genesis 1:27, 'God made them male and female', and 2:24, 'For this reason a man shall leave his father and mother and be joined to his wife, and the two shall become one', and interprets Scripture by Scripture. It is *on the authority of Scripture* that he denies the validity of the interpretation of Deuteronomy 24:1, which gives approval to divorce.

'Eye for an eye'

Even his repudiation of the 'eye for an eye' principle (Mt.
5:38–42), which comes from the Old Testament, cannot fairly
be said to be a repudiation of what in its context the Old Testament taught. In Exodus 21:24, Leviticus 24:20 and Deuteronomy 19:21 we have laws given for the administration of
public justice. The practice of private revenge and family feud
was to be replaced by strictly fair and impartial public administration of justice.[4] In our Lord's day this excellent, if stern,
principle of judicial retribution was being utilized as an excuse
for the very thing that it was instituted to abolish, namely personal revenge. Our Lord gives no hint that he wishes to see the
magistrate relaxing his important social function of witnessing
to the majesty of the Law and to the sanctity of justice, but he
does discourage his disciples from appealing to justice when it
is for the merely selfish purpose of gaining their own rights.
(Similarly in the story of the woman taken in adultery (Jn.
7:53ff.) Jesus does not say what would be the proper treatment
in a legally constituted court. He says in effect, 'I am not here
now as Judge (*cf.* Jn. 3:17). I am here to call men to repentance
while there is time. I call this woman, *and all her accusers*, to
repentance.')

'Hate your enemy'

His final contrast again repudiates a misinterpretation of the
Old Testament. The Old Testament had given the command,
'You shall love your neighbour.' This had been misinterpreted
as involving the corollary, 'You shall hate your enemy.' But of
course in making this addition, which is not a quotation from
the Old Testament, the popular teaching was giving it a

4 We do not know much about the operation of the *lex talionis* in OT
times. It seems unlikely that it was intended, except in the case of
murder, to be taken literally. The whole of Ex. 21:18–36 suggests that
the payment of damages was envisaged. In most forms of Islamic law it
is taken as a limiting concept. The 'heirs of blood' must exact *not more
than* equivalent damage or injury. This normally rules out physical
injury, because there is no way of ensuring exact equivalence. Instead a
tariff of payments is used. The folly of tribal revenge is seen most clearly
when one tribe considers itself superior to another (which it usually
does). It will then demand two or three deaths in return for one.

meaning which is not implied in the context. Leviticus 19:18 was a command originally intended to embrace every member of the Israelite community, and the rest of the verse makes it clear that an Israelite was not to seek for vengeance or harbour grudges against any of his compatriots. Leviticus 19:34 goes further and applies the same principle to the resident alien: 'The stranger who sojourns with you shall be to you as the native among you, and you shall love him as yourself.' 'Love your neighbour' in the Levitical rule already implied 'Love your enemies'.

It is true that the Old Testament in some sense expects the godly man to hate the enemies of God and the enemies of the people of God (*cf.* Dt. 20:16–18; 23:6; 25:17–19; Pss. 109; 139:21–24), but so in some sense does our Lord. The disciple must be prepared to 'hate his own father and mother and wife and children' (Lk. 14:26). The Son of man himself will one day utter the words, 'Depart from me, you cursed, into the eternal fire' (Mt. 25:41). He underlined and completely identified himself with the just judgments of God against sinners recorded in the Old Testament and with those foretold as yet to come, and at the same time he forgave his enemies and loved them even to the cross. The fact that at a certain period in his ministry he forbad James and John to follow the example of Elijah in calling down fire from heaven to consume his opponents is not to deny the reality of divine judgment on a very different occasion (Lk. 9:51–56; 2 Ki. 1:10, 12).

Cumulative evidence

It has been said with truth that the attempt to evade the evidence for our Lord's teaching as to the God-givenness of Scripture is as futile as a mathematician's attempt to prove that it is possible to dodge an avalanche.[5] He may satisfy himself that the trajectory of each boulder is calculable and that an agile man could step out of the way of any one of them. So, taken one at a time, ingenuity may satisfy itself that it can find ways of disposing of many of our Lord's statements about the Old Testament. But these statements do not come one at a time, they form

[5] B. B. Warfield, *The Inspiration and Authority of the Bible* (London, 1959), pp. 119f.

a great avalanche of items of cumulative evidence which cannot in honesty be evaded. Furthermore, the consistency of the results which are obtained by taking the Gospel evidence as it stands is itself a vindication of our method of approach. The items of evidence support one another, suggesting that they derive from one mind, not from a miscellany of dubious church traditions.[6]

There are many who profess that they would be willing to accept our Lord's teaching about the Bible, if only they could know for certain what that teaching was. But the accumulated errors of translation, of oral tradition, and of scribal transmission, leave them – they say – quite uncertain as to what he did teach. Taking refuge behind this belief, they do not grapple with the Gospel evidence, and they feel free to build their theology with a view of Scripture different from that which ordinary historical investigation shows to have been taught by Christ. But however much one may nibble at details of the Gospel record on critical grounds, the over-all picture can be affected only by a wholesale rejection of practically all of it, and this is a length to which few critics, however radical, are prepared to go. The evidence is clear :

To Christ the Old Testament was true, authoritative, inspired.

To him the God of the Old Testament was the living God, and the teaching of the Old Testament was the teaching of the living God.

To him, what Scripture said, God said.

---

[6] This point is made in R. T. France's *Jesus and the Old Testament* (London, 1971), which deals with the whole subject carefully and in detail, and to which I am greatly indebted in the Additional Note which follows.

RADICAL CRITICISM OF THE GOSPELS

It may seem strange to qualify the term 'Christian' by adding the clause 'who regards the Gospels as substantially true'. It must be rare, as we have seen, for a convert from a non-Christian religion to declare his faith in Christ if he has not first come to believe the Gospels to be substantially true. Conversion is normally the end of a process of growing belief that the Gospel story is true and that Jesus was what he claimed to be. For those brought up in a Christian culture, however, the matter is often not so simple. A second-hand Christian belief subjected to criticism may become progressively less sure, while yet never reaching the point of explicit abandonment. It is not abandoned, but radically re-interpreted. Faith in Christ is affirmed, while knowledge of the Jesus of history is disclaimed. This is the position of many New Testament critics today as a result of their study of source and form and redaction criticism. The Gospels, they believe, tell us much about the faith of the early church, but little about Jesus. It is our belief that such a position has been arrived at by abandoning the centrality of God and revelation and by adopting a naturalistic approach to the Gospels. It is outside the scope of this book to deal with this question, but one or two remarks may be in place.

H. E. W. Turner[7] has distinguished two basic approaches to the Gospels: the historical and the interpretative. The former believes that the Gospels were intended to be historical records, the latter that they were essentially propaganda, written to present a particular view of Jesus. The former assumes that the records are true unless good reason can be shown to the contrary; the latter assumes the opposite. The attitude of Bultmann and his school to a Gospel-saying has been summarized as follows : '(1) If it reflects the faith of the church after the resurrection, it must be regarded as a creation of the church, rather than an authentic saying of Jesus. (2) If there is a parallel saying attributed to a Rabbi, it must be held as a Jewish tradition which has erroneously been attributed to Jesus. But if it is neither – if it is clearly distinct both from the faith of the church

[7] H. E. W. Turner, *Historicity and the Gospels* (London, 1963).

and from Judaism – then it may be safely accepted as authentic.'[8] This means, of course, that any appeal to Scripture by Jesus is at once suspect. This approach produces an improbable view of both Jesus and the early church. Jesus becomes an eccentric who took almost nothing from his environment. The church becomes inexplicable, since it took almost nothing from its master. Rather it so altered what it received from him that its teaching can be seen in sharp contrast to the few genuine sayings which it preserved.

Such an approach is possible only on the supposition (a) of a long interval between the uttering of Christ's words and their committal to writing; and (b) of a general lack of interest in preserving his words accurately. The widely accepted notion that the church was almost entirely dependent on oral tradition for forty or more years is itself highly questionable. Indeed the idea that it had little concern to preserve an accurate account of the words and deeds of Jesus is highly improbable. In Judaism oral material was learnt verbatim and passed on verbatim, as 'holy tradition'. There is nothing to suggest that Christians learnt vast lengths of tradition mechanically, but there is much to suggest that the salient material was memorized and carefully handed on. Much of the teaching of Jesus is in poetic or easily memorized form. A special respect is shown for the sayings of Jesus. For instance in 1 Corinthians 7:8, 10, 12, 25, 40 Paul declares his own words to be authoritative, yet puts the words of the Lord on a special plane. 'Where Paul has no saying of Jesus to quote, he does not presume to invent one. While quotations of the words of Jesus in the epistles are not common, we have no evidence of the attribution to Jesus in the epistles of sayings invented to meet contemporary needs, nor do we find in the sayings attributed to Jesus in the gospels material culled from Pauline or other known Christian writings. The words of Jesus were treated as *sui generis*.'[9] The terminology of tradition is used to describe the process of transmission. The apostles are regarded as its guardians.

To one who has been captured in heart and mind by the

[8] R. H. Fuller, *Interpreting the Miracles* (London, 1963), pp. 26f.
[9] R. T. France, *The Use of the Old Testament by Jesus according to the Synoptic Gospels* (Bristol University Ph.D. thesis, 1966), p. 326.

Jesus of the Gospels, there appears to be a host of reasons for believing in the authenticity of the records. To regard the great mass of Gospel teaching as the creation of the Christian community seems to posit a marvellous effect without a plausible cause. Here is what may fairly be claimed as the greatest literature of all time, yet supposedly created by the imagination of an undistinguished community. It seems far easier to suppose that the Jesus of the Gospels created the community than that the community created the Jesus of the Gospels. Many features in the Gospels have an appearance of primitiveness: features have been retained which are liable to offend or perplex; the term 'Son of man' (though hardly used in the early church) is a favourite title; the theme of the kingdom of God has far greater prominence in the Gospels than in the New Testament as a whole; Aramaisms abound. There is complete lack of material in the Gospels on such burning issues in the apostolic church as circumcision or charismatic gifts; there is little on baptism, the Gentile mission, food laws, and relations between church and state – and what little there is refers to the concerns of the period of Jesus' ministry and not to the form in which these issues confronted the church thirty years later. The question of Sabbath observance and of Corban were not apparently live issues at a later period. It seems hard to conceive that a religious movement living so close to the life and death of its founder could have failed to be interested in his words and deeds. The prologue of Luke claims accurate research and eye-witness authority. To one who believes in the authenticity of the Gospels the person of Jesus has depth and breadth and balance and richness. He is real. He is known.

For one who does not see him so, there is no invincible argument. It may be, on the contrary, that for him it is the demands of a scientific approach which seem invincible in the twentieth century, and that therefore, if a scientific approach means a sceptical approach to miracle, then only a sceptical approach to the Gospels will do; and only a sceptical approach to the Christ of the Gospels will do. When this position is adopted it may be questioned what ground is left for faith in Christ and whether belief in the incarnation has not become something quite different from that of historic Christianity. But this anti-miraculous, supposedly scientific approach is itself based on the unproved and unprovable dogma that Nature behaves with invariable uniformity – which we reject. To believe that God has both revealed himself in Christ and has given us a true portrait of Christ in the Gospels is on the purely human level no more contrary to reason than scepticism. If, however, this belief is true and God-given, then it is infinitely more reasonable, for it is to think God's thoughts after him.

Further reading

The question of miracle is helpfully discussed by C. S. Lewis, *Miracles* (Bles, London, 1947). As far as the Gospels are concerned, the key is the resurrection. If this took place, there is no difficulty in principle about the other miracles. J. N. D. Anderson deals with *The Evidence for the Resurrection* (Inter-Varsity Press, London, 1950) concisely and clearly. D. P. Fuller's *Easter Faith and History* (Tyndale Press, London, 1968) discusses the critical and theological questions. I hope to deal with the harmony of the resurrection narratives (together with the dating and inter-relation of the four Gospels) in a later volume.

At the most popular level, the following are useful on the authenticity of the Gospels:

J. B. Phillips, *Ring of Truth* (Hodder, London, 1967).

E. M. B. Green, *Runaway World* (Inter-Varsity Press, London, 1968), chapter 1.

F. F. Bruce, *The New Testament Documents: Are They Reliable?* 5th ed. (Inter-Varsity Press, London, 1960).

Of more scholarly books, written from a variety of standpoints, the following contain valuable material:

D. Guthrie, *New Testament Introduction*, 2nd ed. (Tyndale Press, London, 1970) – the standard conservative introduction.

F. F. Bruce, *New Testament History* (Nelson, London, 1969) – the standard conservative history.

R. T. France, *Jesus and the Old Testament* (Tyndale Press, London, 1971).

E. B. Redlich, *Form Criticism: Its Value and Limitations* (Duckworth, London, 1939) – a useful critique of the formative period of the *Formgeschichte* movement.

C. F. D. Moule, *The Birth of the New Testament*, 2nd ed. (Black, London, 1966).

X. Léon-Dufour, *The Gospels and the Jesus of History* (Collins, London, 1968).

J. A. Baird, *The Justice of God in the Teaching of Jesus* (SCM Press, London, 1963), ch. 1: 'The Question of the Historical Jesus.'

J. Jeremias, *New Testament Theology*, Vol. 1 (SCM Press, London, 1971), ch. 1: 'How reliable is the tradition of the sayings of Jesus?'

A. T. Hanson (ed.), *Vindications* (SCM Press, London, 1966) – the authors and most of the contributors are form critics who do not share the sceptical attitude to Gospel history held by many of the school.

L. Morris, *Studies in the Fourth Gospel* (Paternoster Press, Exeter, 1969).

O. Borchert, *The Original Jesus* (Lutterworth, London, 1933) – argues the difficulty of believing that first-century thought could have invented the Jesus of the Gospels.

THE AUTHORITY
OF JESUS AS
A TEACHER

2

But can we use Christ's authority in this way to establish a twentieth-century doctrine of Scripture? If he was truly Man, must he not to some extent have shared the ignorance and errors of his contemporaries?

Tremendous practical issues are here at stake. The question is whether the teaching of Jesus – about heaven and hell, about angels, demons and the devil, about the Scriptures, about rewards and punishments and judgment, about his second coming, and even about the very nature of God himself – is God's teaching, or just the teaching of an unusually enlightened first-century Jew. This is a question which affects every Christian layman as soon as he opens his Gospels, and every preacher the moment he tries to teach. It is indeed the most crucial question in the world : can we or can we not trust our Lord's teaching?

Believing that Jesus was both God and man, how are we to deal with this problem? Neither psychology nor dogmatics can help us much. The psychology of incarnation is baffling. The attributes of perfect Divinity, such as impeccability, infallibility, omnipotence and omnipresence, logically exclude the corresponding attributes of perfect humanity : peccability, fallibility, limitation of power and locality. Psychologists, arguing from phenomena (normal and abnormal) observed in ordinary men, have made interesting suggestions. But in the end no analogy is satisfactory, because we have no experience analogous to that of Divinity and humanity uniting in a single person.

And dogmatics cannot materially help us, because dogmatics is derived from the historical data recorded in Scripture, and cannot finally get beyond those data. It cannot from outside impose new elements upon the historical record which are not already latent in it. It cannot be argued, for instance, that one who ascribes freedom from error to our Lord denies his full humanity and is therefore a Docetist or an Apollinarian, unless it can be proved that the scriptural data upon which the orthodox condemnations of these heresies were based either explicitly or implicitly deny it. Careful attention to the Chalcedonian definition concerning the person and natures of Christ may indeed draw attention to certain characteristics of the Gospel portrayal which might otherwise be overlooked, but it can add nothing new. If it does, it has gone astray.

THE METHOD OF APPROACH

The one hope of reaching assured conclusions lies in examining our Lord's own statements concerning the authority of his teaching. It is reasonable to believe that in whatever else he might have been mistaken he could not have been God Incarnate and yet unaware of the limitations which the incarnation put upon his Deity. He could scarcely have spoken as though he were omniscient if his knowledge had been limited. He could not have spoken as if his teaching was inerrant if he had been liable to mistakes. As G. Vos says : 'No one can take a Saviour to his heart in that absolute, unqualified sense which constitutes the glory of religious trust, if there persists in the background of his mind the thought that this Saviour failed to understand himself.'[1] If we cannot trust Jesus in what he said about himself, there is no reason to trust him in anything else. The question is, Have we sufficient data to determine our Lord's own view?

Let us again take the Gospel evidence as it stands (allowing each reader to make such subtractions as he feels necessary because of critical uncertainty or doubtfulness of interpretation) and ask : Did our Lord regard the incarnation as having im-

[1] G. Vos, *The Self-Disclosure of Jesus* (Grand Rapids, 1954), p. 16.

posed any limitations (a) upon the extent of his knowledge and (b) upon the authority of his teaching? The two questions must be carefully distinguished, since failure to do so has been a frequent cause of confusion. It is sometimes said that our Lord expressly repudiated inerrancy. But this is based on the assumption that a denial by our Lord of omniscience involves a denial of inerrancy, and that because the one can be proved, the other necessarily follows. A student, however, may well disclaim mathematical omniscience and yet pass an examination without error. That is to say, in a certain limited field and over a certain limited period of time, he expressed himself without error. Similarly it is possible that in the limited fields covered by his teaching and over the limited period of his ministry, our Lord taught without error, even though in his incarnate state he was not omniscient. Error prejudices authority, whereas ignorance merely limits it. There can be little doubt that we have a sufficient number of clear references to give us an accurate view of his teaching on both questions.

DID HE CLAIM TO BE OMNISCIENT?

In his incarnate state our Lord evidently was not omniscient. As a child he 'increased in wisdom' (Lk. 2:52) and there is no evidence that at any stage in his career he was suddenly granted completeness of knowledge. He spent the night in prayer before choosing the twelve (Lk. 6:12f.). On occasions he asked questions apparently for the sake of gaining information. It is probable that, like any good teacher, he would often have asked questions even had he known the answers, but his 'How many loaves have you?' (Mk. 6:38), 'What is your name?' (Mk. 5:9), 'Who touched my garments?' (Mk 5:30), 'How long has he had this?' (Mk. 9:21) seem most natural as spontaneous questions. There is possibly an element of nescience in 'he marvelled because of their unbelief' (Mk. 6:6); he was astonished at Philip's continuing ignorance (Jn. 14:9); he invited the disciples to a lonely place, only to be greeted by the five thousand (Mk. 6:30-34); he looked for figs on a barren tree (Mk. 11:13). The one decisive reference, however, is in the Mount of Olives discourse where he expressly repudiates knowledge of the time of his coming again (Mt. 24:36; Mk. 13:32). Though this is the only recorded denial of omniscience by our Lord in the course of his ministry, its evidential value must be rated very high, scarcely being the sort of saying that the early church would have invented. This saying, together with the confirmation provided by the other evidence cited, seems sufficient justification for affirming our Lord's denial of omniscience. It also shows that Jesus 'was not ignorant of his ignorance'.[2]

This does not, however, mean that the incarnation put supernormal, if not superhuman, knowledge (like that ascribed to the prophets) beyond his reach. The account of the catch of fish in Luke 5:4 (and probably also that in John 21:6) shows something more than shrewd guess-work by our Lord – the experts did not know, Jesus did. Matthew records the incident about the coin to be found in the fish's mouth (17:27). John 1:48 records our Lord's understanding of Nathanael's thoughts, John 4:18 his knowledge of the Samaritan woman's husbands, and John 11:11 his knowledge of Lazarus' condition. All four Gospels record that he knew beforehand about Peter's denials and the cock-crowing. More striking still are his many statements about the more distant future. He frequently looks forward, knowing (at least in outline) the course of his passion, death and resurrection (e.g. Mk. 8:31; 9:31), and the subsequent sending of the Spirit (Jn. 14:26; 16:7). He speaks with the utmost confidence of the destruction of Jerusalem and his Parousia and of the happenings connected with these events (see Matthew 24; Mark 13; Luke 21). He speaks with authority about the judgment and the life to come (e.g. the parables of the Wheat and Tares, of the Sheep and the Goats, and of Dives and Lazarus). In the Q saying of Matthew 11:27 and Luke 10:22 he claims, and claims for himself alone, the power to reveal the Father to men. Stanley Leathes[3] lists nearly 150 references in the Synoptic Gospels alone (more than 200 if the Fourth Gospel is added) in which Christ, either explicitly or by implication, claims supernatural knowledge. But did he claim that his teaching was entirely unvitiated by human error?

---

[2] J. R. W. Stott, in *Guidelines*, ed. J. I. Packer (London, 1967), p. 44.
[3] S. Leathes, *The Law in the Prophets* (London, 1891), pp. 244–259.

DID HE CLAIM COMPLETE TRUTH FOR HIS TEACHING?

The Synoptic Gospels

We find nine Synoptic references (or groups of references) to this matter, well distributed through the various strata.

1. There is the saying recorded in all three Synoptic Gospels : 'Heaven and earth will pass away, but my words will not pass away' (Mt. 24:35; Mk. 13:31; Lk. 21:33). The second part of the statement (as the RV 'shall in no wise pass away' rightly indicates) is emphatic, making the whole saying almost as strong as one could conceive : 'Heaven and earth – the most durable things of time – will pass away, but my words – the eternal truth of God – will never pass away.' It is followed in Mark by the saying about our Lord's ignorance of the time of his advent; and the one intensifies the other by contrast. It is a strange and unexpected thing that *even the Son* should not know about this matter. His teaching was always with complete assurance and commanding authority and often he had shown knowledge of the future, but here is something hidden from him. It heightens the implicit authority of all his other unqualified statements. This is latent in 'not even ... the Son'; but, as if to avoid all misunderstanding, the saying is prefaced by an express statement of the eternal truth of his words : 'Heaven and earth shall pass away, but my words shall in no wise pass away.'

2. In the Sermon on the Mount there are repeated statements introduced by 'But I say to you ...'.[4] It is against the background of his statement 'not an iota, not a dot, will pass from the law' (Mt. 5:18) that we have to understand these sayings. He consistently treats the Scriptures as though their words were the very words of God; yet, despite this, his words carry all the authority of God's words so that he can interpret or even revoke the Old Testament law. He delivered this teaching in his own right. There is none of the Pentateuchal 'The Lord spoke to ...', or the prophetic 'Thus says the Lord'; he simply says, 'I say to you'. To a Jewish audience, the implication was clear : he was either speaking as God or he was blaspheming.

3. The above usage highlights the force of one of our Lord's

---

4 He uses almost the same expression in Mt. 19:9.

favourite expressions : 'Amen', *i.e.* 'truly I say to you', found
thirty-one times in Matthew, thirteen times in Mark, and six
times in Luke. ('Truly, truly, I say to you' is found twenty-five
times in John.) The introductory 'Amen' solemnly attests the
truth of what is about to be said.

4. In the Q passage which forms the conclusion and climax
to the Sermon on the Mount, Jesus has been speaking of the
issues of the final judgment, of those who would and of those who
would not enter into the kingdom of heaven. He concludes with
a striking simile in which he shows that a man's very destiny is
governed by his attitude to Christ's words : 'Every one then
who hears these words of mine and does them will be like a wise
man who built his house upon the rock ... And every one who
hears these words of mine and does not do them will be like a
foolish man who built his house upon the sand' (Mt. 7:24–26;
cf. Lk. 6:46–49). To accept and obey Christ's words is to build
on a rock which cannot be shaken either in this age or the age
to come.

5. Similarly, at Mark 8:38 (paralleled by Lk. 9:26) he says :
'Whoever is ashamed of me *and of my words* in this adulterous
and sinful generation, of him will the Son of man also be
ashamed, when he comes in the glory of his Father.'

6. Another passage, bringing out the tremendous issues involved in the hearer's manner of response to our Lord's teaching, is the interpretation of the parable of the Sower, recorded
by all three Evangelists (Mk. 4:3–20; *cf.* Mt. 13:3–23; Lk.
8:5–15). He explains : 'The sower sows the word ... Satan immediately comes and takes away the word ... persecution arises
on account of the word ... the delight in riches, and the desire
for other things, enter in and choke the word ... those that were
sown upon the good soil ... hear the word and accept it.' 'The
word' is clearly the message he has been proclaiming to them.
His teaching is God's Word and thus carries with it the alternative of life or judgment.

7. In Matthew the interpretation of this parable is prefaced
by a short Q section which reinforces the testimony to the significance of his words : 'Blessed are your eyes, for they see, and
your ears, for they hear. Truly, I say to you, many prophets and
righteous men longed to see what you see, and did not see it,

and to hear what you hear, and did not hear it' (Mt. 13:16f.;
cf. Lk. 10:23f).

8. Immediately preceding Luke's version of this saying is the
Q passage in which our Lord gives thanks for the concealment
of truth from the wise and understanding and his revelation to
babes (Mt. 11:25–27; Lk. 10:21f.). He says, 'All things have
been delivered to me by my Father', and he claims a special
relation between the Father and the Son, 'No one knows the
Son except the Father, and no one knows the Father except the
Son,' and he claims that to himself alone is given the right of
choosing to whom the Father shall be revealed.

9. This saying in turn points ahead to the last words of the
risen Lord recorded by Matthew : 'All authority in heaven
and on earth has been given to me. Go therefore and make
disciples of all nations, baptizing them in the name of the Father
and of the Son and of the Holy Spirit, teaching them to observe all that I have commanded you; and lo, I am with you
always, to the close of the age' (Mt. 28:18–20). As in the former
passage, Jesus here clearly claims his place within the Deity,
and his place as Mediator in subordination to the Father. The
immediate focus of interest is the veracity of his teaching and
the authority of his commandments, but this is set in the context of his vicegerency over all creation.

John's Gospel

John's Gospel reinforces the Synoptic teaching with great in-
sistence, emphasizing two main points : his teaching and his
words are the teaching and words of God; and upon a man's
response to his word depends eternal life.

'Truly, truly, I say to you, he who hears my word and believes in him who sent me, has eternal life' (5:24f.). 'The words
that I have spoken to you are spirit and life' (6:63.) 'How is it
that this man has learning, when he has never studied? ... My
teaching is not mine, but his who sent me; if any man's will is to
do his will, he shall know whether the teaching is from God or
whether I am speaking on my own authority' (7:15–17). 'He
who sent me is true, and I declare to the world what I have
heard from him ... as the Father taught me' (8:26–28). 'I know
that you are descendants of Abraham; yet you seek to kill me,

because my word finds no place in you. I speak of what I have seen with my Father, and you do what you have heard from your father' (8:37, 38). 'But now you seek to kill me, a man who has told you the truth which I heard from God' (8:40). 'Why do you not understand what I say? It is because you cannot bear to hear my word. You are of your father the devil, and your will is to do your father's desires. He was a murderer from the beginning, and has nothing to do with the truth, because there is no truth in him. When he lies, he speaks according to his own nature, for he is a liar and the father of lies. But, because I tell you the truth, you do not believe me. Which of you convicts me of sin? If I tell the truth, why do you not believe me? He who is of God hears the words of God; the reason why you do not hear them is that you are not of God' (8:43–47). 'He who rejects me and does not receive my sayings has a judge; the word that I have spoken will be his judge on the last day. For I have not spoken on my own authority; the Father who sent me has himself given me commandment what to say and what to speak. And I know that his commandment is eternal life. What I say, therefore, I say as the Father has bidden me' (12:48–50). 'Do you not believe that I am in the Father and the Father in me? The words that I say to you I do not speak on my own authority; but the Father who dwells in me does his works' (14:10). 'You are already made clean by the word which I have spoken to you' (15:3). 'If you abide in me, and my words abide in you, ask whatever you will, and it shall be done for you' (15:7). 'For all that I have heard from my Father I have made known to you' (15:15). 'For I have given them the words which thou gavest me' (17:8). 'For this I have come into the world, to bear witness to the truth. Every one who is of the truth hears my voice' (18:37).

HIS AUTHORITY OF MANNER

Besides the direct statements of Jesus we need also to add the evidence of his whole manner and attitude. Our Gospel-writers are all impressed by the sense of authority with which he spoke, which made a deep impression on the crowd. It is true that any great teacher will speak with authority, but the authority of Jesus is quite peculiarly unqualified. The greatest human teacher is humbly conscious of his own fallibility and ignorance; at times his statements are tentative, his predictions are always cautious, and (if he is really great) he will at times confess his errors. But with Jesus there is no trace of this. His statements are never tentative; his predictions are made with unqualified confidence; there is no sign of the slightest confession of error in anything he taught. Without qualification his teaching is the teaching of God.

N. B. Stonehouse, writing about the First Gospel, accurately summarizes the outlook of all the Gospels in reference to our Lord's teaching authority, and then goes a stage further: 'Matthew presents Christ as constituting a new authority alongside that of the Old Testament. While he affirms the revelation of the law and the prophets, and is even subservient to it, yet paradoxically his own authority is not derived from the revelation that had gone before, and even completes and transcends it. As not derived from the Old Testament or from any other extraneous source, his authority is seen to inhere in his own person, that is, in his sheer right, simply because of who and what he is, to speak as he spoke. Consequently, one may not isolate his teaching from his person. The former cannot be affirmed without the latter. Consequently, not his words only but his person and life also come as a new revelation ... to fail to comprehend him as constituting a divine disclosure is to fail utterly to understand him at all.'[5]

MORE THAN A PROPHET

Jesus is the Prophet *par excellence*. But he is infinitely more than a prophet. John the Baptist indeed was more than a prophet (Mt. 11 :9; Lk. 7 :26). Yet he was the slave who was unworthy to carry his master's sandals. He was simply a voice to proclaim the Coming One. Jesus, however, unlike the prophets who pointed away from themselves, called men to himself, demanding of them a religious devotion to his own person. Where the prophets would have said, 'Let us return to the Lord our God', Jesus said, 'Come to me ... I will give you rest. Take my yoke upon you, and learn from me' (Mt. 11 :28f.). 'I am the

[5] N. B. Stonehouse, *The Witness of Matthew and Mark to Christ*, 2nd ed. (London, 1959), pp. 210f.

bread of life; he who comes to me shall not hunger ... All that
the Father gives me will come to me; and him who comes to me
I will not cast out. For I have come down from heaven ... and
I will raise him up at the last day' (Jn. 6:35–40). 'Follow me
and I will make you become fishers of men' (Mk. 1:17). 'Blessed
are you when men revile you ... on my account ... your reward
is great in heaven' (Mt. 5:11f.). 'Every one who acknowledges
me before men, I also will acknowledge before my Father who
is in heaven; but whoever denies me before men, I also will
deny before my Father who is in heaven ... I have come to set
a man against his father ... He who loves father or mother
more than me is not worthy of me ... he who does not take his
cross and follow me is not worthy of me ... he who loses his
life for my sake will find it' (Mt. 10:32–39; cf. Mk. 8:34–38;
Lk. 9:23–26; 12:8f.; 14:26–33). Stretching out his hand toward
his disciples, he said, 'Here are my mother and my brothers!'
(Mt. 12:49; cf. Mk. 3:34; Lk. 8:21). 'She has done a beautiful
thing to me ... wherever the gospel is preached in the whole
world, what she has done will be told in memory of her'
(Mk. 14:6–9). I am the bread of life, which came down from
heaven, the living bread; the light of the world; the door of the
sheep, the good shepherd; the resurrection and the life; the
way, and the truth, and the life; the true vine; the Christ, the
Son of the Blessed (see Jn. 6:35–51; 8:12; 10:7–14; 11:25;
14:6; 15:1; Mk. 14:61f.). 'This cup is the new covenant in my
blood' (1 Cor. 11:25). 'Where two or three are gathered in my
name, there am I in the midst of them' (Mt. 18:20).

THE MESSIAH KING

Jesus showed himself the Prophet *par excellence* by his words
and the King *par excellence* by his deeds. His mighty works, as
he told the synagogue at Nazareth and the messengers of John,
were Messianic signs (Lk. 4:18ff.; Mt. 11:2ff.). The Messiah of
contemporary Jewish expectation was one who had a special
relationship to God, who would usher in the end of the age and
establish the kingdom of God; his deeds would be the deeds
of God himself. This was further currently interpreted as
meaning the overthrow of the hated Romans and the establishment of a great Jewish empire. Jesus accepted the first part

of this equation, and extended it to its utmost limits, but the second part he totally rejected. The Messiah King was both Lord and God, in spite of the fact that he was lowly and rejected, the Suffering Servant. By word and deed he showed himself Lord over wind and wave, over beast and tree, over food and drink, over sickness and death, over demons and Devil. He read the hearts of men (Jn. 2:25).

He accepted the title Lord : 'You call me Teacher and Lord; and you are right, for so I am ... he who receives me receives him who sent me' (Jn. 13:13–20). The sincerity of the use of this term 'Lord' will determine a man's destiny on the day of judgment (Mt. 7:21–23; Lk. 6:46–49). He was 'Lord of the Sabbath' (Mk. 2:28; Lk. 6:5). Jesus incurred the charge of blasphemy for forgiving sins (Mt. 9:1–8; Mk. 2:1–12; Lk. 5:17–26). Nine times it is recorded that he allowed men to worship him unrebuked [6] (Mt. 8:2; 9:18; 14:33; 15:25; 20:20; 28 :9,17;Mk.5 :6;Jn. 9 :38). He described himself as the ladder between earth and heaven (Jn. 1:51). He spoke of himself as Saviour – Saviour of the lost (Lk. 19:10; Jn. 10:9), Saviour of the world (Jn. 12:47). He spoke of his coming on the clouds with the angels, with power and great glory, 'as the lightning flashes and lights up the sky from one side to the other', causing the tribes of the earth to mourn – again incurring the charge of blasphemy (Mt. 16:27; 24:30; 25:31; 26:64; Mk. 13:26; 14:62; Lk. 17:24; 21:27; 22:69). His voice would raise the dead : 'All who are in the tombs will hear his voice and come forth, those who have done good, to the resurrection of life, and those who have done evil, to the resurrection of judgment' (Jn. 5:28f.). He was going to his Father's house to prepare a place for his disciples (Jn. 14:2). On the judgment day, he would be judge. 'The Son of man shall sit on his glorious throne ... judging' (Mt. 19:28). They must pray for strength 'to stand before the Son of man' (Lk. 21:36). As King he will say, 'Come, O blessed ... Depart from me, you cursed' (Mt. 25:31–46). 'The Son of man will send his angels, and they will gather out of his kingdom all causes of sin and all evildoers, and throw them into the furnace of fire' (Mt. 13:41f.).

6 Contrast Paul and Barnabas at Lystra (Acts 14:8–18) and John in the Apocalypse (Rev. 19:10; 22:8f.).

HIS DIVINITY

He spoke with great solemnity of himself as *eternally* pre-existent : 'Truly, truly, I say to you, before Abraham was, I *am*' (Jn. 8:58) – at which they tried to stone him. He was the Son of man who *came* to give his life (Mk. 10:45), who *came* to fulfil the law (Mt. 5:17). He used the language of an eye-witness when speaking of unseen realities : 'Truly, truly, I say to you, we speak of what we know, and bear witness to what we have seen . . . No one has ascended into heaven but he who des-cended from heaven, the Son of man' (Jn. 3:11–13). 'Glorify thou me in thy own presence with the glory which I had with thee before the world was made' (Jn. 17:5). God, heaven and the angels are a familiar environment to him. He spoke of him-self (using the definite article) as 'The Son of God' (Jn. 5:25; 11:4). (On a number of other occasions 'Son of God' is used (for grammatical reasons, without article), but the sense is equally definite. Noteworthy is the account of the temptation, which, if it is not pure invention, must have come from Jesus himself.)

Both John and the Synoptists stress that Jesus was crucified for affirming that he was the Son of God, and so equal with God (Jn. 5:18; 19:7; Mt. 26:63–68; Mk. 14:61–64; Lk. 22:70f.). Almost more significant than the designation 'the Son of God' is Jesus' use of the simple terms 'the Son' and 'the Father' found very frequently in John and on occasions in the Synoptists. The Son is clearly the Son of God the Father, but neither 'the Son' nor 'the Son of God' stands in contrast to 'the Son of man', a designation often used in contexts where his uniqueness and authority is emphasized. Within two consecu-tive sentences, Jesus uses all three terms (Jn. 5:25–27). He makes the significance of the terms 'the Son' and 'the Father' quite plain : 'I and the Father are one' (Jn. 10:30). 'He who has seen me has seen the Father ... I am in the Father and the Father in me' (Jn. 14:9f.). It is true that he never explicitly declared himself to be God, yet implicit in his words and deeds was an inescapable claim to deity. To him and to his hearers there was One God, Eternal, Creator, Revealer, Judge, Re-deemer, Saviour, Forgiver, who alone might be worshipped –

and Jesus was that One.[7] He accepted from Thomas the address : 'My Lord and my God !' (Jn. 20 :28). The claims that he made for the authority of his teaching were not simply the claims of a prophet of God to speak the words of God. His words were God's words, because he was God. 'I say to you' is final authority.

THE PARADOX

This is the testimony of the Gospels : God, yet man; infallible, yet limited in knowledge. Is not this a paradox too stark to be endured? Is it conceivable that a being could rightly claim so much and still be a true man? Is it not better to cut the knot and attribute his humanity to history and his divinity to the early church? There is of course an element of paradox in this combination of unqualified authority with some measure of ignorance. But there is an element of paradox in all that concerns the incarnation. Jesus 'weeps at the grave of the friend whom he raises; he sleeps in the storm, which by his power he stills; he in vain seeks figs on the tree, which he causes to wither at a word'.[8] There are, however, a number of considerations which ease the paradox.

  1. *There is a beautiful consistency about the paradox*. That the humanity of Christ is depicted in the Gospels as fully and clearly as his divinity needs no documentation. Jesus is seen as

[7] There are a number of passages in which it is probable that Jesus deliberately recalled and applied to himself passages in the OT which refer to Yahweh, *e.g.*: in Dn. 7:9 the Ancient of Days occupies the throne; in Mt. 19:28; 25:31ff. the Son of man is the King who occupies the throne. In Mal. 3:1 ; 4:5 the forerunner (=John the Baptist) is to prepare the way for the Lord (=Jesus) (Mt. 11:10,14; 17:11f.; Mk. 9:12f.; Lk. 7:27). The one who seeks and saves the lost is the Lord (Lk. 19:10; Ezk. 34:16,22). It is the Lord who sweeps away stumbling-blocks (Mt. 13:41; Zp. 3:1, Hebrew). See also Mt. 24:35; Mk. 13:31; Lk. 21:33; Is. 40:8. Mt. 21:16; Ps. 8:2. Lk. 10:19; Ps. 91:13. Lk. 20:18; Is. 8:14f. That Jesus the Son was distinct from the Father (and from the 'other Counsellor') is also presupposed and asserted with the utmost clarity. He was the Son come forth from the Holy Trinity into the world. It is one of the remarkable features of the NT that from beginning to end it is solidly Trinitarian. That this strange doctrine captured the mind of the whole church so completely cannot be explained except by the recognition that Jesus himself gave his disciples some such teaching as that recorded in John 14–16.
[8] J. J. van Oosterzee, *Christian Dogmatics* (London, 1900), p. 496.

the Last Adam, as Ideal Man in perfect communion with God.[9] God, on the one hand, is all powerful, all holy, all knowing; unable to fail, unable to sin, unable to err. Fallen man, on the other hand, fails, sins, errs. Ideal Man, however, could-but-does-not-fail, could-but-does-not-sin, could-but-does-not-err. Jesus tasted human weakness to the limit, but did not fail; experienced temptation at its fiercest, but did not sin; shared human ignorance to the full, but taught no error.

2. *There is a unity about the personality of the paradoxical Person.* His divinity and humanity are not depicted as incompatibles. The whole portrayal of Christ is of an entirely unified personality, and any attempt to eliminate the divine elements from it is to leave a Christ incredible as source and inspiration of the infant church.

3. *There is a rationale to the relation of the incarnate Son and the heavenly Father. It was a relation of subordination.* If Jesus was liable to fail, to sin, to err, why did he not do so? The answer lay in the voluntary surrender of his human nature to God, with the consequent unimpeded flow into his body, into his will and into his mind of all that the Father willed to impart. He claimed sinlessness, yet attributed all goodness to God (Jn. 8:46; Mk. 10:17f.; Lk. 18:18f.). He claimed freedom from error, yet attributed all truth to the Father. 'Truly, truly, I say to you, the Son can do nothing of his own accord, but only what he sees the Father doing; for whatever he does, that the Son does likewise ... I can do nothing on my own authority; as I hear, I judge; and my judgment is just, because I seek not my own will but the will of him who sent me' (Jn. 5:19, 30).

4. *The purpose of the incarnation is clearly defined: God became man, so that as Man he might save man.* The Son not only became man, accepting human limitations, but he also became Servant, setting aside his own will. He not only became Servant, he also accepted as his vocation death on the cross. Though his Messiahship and supernatural status are proclaimed from beginning to end of all the Gospels, they are partly veiled by his perfect humility. In the temptation he faced the issue as to how he was to use the powers which he knew to be latent within him as the Son of God. He determined to go the

[9] In what follows I am indebted to some notes by J. R. W. Stott.

way of entire subservience to the Father's will. G. Vos says : 'No array of explicit statements in which he acknowledges his acceptance of the Old Testament Scriptures as the word of God can equal in force this implied subordination of himself and of his work to the one great scheme of which the ancient revelation given to Israel formed the preparatory stage. Indeed in appropriating for himself the function of bringing the kingdom, in laying claim to the Messianic dignity, Jesus seized upon that in the Old Testament which enabled him at one stroke to make its whole historic movement converge upon and terminate in himself. Jesus knew himself as at once the goal of history and the servant of history.'[1]

The self-designation 'Son of man' which he chose for himself presumably recalled the transcendental figure 'like a son of man' of Daniel 7:13, to whom everlasting dominion was given. To his mind it was no doubt a Messianic title, but it suggested a kingdom which was not of this world. Jesus presented himself as Messiah, yet in such a way as to provoke expectation and questioning rather than immediate and outright acceptance or rejection.[2] But the title 'Son of man' was also peculiarly suitable for the Last Adam, who had come to die. Throughout his ministry Jesus was driven by a sense of the predestined necessity that he should suffer and die for the sins of men. This he revealed progressively as time went on. As early as the Sermon on the Mount he said, 'Blessed are you when men revile you and persecute you and utter all kinds of evil against you falsely on my account' (Mt. 5:11). He warned his disciples that identification with him meant a sharing in his sufferings. Then, after the disciples' belief in his Messiahship had become a settled conviction, he began to tell them repeatedly that he 'must' (not only suffer, but) die, giving his life a 'ransom for many' (Mt. 16:21; 20:28). Finally, on the night of his arrest he solemnly spoke of the new covenant established in his blood

---

[1] G. Vos, *The Teaching of Jesus concerning the Kingdom of God and the Church*, pp. 14f.

[2] He used the term Messiah (or Christ) privately to the Samaritan woman (Jn. 4:25f.), but he does not appear to have done so to the disciples until after Peter's confession at Caesarea Philippi (Mk. 8:29; 9:41), and he did not acknowledge the title publicly till he was challenged by Caiaphas on the eve of his crucifixion (Mk. 14:61f.).

for the remission of men's sins, and he instituted the Lord's Supper as a perpetual commemoration of his sacrificial death (Mt. 26:26–28; Mk. 14:22–24; Lk. 22:14–22; 1 Cor. 11:23–26). The first man's disobedience brought death to all his seed; by his death on the cross the Second Man's obedience brought life to all believers.

THE GROWTH OF OUR LORD'S SELF-CONSCIOUSNESS

It would ease the difficulty of belief in the incarnation if it were possible to conceive in some measure how a consciousness of divinity could develop in a human personality without destroying its humanity. The Gospels do not explain the process, they merely give glimpses of Christ's self-consciousness at different stages of its development. But some helpful suggestions have been made. E. Stauffer[3] recalls that Jewish tradition always maintained that Jesus was immorally born : 'In a Jewish genealogical table from the period before 70, Jesus appears as "the bastard of a wedded wife" ... The later rabbis, without further ado, call Jesus the son of the adulteress, the son of the prostitute ... Celsus's Jew knows as early as 160 all sorts of gossipy tales about Mary and the Roman legionary Panthera. Amongst the Samaritans and Mandaeans also, Jesus is designated offensively as the Son of Mary.' There is evidence that this belief goes right back into the time of our Lord's ministry. The innocent-sounding expression 'Son of Mary' is used in Mark 6:3, and Stauffer makes it clear that by it the Jews meant : 'Jesus is the son of Mary, and of Mary alone, not of Joseph.' And may not the scornful remark : '*We* were not born of fornication' (Jn. 8:41) be intended to carry a barbed innuendo? W. Childs Robinson[4] has suggested that this ugly tradition goes right back into the days of his childhood. We could picture the heart-broken boy coming home from school one day, asking his mother to deny the filthy lie about Joseph not being his father. Then she and Joseph tell him the truth. Perhaps they tell him only a little at first, but he learns that God, not Joseph, is his Father, and henceforth 'Abba, Father' becomes his mode of address in prayer. 'Abba' is on his lips at death as it was in his

---

[3] E. Stauffer, *Jesus and His Story* (London, 1960), pp. 24f.
[4] *Christianity Today*, 10 (May 13, 1966), p. 10.

first recorded words. At the age of twelve he gently rebukes them for not realizing that there is a necessity laid upon him to be 'in the things of my Father'. The sense of his predestined mission is already with him, and he understands it better than they. But he returns to Nazareth, submitting himself to their authority, and grows in wisdom and stature, and in favour with God and man (Lk. 2:41–52).

While always subservient to his Father's will, and sensitive to his parents' reserve, there seems no reason to doubt that his eager mind would have pieced together many of the wonderful circumstances said to have surrounded his birth; nor does there seem any reason to doubt that his parents would have told him everything in detail when they considered that the time had come when he should know. And what a tale they had to tell of his dignity and mission – unbearable to any lesser person than the lowly Emmanuel!

Witness to him came from Joseph and Mary, from shepherds and worshipping wise men, from Zechariah and Elizabeth, Simeon and Anna, from angelic visits and repeated dreams; it came in the awe of a priest struck dumb in the Holy Place in Jerusalem, and in the terror of the butchered infants in the city of David; in the fulfilment of prophecy both through humble god-fearing Israelites and through the ungodly king and the pagan emperor; in the wonder of John's birth to aged parents and in the miracle of Christ's conception by the Holy Spirit. During those unforgettable months during the reign of Caesar Augustus, the veil which divided earth and heaven seemed to be drawn aside and God 'visited his people'. The Holy Spirit came upon one and another to bear their witness to what God was doing; and the Holy Spirit came upon Mary, and the power of the Most High overshadowed her in the birth of her holy child, 'the Son of God'.

Words were heaped upon words to indicate the dignity and the glory of his work. 'He will be great, and will be called the Son of the Most High' (his unique Sonship); 'and the Lord God will give to him the throne of his father David' (his Messiahship), 'and he will reign over the house of Jacob for ever; and of his kingdom there will be no end' (his eternal Dominion) (Lk. 1:32f.). Elizabeth, filled with the Holy Spirit, called Mary 'the mother of my Lord' (Lk. 1:43). John was to go before Jesus 'to make ready *for the Lord* a people prepared' (Lk. 1:17). He was to be 'ruler', 'King of the Jews', 'Christ the Lord', 'Saviour', 'a light for revelation to the Gentiles, and for glory to thy people Israel'. He was to bring 'mercy', 'redemption', 'salvation', 'forgiveness of sins', 'good news of a great joy'; he was to fulfil the words of the prophets and implement the covenant promises to Abraham and his posterity for ever.

God had visited his people. For a short time only the veil was drawn aside; the angels ascended and descended; a glimpse was caught of the glory of God and his celestial hosts; then the veil was drawn back, and there was silence. But Mary kept all these things, pondering them in her heart. When the time came for his parents to tell Jesus, he must have drunk in every syllable they told him – including the fact that he was to be a sign spoken against and that his mother's soul was to be pierced through. These tremendous things established themselves in his maturing mind. With this knowledge as his guide to the study of the holy Scriptures and with his own deep communion with God (certainly no less wonderful than that of a Paul who was caught up to the third heaven and 'heard things that cannot be told', 2 Cor. 12:4), Jesus bided his Father's time in Nazareth. Scripture dominated his mind. It was not the idea of Davidic kingship, which formed the mainstream of Old Testament prophecy (Is. 9:1; Mi. 5; Je. 23:5f., *etc.*) and which dominated popular expectation, that rivetted itself upon him. It was the Suffering Servant of Isaiah 52:13 – 53:12[5] and the smitten Shepherd-King of Zechariah 10–14 that showed him his vocation. His kingship was to be lowly (Zc. 9:9f.). The Son of man must first suffer for men's sins, before being vindicated in accordance with Daniel 7 and Psalm 110. His ministry would inaugurate the kingdom of God and usher in the last days. The last days would be consummated when God's age-long purposes for Jew and Gentile were complete and the last judgment over. When the moment came for his ministry to begin, he knew who he was, what his task was

[5] That Jesus saw himself as the Suffering Servant of Isaiah has been contested in modern times, notably by M. D. Hooker, *Jesus and the Servant* (London, 1959). A defence will be found in R. T. France, *Jesus and the Old Testament* (London, 1971), pp. 110–132.

and what were the limitations of his human nature. With this authority he summoned his hearers to obedience to his word; with this authority he authenticated the Old Testament.

OBJECTIONS
TO THE
CLAIMS OF
JESUS

3

ERRORS OF CONDITIONING

The falsity of the general objection that an incarnation must be conditioned by the errors of the age should by now be clear. It is indeed hard to conceive that a true incarnation could have taken place, say, amongst the Greeks without the child growing up with Greek beliefs, or amongst the Hindus without him becoming a Hindu. But of course the whole Bible presupposes that the *milieu* of the incarnation was not arbitrary. Israel was chosen and trained for many centuries through direct revelation in preparation for the Messiah. Though all Christ's contemporaries to some extent misrepresented the Scriptures, the Scriptures themselves were God-given and perspicuously clear in their message to one who was pure in heart. They provided a conditioning in the truth. To this extent our Lord was a child of his age. But in his power to detect and reject the errors of his contemporaries and in his own unique understanding of Scripture, he transcended his age. To Jesus these very Scriptures provided the key to the understanding of his own role: the Old Testament revelation was consummated by him, the Old Testament prophecies were fulfilled in him, and the mighty works of the Messiah were wrought through him. The incarnation took place at God's time and in God's place according to his predetermined plan.

IGNORANCE OF SCIENTIFIC THOUGHT:
RIGHT ON RELIGION, WRONG ON FACT?

Jesus' 'universe of discourse' was first-century Jewish piety and not post-Enlightenment thought. He seemed totally unaware of the mass of alleged contradictions discovered by modern 'scientific' historical criticism, and even of the supposed horrors of Old Testament morals, and he is thought to have made statements of fact about the Old Testament which are now known to be untrue. This poignantly illustrates the kenotic dilemma. Jesus had an Old Testament, which he knew to have been copied by fallible hands, which had in it, plainly for all to read, the same apparent inconsistencies that we see today, and which had the same moral difficulties as our present Old Testament. If his divine nature influenced his human nature so little that he accepted without more than ordinary scrutiny the ideas prevailing around him, is it possible to regard him as having even a unique moral sense, let alone a unique intelligence, seeing he regarded the whole Old Testament as inspired? It is doubtful whether we have any right to call him the best of men, let alone the perfect Man. C. J. Cadoux penetratingly says: 'Of those Christians who see that the intellectual infallibility of Jesus cannot be maintained, many try to guard themselves by urging that the limitations of his knowledge affected only those matters which are of no moral or religious importance. The supposition is arbitrary. For the limitations in question arose from the impression made upon his thoughts by the teaching to which as a Jewish boy he had been subjected. That teaching clearly embodies ideas about the character of God as well as beliefs concerning the authorship of the Pentateuch and the Psalms and concerning the life after death.'[1]

There is no trace in the teaching of Jesus of a dichotomy between the non-moral world of fact, concerning which he was fallible, and the world of religious experience, concerning which he was infallible. This dichotomy of thought, which goes right back to the medieval disjunction of natural and revealed theology, is (as F. A. Schaeffer is never tired of proclaiming) quite unbiblical. The world of science and history is as truly God's world as the world of religious experience, and is the very medium of revelation. There is no reason to think that the Father allowed Jesus to go wrong in the one sphere, but kept him right in the other. Indeed, the difficulties in the sphere of morals are far weightier than those in the sphere of history.

[1] C. J. Cadoux, *The Historic Mission of Jesus* (London, 1941), p. 343.

Whether in fact modern thought shows a better understanding than he of the problems of Old Testament criticism and of Old Testament morality is to be explored in later volumes.

DEMONOLOGY

The twentieth century pooh-poohs his belief in Satan, in angels and in demons. But not on rational grounds. There is no rational ground for believing that man is the only spiritual entity in God's world. There is nothing intrinsically unreasonable in a belief in mighty forces of spiritual evil as 'world rulers of this present darkness', led by 'the ruler of this world' (Eph. 6:12; Jn. 14:30; Mt. 4:8), who had power to give our Lord 'all the kingdoms of the world'. The world is piled high with insoluble problems which ensure some unhappiness to all and almost unending misery to millions. The whole system looks diabolically efficient. Whether we think this is simply man's inhumanity to man, or something more, will depend on the view we take of the authority of Christ's belief and teaching. So with belief in angels. If he believed in them, we shall have no hesitation in accepting other sober records in the Bible of heavenly messengers. So with demons. It is quite clear that hallucinations about devil-possession are a frequent feature of mental illness, but that all such beliefs (including our Lord's) have been hallucinations is no more than an *a priori* judgment.

THE TIME OF THE SECOND COMING

Jesus is said to have misled the early church into believing in his near return. There is a twofold strain in the New Testament, on the one hand urging expectant watchfulness and on the other warning against disheartenment over apparent delay. This double element goes back to the teaching attributed to our Lord in the Gospels. There are such sayings as 'The kingdom of God is at hand' (Mk. 1:15); 'You will not have gone through all the towns of Israel, before the Son of man comes' (Mt. 10:23); 'there are some standing here who will not taste death before they see the kingdom of God' (Lk. 9:27). And also, 'The bridegroom was delayed'; 'after a long time the master comes' (Mt. 25:5, 19; *cf.* Lk. 12:45); 'the end is not yet . . . all this is but the beginning of the sufferings . . . this gospel of the kingdom will be

preached throughout the whole world, as a testimony to all
nations; and then the end will come' (Mt. 24:3–14); 'Jerusalem
will be trodden down by the Gentiles, until the times of the
Gentiles are fulfilled' (Lk. 21:24).

It would take us too far afield to discuss the coming of the
kingdom in detail. Suffice it to say that the key which produces
order out of the apparently discordant references is the recognition that the manifestation of the kingdom has many stages
including our Lord's baptism, transfiguration, crucifixion, resurrection and ascension, Pentecost, the destruction of Jerusalem
and the Parousia. The transfiguration, ascension, giving of the
Spirit and the destruction of Jerusalem, with their themes of
glory, kingship, power and judgment, have rightly been described as 'proleptic elements of the Last Day'.

'This generation will not pass'

The focus of acutest difficulty is the long Mount of Olives discourse (Mt. 24; 25; Mk. 13; Lk. 21), given on the Tuesday
before Christ's death, in which our Lord says, 'Truly, I say to
you, this generation will not pass away till all these things take
place.' The wider content of the discussion includes a warning
to the Jewish people of fearful judgment. The ministry began
with the Baptist's call to repentance: ' "You brood of vipers!
Who warned you to flee from the wrath to come? . . . do not
presume to say to yourselves, 'We have Abraham as our father'
. . . Even now the axe is laid to the root of the trees; every tree
therefore that does not bear good fruit is cut down and thrown
into the fire" ' (Mt. 3:7–10). During the final week in Jerusalem
the doom of the nation is pronounced in absolute terms: 'The
tax collectors and the harlots go into the kingdom of God before
you. For John came to you in the way of righteousness, and you
did not believe him . . . Therefore I tell you, the kingdom of
God will be taken away from you and given to a nation pro-
ducing the fruits of it' (Mt. 21:31–43). Those who kill the Son
deserve a miserable death. A great crisis is predicted within the
lifetime of some of those present: 'There are some standing here
who will not taste death before they see the Son of man coming
in his kingdom' (Mt. 16:28); 'Daughters of Jerusalem . . . weep
for yourselves and your children. For behold, the days are com-

ing when . . . they will begin to say to the mountains, "Fall on us" ' (Lk. 23:28–30).

In the immediate context is a chapter of terrible denunciations, leading up to: 'You serpents, you brood of vipers, how are you to escape being sentenced to hell? Therefore I send you prophets and wise men and scribes, some of whom you will kill and crucify, and some you will scourge in your synagogues and persecute from town to town, that upon you may come all the righteous blood shed on earth, from the blood of innocent Abel to the blood of Zechariah the son of Barachiah, whom you murdered between the sanctuary and the altar. Truly, I say to you, all this will come upon this generation. O Jerusalem, Jerusalem, killing the prophets and stoning those who are sent to you! How often would I have gathered your children together as a hen gathers her brood under her wings, and you would not! Behold, your house is forsaken and desolate' (Mt. 23:33–38). Upon that particular generation was to fall the judgment for the piled-up guilt of the nation's age-long rejection of God. The Temple, which had been the dwelling-place of the Lord, was to be forsaken by God – no longer '*my* house' (Mt. 21:13), but '*your* house'. Thus was declared the judicial rejection of Jewry as the people of God. Such rejection was almost unthinkable to the disciples. Was not the Temple to be the glory and beauty of the earth in the days of the Messiah and would it not stand till the end of time? (*Cf.* 1 Ki. 9:3; 2 Ch. 7:16.) 'The destruction of the Temple was for them the end of the world.'[2] Christ had already spoken often about the Coming of the Son of man, including a lengthy discourse during the final journey to Jerusalem (Lk. 17:11–37), but now he added this shocking further prediction. The disciples ask for clarification. There are two possible ways of understanding his reply which make coherent sense of the discourse.[3]

---

[2] J. M. Kik, *Matthew Twenty-Four* (Swengel, Pa., USA, 1948), p. 28.
[3] There have of course been many other, less satisfactory, interpretations of this passage. These are discussed by G. R. Beasley-Murray, *Jesus and the Future* (London, 1954) and *A Commentary on Mark Thirteen* (London, 1957); A. L. Moore, *The Parousia in the New Testament* (Leiden, 1966); R. T. France, *Jesus and the Old Testament* (London, 1971). Kik's book, mentioned in the previous footnote, though a popular exposition, is argued exceptionally clearly.

Interpretation A

The disciples asked (or thought they asked) two questions: 'When will these things be, and what will be the sign of your coming?' But there were really four questions:

1. *What will be the sign that the destruction of the Temple is near?* Answer: It will not be for some time. There is to be much trouble and a world-wide preaching of the gospel first (*cf.* Acts 2:5; Rom. 1:5, 8; Col. 1:6). When 'the abomination of desolation' (Matthew and Mark) spoken of by Daniel stands 'in holy place' (Matthew), or when Jerusalem begins to be encircled by armies (Luke), that will be the sign for those in Judea to flee.[4] There will be great tribulation; there will be no Parousia; Jerusalem will be like a rotting carcase set upon by vultures (Mt. 24:4–28; Mk. 13:5–23; Lk. 21:8–24a).

2. *What will be the sign of the coming?* Answer: After its fall Jerusalem will be trodden underfoot until the 'times of the Gentiles' have been fulfilled, and there will be portents in the heavens and distress on earth. But the coming itself will be unheralded and unmistakable, like lightning, for all to see (Mt. 24:29–31; Mk. 13:24–27; Lk. 21:24b–27).

3. *When will the destruction be?* Answer: They are to pay careful attention to 'all these things' which he has spelt out in detail, knowing that their ultimate deliverance is steadily draw-

---

[4] Dn. 9:27; 11:31; 12:11. The cryptic reference to the desolating sacrilege standing 'in holy place' cannot mean literally an entering of the Temple or city by the Romans, as this would be too late as a warning to those in Judea, though it would adequately represent the Jewish sense of horror towards the Roman ensigns as described by Josephus (*Antiquities* xviii.3). Luke's more straightforward description of the encircling armies might conceivably be understood of the invasion of the holy *land*, but this is not how a reader of the book of Daniel would naturally take it. R. T. France (following M.-J. Lagrange, *Matthieu*, Paris, 1923, pp. 461f.) thinks that the profanation of the Temple by the Zealots as described by Josephus (*Wars* iv.3) fits the prediction best. In the winter of AD 67/68, as Roman pressure against the Jewish rebels was increasing, Zealots took control of the city, set up their headquarters in the Holy Place and held a mock ceremony to instal a bumpkin as High Priest. Carnage followed and the holy city was defiled with blood. The approach of the Roman armies tallies with Luke, and the desecration of the Holy Place tallies with Matthew (and Mark). Either of these would have provided an adequate warning to the Christians that it was time to flee. (See *Jesus and the Old Testament*, p. 72 n. 102.)

ing nearer. He solemnly assures them that they will take place
before the present generation has passed away (Mt. 24:32–35;
Mk. 13:28–31; Lk. 21:28–33).

4. *When will the coming be?* Answer: Of 'that day' no-one
knows except the Father. It may seem to be a very long time.
They must watch (Mt. 24:36 – 25:46; Mk. 13:32–37; Lk.
21:34–36).

The greatest difficulty in this interpretation is Matthew's
'*Immediately* after the tribulation of those days . . . *then* will
appear . . .' (24:29, 30) which seems to hold closely together in
time the city's destruction and the 'coming' of the Son of man.
Both 'immediately' and 'then', however, are often used with
very little force,[5] and it seems feasible to interpret the passage of
the whole period from AD 70 to the end. It would indicate that
without any break troubled times will continue till that moment
when the sign of the Son of man appears.

Interpretation B

A bolder, and at first sight more difficult, solution has been
adopted by J. M. Kik, R. T. France, and others. It differs only
in its interpretation of Section 3. It sees the *whole* of Matthew
24:4–35 as referring to the destruction of the Temple and the
divine rejection of the Jewish nation, and the whole of Matthew
24:36 – 25:46 as referring to the last judgment. In the former
come verses 29–31 : 'Immediately after the tribulation of those
days the sun will be darkened, and the moon will not give its
light, and the stars will fall from heaven, and the powers of the
heavens will be shaken; then will appear the sign of the Son of
man in heaven, and then all the tribes of the earth will mourn,
and they will see the Son of man coming on the clouds of heaven
with power and great glory; and he will send out his angels with
a loud trumpet call, and they will gather his elect from the four
winds, from one end of heaven to the other.'

At first sight it seems obvious that the shaking of the heavens,
the mourning of the tribes, the coming of the Son of man, the
sending out of the angels, the trumpet call and the gathering in

---

[5] The weak 'then' is very common in Matthew, but the weak 'immediately' is a characteristically Marcan, rather than Matthean, use.

of the elect all refer to the final coming of Christ. Interpretation B, however, takes the passage somewhat as follows: The 'tribes of the land' (echoing Zc. 12:12) are the tribes of Israel. 'The Son of man coming' (which does not use the special word Parousia, but a common participle) refers to his coming in judgment to Israel. The 'sending out' is of 'messengers' of the gospel to gather in the elect, and refers to the accelerated evangelization of the Gentile world which followed the church's decisive break with Judaism.

The detailed arguing of this case (with all its implications for the interpretation of other parts of the New Testament) must be left to the specialists, but the following points may be made.

Sun, moon and stars: the passing of the old order

The language of sun and moon darkened and stars falling from heaven may seem extravagant for the destruction of Jerusalem, but it was in fact an event of cosmic importance. The history of redemption consists of two dispensations – the old dispensation during which Israel was God's chosen people and the new dispensation during which God's chosen people were drawn from all nations. The end of one dispensation overlapped with the beginning of the other. The beginning of the end of the old dispensation was proclaimed by John the Baptist and the final end of the old dispensation was proclaimed by God in the sweeping away of Jerusalem. It is difficult to exaggerate the significance of this event. Furthermore, it is difficult to exaggerate the horror of Jerusalem's end. Judging by the description of Josephus,[6] the language is not extravagant. Our Lord's prophecy may be taken literally, it was 'great tribulation, such as has not been from the beginning of the world until now, no, and never will be'. Further, the language here used is almost precisely that of the prophets when they speak of temporal judgments on heathen nations, such as Babylon, Idumea and Egypt. If it was suitable for them, it was suitable for the far more significant judgment upon Jerusalem. Furthermore, Peter (quoting Joel) can use the same sort of language with reference to Pentecost.[7]

6 *Wars*, Books 5 and 6.
7 Is. 13:10; 34:4f.; Ezk. 32:7f.; Joel 2:28–32; Acts 2:16–21.

The pouring out of the Spirit and the turning of the sun to darkness and the moon to blood, which Joel speaks of as a prelude to the day of the Lord, are (he says) being fulfilled. The new order is being ushered in with power, the old order is passing away under judgment. This figurative language is suitable to Pentecost and other great acts of God and not only for the day of judgment.

Clouds

The original description of Daniel, 'with the clouds of heaven there came one like a son of man', concerns an action in heaven. Dominion is taken from the rulers of earth and is given to the Messiah and to the saints of the Most High (Dn. 7:13, 14, 18). It is thus a suitable figure for the destruction of Jerusalem[8] — the final act in which God showed his rejection of the nation which rejected the Messiah and in which he finally and exclusively identified the disciples of Jesus as his chosen people. This final act was, however, the culmination of a process. The saying of Jesus to Caiaphas, addressed in the plural to all those present,

---

[8] God's judgment upon Egypt, which was plainly no literal, visible 'coming', is described in these terms in Is. 19:1: 'The Lord is riding on a swift cloud and comes to Egypt.' Then follows a particularized account of the political and social woes which are to come on the land. *Cf.* Ps. 97:2, 3. The cloud image is not intended to be a very precise one — 'cloud' or 'clouds'; 'in', 'with' or 'on' are used interchangeably. 'A bright cloud overshadowed them' (Mt. 17:5) in the Mount of Transfiguration when the Father declared the Sonship of Jesus. Having declared 'All authority in heaven and on earth has been given to me' (Mt. 28:18), Jesus 'was lifted up, and a cloud took him out of their sight' (Acts 1:9). At the Parousia (according to 1 Thes. 4:15–17) the Lord will come down from heaven (it does not say 'to the earth') and the saints will be caught up 'in the clouds . . . in the air'. The wording of Acts 1:11 (RV): 'in like manner' could suggest a return to earth in a cloud, but the language is far too imprecise to require it. Rev. 14:14–16 with 'one like a son of man . . . who sat upon the cloud' and 'swung his sickle on the earth' is imagery which does not lend itself to prosaically literal interpretation. Rev. 1:7 alone takes up the language of Mt. 24:30 to apply it (apparently) to the final coming: 'he is coming with the clouds, and every eye will see him . . . and all tribes of the earth will wail on account of him.' If by any chance the Apocalypse is of Neronian date, prior to the destruction of Jerusalem, this need not refer specifically to the Parousia. The language of Mt. 24:30 is thus suitable either for the Parousia or for other great acts of God.

'You will see[9] the Son of man seated at the right hand of Power, and coming on the clouds of heaven' (Mt. 26:64) is prefaced by the words 'From now on' (Lk. 22:69). The passion and crucifixion (with the rending of the curtain which hid the Holy of Holies), the stoning of Stephen (which caused the scattering of the gospel-preaching church) and the destruction of Jerusalem were stages by which the old order was judged and the new ushered in.

The trumpet and the angels

Although the blowing of the trumpet is used of the Parousia,[1] it is also used more generally for the proclamation of good news. For instance, the year of jubilee, which meant freedom for the slaves, was announced by trumpet blast.[2] Although angels are to be present at the Parousia, the primary meaning of $\ddot{\alpha}\gamma\gamma\varepsilon\lambda o\varsigma$ is 'messenger' and need not refer to supernatural beings.[3] The messengers of the gospel gather the elect from the four winds, so that they 'come from east and west, and from north and south, and sit at table in the kingdom of God' (Lk. 13:29). Quite the reverse of the destruction of Jerusalem being an unmitigated disaster, it is the herald of summer (Mt. 24:32f.) – of a great response to the gospel in the Gentile world.

If this can be accepted, the whole passage has a wonderfully clear structure. Matthew 24:4–35 (apart from an incidental reference in verse 27) is concerned solely with the destruction of Jerusalem. It is precise about the events, the timing and the sign and it gives instructions sufficient to make possible the Christians' escape. 'All these things' will take place before 'this generation' passes away. Matthew 24:36 – 25:46 is concerned solely

[9] 'See' in Greek, as in English, need not refer to a particular sense perception; it can apply to a progressive experience. 'They will see for themselves that their time of power is finished' (R. T. France, *Jesus and the Old Testament*, p. 236). 'The coming of the Son of Man on the clouds of heaven was never conceived as a primitive form of space travel, but as a symbol for a mighty reversal of fortunes within history and at a national level' (G. B. Caird, *Jesus and the Jewish Nation*, London, 1965, p. 20).
[1] 1 Cor. 15:52; 1 Thes. 4:16.
[2] Lv. 25:9f. 'To preach good news' is 'to proclaim release to the captives . . . the acceptable year of the Lord' (Lk. 4:18f.=Is. 61:1f.).
[3] Lk. 9:52; 7:24; Jas. 2:25. Of John the Baptist: Mt. 11:10; Mk. 1:2; Lk. 7:27.

with the end. Of 'that day' there will be no signs (a thief gives no
sign) – people will be leading normal lives. Of its timing, no
indication is given, except that it may be a long time and that
'Jerusalem will be trodden down by the Gentiles, until the times
of the Gentiles are fulfilled' (Lk. 21:24).

The 'any moment' myth

On neither of the two suggested interpretations does Jesus teach
the end of the world within the lifetime of some of his hearers.
Indeed, it seems to be a modern myth to suggest that it was
believed 'that the Lord would return at any moment to bring in
the Kingdom, and there could be no purpose in writing down a
record for a future age which would never come'.[4] Stephen
appears to have taught openly that Jesus would 'destroy this
place' (Acts 6:14) and the early church did not expect the
Lord's return until that prophecy had been fulfilled. There is no
indication that the Christians lived at first in momentary expectation of his coming and that in course of time the hope
gradually faded. The topic is very much alive in a number of
the later writings, such as Revelation, 2 Peter, Jude and the
Pastorals.[5] The amount of space given to the subject of the
Parousia of course varies from book to book, but this is simply
because the subject-matter varies from book to book.

Paul and the Parousia

To Paul in particular the approach of the last day was an ever-
present reality: 'salvation is nearer to us now than when we
first believed; the night is far gone, the day is at hand' (Rom.
13:11f.); 'the time we live in will not last long . . . the whole
frame of this world is passing away' (1 Cor. 7:29–31, NEB); yet
he clearly did not believe that it might be at any moment. 'That
day will not come', he taught, 'unless the rebellion comes first,
and the man of lawlessness is revealed' (2 Thes. 2:3). He recognized that 'a hardening has come upon part of Israel', and he
seems (though the passage is not easy to interpret) to envisage a
national turning to God after 'the full number of the Gentiles
come in' (Rom. 11:25f.). Even in 2 Timothy 4:3–6, when he

---

[4] E. F. Scott, *The Validity of the Gospel Record* (London, 1938), p. 2.
[5] 1 Tim. 6:14; 2 Tim. 4:1,8; Tit. 2:13.

knows that he is nearing the end of his life, he warns Timothy to expect a deteriorating situation in the future. There was a programme to be fulfilled. When it is suggested that Paul's expectation of the coming faded in the decade between his letters to the Thessalonians and his letters from captivity in Rome, it is often forgotten that he had been converted some seventeen years when he wrote the former. There are no known circumstances which make it likely that this mature missionary and theologian should have changed his views thus late in life. That he on one occasion couples himself with those that 'are left until the coming of the Lord' (1 Thes. 4:15) signifies nothing. On two occasions he identifies himself with those who will be dead at the second coming: 'God raised the Lord and will also raise us up'; 'he who raised the Lord Jesus will raise us also.' This is language of resurrection rather than rapture.[6] The ease with which the church postponed its expectation of the Lord's coming under the teaching of events tells against the idea that the disciples had been wrongly taught by Jesus.

THE AUTHORSHIP OF PSALM 110

He made David the author of Psalm 110 (Mt. 22:41f.; Mk. 12:35f.; Lk. 20:41f.), which many critics deny, mainly on the ground that 'my lord' in verse 1 is the ordinary mode of address to an Israelite king, more likely to have been used by a prophet of a king than by King David of the Messiah. Royal psalms, it is true, tend to use extravagant language, because they express the ideal of Kingship and so have a secondary Messianic reference. But this psalm has no specifically royal terminology. It is concerned with priesthood – a non-hereditary and everlasting priesthood. Yet no king of the monarchy period was a priest and all the Hasmonean priest-kings were of the line of Aaron. Furthermore, sitting at God's right hand goes beyond the

---

[6] 1 Cor. 6:14; 2 Cor. 4:14. In any case, even if these references did not exist, the 1 Thes. passage would signify little. Paul is talking about the two classes of believers – those asleep and those alive. As he was at the time in the latter class, he uses the first person plural quite naturally of himself and his fellow believers. In 1 Cor. 15:51 he finds a neutral form of words which does not even formally identify him with one group rather than the other: 'We shall not all sleep, but we shall all be changed.'

language of the royal psalms. (The only possible parallel is Dn. 7:9–14, a Messianic passage.) The language is suited to the one of whom Nathan spoke to David whose throne was to be for ever (2 Sa. 7:12–16). It was David's Messianic offspring, not David, who could be described as a priest-king, who would execute judgment among the nations and shatter chiefs over the wide earth and reign for ever. It was certainly regarded as Messianic both by our Lord and by his opponents. It is the most quoted psalm in the New Testament, where it is always regarded Messianically. There is no convincing setting for it except the reign of David, who took Jerusalem and made it his capital and so entered upon the heritage of Melchizedek. The (ancient) psalm-title attributes it to David. Those who deny the Davidic authorship are quite divided as to who wrote it and when. Possession is nine points of the law. There are no good grounds for dispossessing the 'sweet psalmist of Israel'.

THE HISTORICITY OF JONAH

There seems little doubt, as we have seen,[7] that our Lord regarded the story of Jonah as history. There would of course be no objection in principle to receiving a non-historical allegory (illustrating God's care for the heathen) into the Canon. It is widely held that this was its clearly understood original intention. Such a view is of course immensely attractive to the modern Christian, but it is much easier to assert than to prove. It is strange that its original intention was completely forgotten by the time of Christ, and that he, with his intimate knowledge of Jewish ways of thinking, should not have recognized its literary form. It is strange, too, that this story of *unfulfilled* prophecy should have found a place among the canonical prophets. If the miraculous element in the Bible as a whole is accepted, it may well seem best to regard the book as history, written by Jonah

[7] See pp. 14f. The literary *genre* of the book is usefully discussed by G. Ch. Aalders, *The Problem of the Book of Jonah* (London, 1948). See also *The New Bible Dictionary* (London, 1962), arts. 'Book of Jonah', 'Nineveh'; D. E. Hart-Davies, *Jonah: Prophet and Patriot* (London, 1931); H. L. Ellison, *The Prophets of Israel* (Exeter, 1969), pp. 55ff. Ellison remarks: 'Philo of Alexandria, that great master of allegory, who would doubtless have eagerly seized on a symbolic or allegoric explanation had it been known to him, "took great pains to explain the marvel of the fish".'

the prophet (2 Ki. 14:25) in the reign of Jeroboam II, long before the destruction of Nineveh (prophesied by Nahum and Zephaniah) in 612 BC. The prophet recounts his awesome experiences (which brought a great heathen city to its knees) with restrained, yet vivid, detail. From the human standpoint the book presumably found its place in the Canon mainly because of the great miracle. But from the divine standpoint it was also a revelation of divine compassion for the heathen and prophetical of the resurrection of one greater than Jonah. The question hinges on the larger question of biblical miracle, which is to be discussed in a later volume.

'IN THE TIME OF ABIATHAR'

Finally there are said to be two minor errors of history. Jesus appeared to place in the high priesthood of Abiathar an event which took place during the high priesthood of his father Ahimelech (Mk. 2:25f.; 1 Sa. 21:1–6), and he described Zechariah as son of Barachiah, when apparently he was son of Jehoiada (Mt. 23:35; 2 Ch. 24:20–22). It needs to be stated with great emphasis that these are a challenge to our Lord's inerrancy only on the supposition of an extremely accurate transmission of his words. There is a great intrinsic improbability that small, quite inessential and quite obvious, historical errors should have been retained and accurately transmitted in oral tradition for thirty or more years. The Old Testament was demonstrably extremely well known and such errors would have been quickly detected and would have dropped out of the tradition.

It is far better to assume either the intrusion of error at or near the time of writing, or a different understanding of the passages which in fact eliminates error altogether. In other words, these are questions which are concerned directly with the inerrancy of the Evangelists and only indirectly with the inerrancy of Christ. Since, however, the inerrancy of the Evangelists is ultimately one of our concerns, it seems best to deal with these somewhat technical questions at this point.

Jesus said something, presumably in Aramaic, which is reproduced in most of the best MSS of Mark 2:26 as ἐπὶ ᾿Αβιάθαρ ἀρχιερέως, but in some others (with article added) as ἐπὶ

'Αβιάθαρ τοῦ ἀρχιερέως. The most obvious translation of the former is 'when Abiathar was high priest' and of the latter 'in the time of Abiathar the High Priest'. The second expression would involve no mistake, since it is not incorrect to refer to an event in, say, Queen Victoria's childhood as 'in the days of Queen Victoria'. It would seem rash without a thorough study of contemporary usage to affirm categorically that the first expression could not have been used in Hellenistic Greek in the second, less precise sense. This is particularly so since ἀρχιερέως was used in New Testament times not only for the acting High Priest but for the members of the high priestly family generally. In this sense Abiathar was always a high priest, and he was presumably helping with priestly duties during the latter part of his father's life (1 Sa. 22:16–20). At a later stage Abiathar shared the high priesthood with Zadok (2 Sa. 15:35; 17:15; 19:11; 1 Ki. 4:4), so it is possible that he was also joint high priest with Ahimelech before he died. The nearest equivalent to the expression in the New Testament is Luke 3:2, ἐπὶ ἀρχιερέως ᾿Άννα καὶ Καϊαφᾶ, 'in the high priesthood of Annas and Caiaphas', where it will be noted that office and names are in the reverse order. (And only one of them, Annas, was actually reigning high priest.) It is arguable that in the form ἐπὶ 'Αβιάθαρ ἀρχιερέως the stress is upon 'in the time of Abiathar' and that ἀρχιερέως is added as the briefest way of identifying the one who (later) became high priest. The fact that Abiathar's career was much more distinguished than that of his father Ahimelech (as Queen Victoria was more distinguished than her predecessor William IV) could account for the choice of his name to identify the period.

The issue is therefore by no means clear-cut. But that the expression suggested to many the more precise, and historically inaccurate, sense is plain enough. The manuscript evidence strongly favours the shorter form, but there is a considerable number of important authorities (representing nearly all the earliest text types) in which either the article has been added (e.g. A Θ fam. 1 fam. 13 33) or the whole phrase dropped out (e.g. D W a b e sin. syr.; and it is not found in Matthew or Luke). This shows that the Old Testament was sufficiently well known for the apparent error to be readily recognized. And the error (or ambiguity) was so keenly felt that a number of copyists independently took the considerable step of correcting the text. It is a little surprising, therefore, that those who heard the oral tradition tolerated it, and that Mark included it.

There is a further possible explanation. In Mark 12:26 we have another instance of ἐπί with the genitive in the expression ἐπὶ τοῦ βάτου, where it is usually taken to mean 'at the passage of Scripture concerning (or, entitled) the Bush'. (In Luke 20:37 the same construction is preserved.) ἐπὶ Ἀβιάθαρ ἀρχιερέως may have meant 'at the passage of Scripture concerning (or, entitled) Abiathar the High Priest', for the passage comes in the chapter which immediately precedes that recording the first exploits of Abiathar, and chapters 21–23 contain important references to the high priest's family. If so, it would explain the persistence of the phrase amongst the first generation of Christians, and also the tendency for it to be discarded as misleading, if not erroneous, at an early date. And, of course, it would dispose of any question of error by Jesus.

ZECHARIAH THE SON OF BARACHIAH

With regard to 'Zechariah the son of Barachiah, whom you murdered between the sanctuary and the altar' (Mt. 23:35), eight suggestions (of varying worth) have been made.

1. Jesus made an obvious mistake which was faithfully and gratuitously transmitted for some decades and then committed to writing. Incredible.

2. The 'obvious' answer – the Evangelist made a mistake. It is not likely, however, that he would have inserted this phrase on the spur of the moment; and if he had taught it for some time it would have been challenged.

3. It was inserted by a very early copyist and so became the sole source of the whole textual tradition and was almost[8] un-challenged thereafter. This is of course possible. A scribe, not so clever as he thought, might have confused Zechariah the son

---

[8] It is not found in ℵ, Eusebius and a few cursives. But this must be an attempted improvement. If this shorter form of the text had been derived after a number of copyings from the original autograph, it would have affected the textual tradition more widely.

of Jehoiada with the canonical prophet who was son of Berechiah, and have 'improved' the text by this addition. But the
trend of textual criticism (see chapter 7) is to show the unlikeli-
hood of an original reading disappearing from the textual tradition.

4. Zechariah son of Barachiah is to be identified with a
wealthy Jew, Zechariah son of Bareis, Barouchos (*i.e.* Baruch)
or Bariskaios, who according to Josephus was killed in the
Temple *c.* AD 68 by Zealots on a trumped up charge of betray-
ing the Jews to Vespasian. This converts a reference to past
history ('whom you murdered') into a prophecy. Even if it was
an oracle of a Christian prophet, it seems a tortuous misrepre-
sentation to put it into the mouth of Jesus as part of the history
of Holy Week.

5. Zechariah, father of the Baptist, according to the second-
century apocryphal *Book of James*, was killed in the Temple at
the instigation of Herod the Great. A tradition of this sort was
known to Origen and others, but its value is most dubious.
There is no evidence that his father was Barachiah, and it is
strange that he was not recognizably described as 'father of John
the Baptist'. It has been argued that the vivid detail 'between
the sanctuary and the altar' and the use of the second person
'whom *you* murdered' suggests something in living memory. (It
would be odd to speak in our day of Thomas à Becket 'whom
you murdered'.) The latter point is plausible, but certainly not
decisive, for the corporate solidarity of the Jewish race was
strongly felt.

6. The canonical prophet, 'son of Berechiah, son of Iddo'
might by a strange coincidence have also been killed in the
Temple. There are two possible references to this effect given
by Strack-Billerbeck,[9] but the evidence is slender.

7. It may be a case of 'homiletic identification' of two different people with the same name. The rabbis of later times frequently blended together two biblical characters and attributed
the virtues of both to the one, on the principle that it was
homiletically valid to enhance the praise of righteous men,
provided some biblical support (however far-fetched) could be

[9] H. L. Strack and P. Billerbeck, *Kommentar zum Neuen Testament aus
Talmud und Midrasch*, vol. I (München, 1922), pp. 941f.

found for the identification.[1] There is some evidence for this practice as early as the Mishna, and even in 2 Esdras (c. AD 100). At first sight this seems an absurd practice, which, instead of identifying the character from whom a lesson is to be learnt, merely invites confusion. It is difficult to imagine Jesus doing this, especially at a moment of solemn denunciation. If, however, the practice was widely used at this time, it would render easier the idea that the Evangelist or an early copyist slipped the phrase in.

8. Zechariah may have been the grandson of Jehoiada and son of Barachiah. Our Lord's saying points to the fulfilment of all the prayers of the righteous for the vindication of God's justice from one end of the Old Testament to the other. In Genesis 4:10 God had said of Abel: 'The voice of your brother's blood is crying to me from the ground.' Zechariah's dying prayer (2 Ch. 24:22, RV) was: 'The Lord look upon it, and *require it*.' The Lucan parallel to our passage says: 'that the blood of all the prophets, shed from the foundation of the world, *may be required* of this generation' (Lk. 11:50). This saying seems decisively to identify our Lord's 'Zechariah the son of Barachiah' with 'Zechariah the son of Jehoiada' of Chronicles. Thus the great disaster of the destruction of Jerusalem which came upon 'this generation' was a fulfilment of the many prophecies of judgment upon an apostate nation. Our Lord's thought on the one hand moves in the world of scriptural prophecy, and on the other it has a tremendous sense of the unity of Israel. There is, therefore, nothing incongruous in referring to the last murder in the biblical histories,[2] even though it was not the most recent martyrdom (*cf.* Urijah, Je. 26:23), nor in using the terminology 'whom you murdered' of an event long ago.

If we accept this identification, we appear to have a straight conflict between Chronicles ('son of Jehoiada') and Matthew ('son of Barachiah'), *with Matthew's version very strangely going almost unchallenged*. There is, however, no Hebrew word

[1] Z. H. Chajes, *The Student's Guide through the Talmud* (London, East and West Library, 1952), ch. 21: 'The Quoting of Various Persons under One and the Same Name.'
[2] On the position of Chronicles in the Canon, see pp. 134ff.

for 'grandson', and the Chronicler could quite properly have used the term here for a grandson of Jehoiada, and the reference to Barachiah could have been a well-known item of the high priestly genealogy, which happens to have found no place in the biblical records or Josephus. The case for this is not negligible.

a. Though Zechariah the prophet calls himself 'the son of Berechiah, son of Iddo' (Zc. 1:1, 7), elsewhere in the Old Testament he is simply 'the son of Iddo' (Ezr. 5:1; 6:14). This might be because 'Zechariah, the son of Berechiah' was ambiguous. Zechariah or Zachariah was an exceedingly common name; there are about thirty people so named in the Bible. There are some eight Berechiahs or Barachiahs, one Jeberechiah and three Baruchs. These (also Iddo, Benaiah, Jehoiada) are predominantly Levite names, which tend to be repeated in the genealogies of Levite families. There was one (priestly?) Zechariah, son of Jeberechiah (Barachiah in Septuagint) in Isaiah's day (Is. 8:2); it would not be surprising if there had been a Zechariah son of Berechiah (or Baruch) before his time as well as the two after (the prophet and the rich man in the reign of Vespasian).

b. Jehoiada lived to a great age and a good deal happened between his death and the murder of his 'son' Zechariah (2 Ch. 24:15–22).[3] By this time Jehoiada's eldest son, if still alive, would have been an old man. The dynamic Zechariah could well have been a grandson. The biography of Zechariah is condensed into three verses and the mention of an undistinguished or predeceased father would have been an irrelevance.

c. According to the Talmud 'a horror of their impious deed long possessed the Jews, who believed that the blood . . . continued to bubble on the stones of the court, like blood newly shed, until the temple was entered, just prior to its destruction, by Nebuzaradan.'[4] This incident was much discussed by the rabbis, which may account for the recollection in oral tradition of the precise location of the assassination and the name of the martyr's undistinguished father. It may also account for the fact that Matthew's 'error' provoked so little reaction in the textual tradition.

[3] According to the Hebrew, more than one 'son' was killed (24:25).
[4] *Speaker's Commentary*, 2 Ch. 24:21, *cf.* Strack-Billerbeck, I, 940f.

Dogmatism is clearly not called for. Suggestions 3, 5, 6 or 8 would not conflict with a belief in divine authorship. 5, 6 and 7 are remotely possible, worth mentioning as a reminder of how fragmentary our knowledge is, and of how in each case the unexpected recovery of one item of confirmatory information would transform an unlikely possibility into a serious one. 3 or 8 could well be the answer.

Neither individually nor collectively do these objections make a weighty case against the claims made by Jesus as a teacher.

ADDITIONAL NOTE
EXTRA-BIBLICAL TRADITIONS

It is well to remind ourselves that the New Testament supplies
information supplementary to the Old Testament at a number
of places. For example, the hope which sustained Abraham
when offering Isaac (Heb. 11:19); Moses' education and great-
ness in deed (Acts 7:22); his motives in leaving Pharaoh's court
(Heb. 11:24–27); the names of the Egyptian magicians (2 Tim.
3:8); the terror of Moses at Sinai : 'I tremble with fear' (Heb.
12:21); Elijah's prayer and the three and a half year drought
(Jas. 5:17); 'others ... were sawn in two' (Heb. 11:37). Josephus,
too, adds many items of tradition to the scriptural account,
some fanciful, some evidently traditional (and not improbable)
inferences from the Old Testament text, and some quite independent material. What has survived in writing must be only
a fraction of the tradition that was current at any one time.
There were doubtless traditions in circulation concerning all
periods of Old Testament history – and not all of them were
untrue.

It is possible that such a tradition may explain not only
'Zechariah the son of Barachiah', but also a well-known crux
in the speech of Stephen. Stephen says (Acts 7:14ff.) : 'Joseph
sent and called to him Jacob ... and Jacob went down into
Egypt. And he died, himself and our fathers, and they were
carried back to Shechem and laid in the tomb that Abraham
had bought for a sum of silver from the sons of Hamor.' This
is held to be a confusing (or at best a telescoping) of two Old
Testament stories : Abraham's purchase of a burial-cave at
Mach-pelah in Hebron for 400 silver shekels from Ephron the
Hittite (Gn. 23:16; 49:29ff.), and Joseph's burial at Shechem
in a piece of ground which Jacob had bought for 100 pieces of
silver from the sons of Hamor (Gn. 33:19; Jos. 24:32).

Clearly, Stephen's account has much more in common with
the latter than the former, but is itself somewhat ambiguous.
Who died? Jacob or Joseph? Jacob does not readily fit the
story since he was buried with great ceremony at Hebron (Gn.
50:13), whereas the bodies of Joseph and his brothers were
apparently left in Egypt till the Exodus (Ex. 13:19), afterwards

to be buried at Shechem. (Josephus, *Antiquities* ii.8.2, it is true, says that Joseph's brothers were buried at Hebron, but there appears to be no strong tradition associating the sons of Jacob with the burial-place there. Jerome (who also lived in South Palestine) says specifically that they were not buried in (Kiriath–)Arba (= Hebron), but in Sychem (*Letter* 57:10).) If it is accepted that Joseph's death and burial are referred to, all is plain sailing, except that Abraham is said to have bought the tomb, not (as the Old Testament states) Jacob.

There are at least four possible explanations. 1. It could have been a crass mistake by Stephen, the hero of the story. But that this was passed on and not corrected for thirty years in a community which knew Genesis very well seems unlikely. 2. 'Abraham' could have been an early interpolation into Acts, which similarly went uncorrected, or 3. a writing-out of a mis-read abbreviation, say A(BRAAM) for IA(KOBOS). 4. It could have been a fragment of tradition (otherwise unpreserved) to the effect that Jacob in returning to Shechem from his long exile in Haran was in fact re-staking a claim (which had long since lapsed) to a piece of land previously bought by his grand-father when he first came to Canaan (Gn. 12:6). He re-lived his grandfather's entry into the Promised Land, and re-affirmed his belief in the covenant promise by repeating his act of faith. It is perhaps significant that Jacob afterwards continues to re-trace the steps of Abraham by going on to Bethel (12:8; 35:1–6) and Hebron (35:27). In view of the continuing importance of Shechem in the Old Testament, there is no intrinsic improba-bility in the view that Abraham's visit had greater significance than the brief report in Genesis 12:6, 7 might suggest. That is to say, that Abraham not only received his first vision there and a confirmation of the gift of the Promised Land to his descend-ants, but that he also staked out his claim in faith by buying for himself a token piece of land. On the whole this seems the most likely explanation of Stephen's form of words.

THE NEW TESTAMENT
WRITERS AND
THE OLD TESTAMENT

4

UNDERLINING THE TEACHING OF JESUS

The New Testament writers took the same view of the Old Testament as Jesus, at least in general terms. To them, as to him, the Old Testament was true, authoritative, inspired. To them, as to him, the God of the Old Testament was the living God and the teaching of the Old Testament was the teaching of the Living God. To them, as to him, what Scripture said, God said. There are many hundreds of allusions to the Old Testament. We can do no more than glance at a few points of interest, particularly at those where there is something new or perplexing.

THE TRUTH OF OLD TESTAMENT HISTORY

Many of his historical references are taken up again.[1] In addition there are a number of others, including Enoch (Heb. 11:5; Jude 14), Melchizedek (Heb. 5:6ff.), Joseph (Acts 7:9ff.; Heb.

[1] Abel reappears, along with his brother Cain (Heb. 11:4; 12:24; 1 Jn. 3:12; Jude 11). Noah is mentioned in Heb. 11:7; 1 Pet. 3:20; 2 Pet. 2:5. The name Abraham occurs thirty-nine times outside the Gospels; many details about his life and about his wife and family are given. Sodom and Gomorrah and Lot appear again (Rom. 9:29; 2 Pet. 2:6f.; Jude 7). Moses has forty-two references, with a variety of details about the Exodus, the giving of the Law and the wilderness journeys. There are a number of references to David, as psalm-writer, and as ancestor of Christ. Solomon again has his mention (Acts 7:47). Elijah comes again (Rom. 11:2; Jas. 5:17), though not Elisha or Jonah. Just as our Lord spoke often of the persecution of the prophets, so Stephen uses it as his final illustration (Acts 7:52). The sweep of history is brought out, together with a number of interesting historical details, in the genealogies of our Lord in Matthew and Luke. There are the following references to Genesis 1–3: Rom. 5:12–21; 1 Cor. 15:21,22; 2 Cor. 11:3; 1 Tim. 2:13,14; Heb. 4:4; Jas. 3:9; Rev. 20:2.

11:22), Korah (Jude 11), Aaron's rod that budded (Heb. 9:4), Balaam (2 Pet. 2:15; Jude 11), Balak (Rev. 2:14), Joshua (Acts 7:45; Heb. 4:8), the fall of the walls of Jericho (Heb. 11:30), Rahab (Heb. 11:31; Jas. 2:25), God's destruction of the nations of Canaan (Acts 13:19), the judges – Gideon, Barak, Samson, Jephthah (Acts 13:20; Heb. 11:32), Samuel, Saul (Acts 13:20f.; Heb. 11:32); Daniel and his three friends are particularly in mind as those who 'stopped the mouths of lions, quenched raging fire' (Heb. 11:33f.). Job is mentioned by name in James 5:11.

This list is far from exhaustive, but it is sufficient to show how closely the New Testament writers follow the lines laid down by Jesus. Of these writers we could repeat almost verbatim what we said earlier of him.[2] 'Although these quotations are taken more or less at random from different parts of the Old Testament and some periods of the history are covered more fully than others, it is evident that they were familiar with most of our Old Testament and that they treated it all equally as history. Curiously enough, the narratives least acceptable to the "modern mind" are the very ones that they seemed most fond of choosing for their illustrations.' Naturally their greatest familiarity is with the Law and the Prophets (including the Former Prophets – the historical books from Joshua to Kings), which were regularly read in synagogue, but the Writings are also known. While showing no slavish and exclusive adherence to our Lord's own selection of illustrations, they preserve in a very remarkable way the emphases and proportions that we find in his teaching.

The authority of Old Testament teaching

The position is the same with regard to the authority of the Old Testament in matters of doctrine and ethics. Here are a few of the more obvious examples. Paul in the Epistle to the Romans, his most systematic exposition of Christian doctrine, establishes crucial points in the argument by extended scriptural quotation. The extent and source of sin, justification by faith, election, and the validity of the Gentile mission, are argued in detail on the basis of Old Testament teaching.[3] The continuing guilt of

[2] See p. 13.
[3] Rom. 3:10–20; 5:12–21; 4:3–25; chapters 9–11; 15:9–12.

the Jewish people is similarly argued by Stephen in Acts 7. Justification is also argued from Scripture by James (2:21–25). The hardening of unbelievers is established by Paul on the same passage as that used by our Lord, and this passage is taken up again by the fourth Evangelist, and by Paul in Acts.[4] The divine Sonship and the High Priesthood of Jesus are interpreted at considerable length in Hebrews[5] from the Old Testament. The final judgment is proved in Romans 14:11 by Isaiah 45:23. 1 Peter 1:24 appeals to Isaiah 40:6 to show the unfailing character of the word of God.

In establishing ethical principles appeal is also made to the Old Testament. Love, humility, avoidance of revenge, steadfastness in trial, obedience to parents, abstention from idolatry, avoidance of the unequal yoke, freedom from the ceremonial law, faithfulness in marriage – are all upheld by scriptural quotations.[6] To show the proper attitude to the state, and for the regulation of such affairs as the payment of workers and the gift of speaking in tongues, appeal is made to the Old Testament.[7]

The inspiration of the Old Testament writings

With regard to the inspiration of the writings, we find the same pattern of teaching followed with great fidelity. The human authors are sometimes acknowledged,[8] but the authority of the writing arises from the fact that God is the ultimate author. It was he who spoke through Moses and the prophets and the psalm-writers, and it was he who caused their words to become Scripture.[9] The fulfilment of prophecy occupied a central posi-

[4] Is. 6:9; Mk. 4:12; Rom. 11:8; Jn. 12:40; Acts 28:26.
[5] Heb. 1:5 – 2:9; 5:6 – 7:28.
[6] Rom. 13:8–10; Jas. 2:8; Jas. 4:6; Rom. 12:19; Heb. 11:4 – 12:1; Eph. 6:2; 1 Cor. 10:7; 2 Cor. 6:17; Gal. 4:21–30; Eph. 5:31; cf. 1 Cor. 6:16.
[7] 1 Pet. 2:17; 1 Cor. 9:9; 1 Tim. 5:18; 1 Cor. 14:21.
[8] E.g. Moses (Rom. 10:5, 19); David (Rom. 4:6); Isaiah (Rom. 10:20); Hosea (Rom. 9:25).
[9] E.g. Moses and the prophets (1 Cor. 9:9; Acts 26:22; 28:23). 'The scripture had to be fulfilled, which the Holy Spirit spoke beforehand by the mouth of David' (Acts 1:16; cf. 4:25). 'The Holy Spirit was right in saying to your fathers through Isaiah the prophet' (Acts 28:25). 'That which was spoken through Jeremiah the prophet'; 'by the prophet Joel' (Mt. 2:17; Acts 2:16).

tion in the church's teaching, particularly in the early days, when its main task was the presentation of Jesus to the Jewish people as Messiah. Indeed the whole relation of New Testament to Old is summed up in the one word 'fulfilment'.

Each Evangelist takes up the theme in turn. In Matthew the narrative is repeatedly punctuated with prophetic Scriptures, which the writer says were fulfilled in the life of Jesus. Mark's very first words after the title are : 'As it is written. . . .' Luke's Prologue announces 'a narrative of the things which have been accomplished among us'; his infancy narratives are steeped in Old Testament phraseology; and his Gospel reaches its climax with the farewell words of Christ : 'These are my words which I spoke to you, while I was still with you, that everything written about me in the law of Moses and the prophets and the psalms must be fulfilled' (Lk. 24:44). John's first chapter introduces the Baptist with the same text from Isaiah that Mark had used, 'I am the voice of one crying in the wilderness' (1:23), and chapter 20 includes this comment : 'for as yet they did not know the scripture, that he must rise from the dead' (20:9).

Again, as with our Lord, there is frequent use of the term 'Scripture' and of the formula 'it is written'. We have already mentioned the substitution of 'scripture' for 'God' in Romans 9:17 and Galatians 3:8 and of 'God' for 'scripture' in Matthew 19:4, 5. There are a number of further instances of this latter use, where Old Testament texts, not originally put into the mouth of God, are referred to him. 'Sovereign Lord, who didst make the heaven ... who by the mouth of our father David, thy servant, didst say by the Holy Spirit, "Why did the Gentiles rage?"' (Acts 4:24f.). 'Therefore he (God) says also in another psalm, "Thou wilt not let thy Holy One see corruption"' (Acts 13 :35). 'And again when he brings the firstborn into the world, he says, "Let all God's angels worship him". Of the angels he says, "Who makes his angels winds, and his servants flames of fire". But of the Son he says, "Thy throne, O God, is for ever and ever ..." And, "Thou, Lord, didst found the earth in the beginning"' (Heb. 1:6–10). 'Therefore, as the Holy Spirit says, "Today, when you hear his voice"' (Heb. 3:7). Again, where there are no formal quotations, there are often allusions to the Old Testament. The supreme example is the

Apocalypse, where, according to H. B. Swete,[1] no fewer than
278 out of its 404 verses contain references to the Jewish Scriptures.

'It says', 'he says'

In addition to these features which can be directly paralleled
from our Lord's teaching, there are some interesting new expressions which do not add anything in principle to his teaching, yet underline it in fresh and striking colours. Of very great
interest is the expression λέγει, 'it says' or 'he says', which
is particularly characteristic of Hebrews. λέγει and various
other similar expressions (e.g. φησί, εἴρηκε are commonly
used without any subject expressed to introduce quotations
from the Old Testament.[2] It has been argued that λέγει is
sometimes strictly impersonal, meaning merely 'it is said (by
someone somewhere)'. In view of Warfield's extremely thorough
investigation of the subject,[3] such an interpretation can scarcely
be sustained. Far from the subject of λέγει being indefinite,
it is nearly always a most solemn appeal to the living voice of
God. The subject is God, or (what amounts to the same thing
in this context) Scripture. As Warfield says : 'We may well be
content in the New Testament as in Philo to translate the
phrase wherever it occurs, "It says" – with the implication that
this "It says" is the same as "Scripture says", and that this
"Scripture says" is the same as "God says".'[4]

---

[1] H. B. Swete, *Apocalypse of St. John* (London, 1907), pp. cxxxvff.
[2] *E.g.* 1 Cor. 6:16; 2 Cor. 6:2; Eph. 4:8; Heb. 8:5.
[3] Fifty pages of *The Inspiration and Authority of the Bible* (pp. 299ff.)
are devoted to 'It says', 'Scripture says', 'God says'.
[4] *Ibid.*, p. 348. Eph. 5:14 may be a special case. 'Therefore it is said,
"Awake, O sleeper, and arise from the dead, and Christ shall give you
light".' There are perhaps echoes of Is. 26:19 and 60:1, but few will
follow Warfield in regarding it as an OT quotation. At most it could be
a free statement of a general scriptural injunction (Jn. 7:38; Jas. 4:15
and possibly 1 Cor. 2:9 appear to be examples of free paraphrases of Old
Testament teaching, perhaps recalling more than one passage). Nor is
there solid evidence that a non-canonical writing is being quoted. It
reads like an extract from a Christian hymn. E. E. Ellis, in an article on
the use of the phrase 'Saith the Lord' in quotations that already have an
introductory formula (*Evangelical Quarterly*, 29 (1957), p. 23), thinks

The oracles of God

Another striking description of the Old Testament is to be found in Paul's statement that the Jews 'are entrusted with the oracles of God' (Rom. 3:2). Oracles are divine utterances. It is a favourite use of Philo's, and it is clear that for him, and presumably also for Paul, the oracles include the whole of Scripture-narrative and words of men, as well as words put directly into the mouth of God. This last point is important, because the concept of divine oracles is prominent in the Old Testament prophets. The expression *ne'um Yahweh*, 'saith the Lord', is an oft-repeated oracular formula, preceding or following an utterance directly given by God. Thus the Old Testament contains a wealth of oracular material, cast in propositional form and regarded as words direct from the very mouth of God. But this does not cover the long stretches of narrative and poetry and human discourse that are also contained in it. Philo without any question regards the whole of Scripture as oracular, and there can be little doubt that Paul here is referring to the whole body of sacred writings. In Hebrews 5:12 and Acts 7:38 the term is used in the same, or in a closely related, sense. In 1 Peter 4:11, those who speak, that is, those who minister the Word in public, are to speak 'as it were' oracles of God. This of course is not an injunction to summon some gift of infallibility that would make every sentence literally an oracle. They are to speak 'as it were oracles of God', that is to say (presumably), without adulterating the Word with man-made teaching, and

---

that these may be derived from Christian prophecy. The same explanation is possible here. This may be truly a divine oracle, though not an OT one. Those filled with the Spirit spoke in psalms and hymns and spiritual songs, some of which could have been truly oracular (Eph. 5:18, 19; *cf.* 1 Cor. 14:26–33). See also E. G. Selwyn, *1 Peter* (Macmillan, London, 1946), pp. 266f. But in any case language must not be treated mechanically. Because NT writers habitually use common expressions such as 'it is written' or 'it says' as formulas of quotation solemnly to attest the divine authority of what is quoted, it does not mean that they are always bound to do so. If Paul wanted to quote a well-known, but not oracular, hymn, he could use the expression 'therefore it says' to mean 'it is in illustration of this point that the hymn says'. Context must determine whether the use is technical or not.

with the solemnity that is due to teaching that is in truth the Word of God.[5]

'God-breathed', 'moved by the Spirit'

2 Timothy 3 : 16, 'All scripture is inspired by God', contains another interesting word : θεόπνευστος. Warfield concludes an elaborate study of it thus : 'What is θεόπνευστος is "God-breathed" ... the product of Divine spiration ... It does not express a breathing *into* the Scriptures by God ... What it affirms is that the Scriptures owe their origin to an activity of God the Holy Ghost and are in the highest and truest sense His creation.'[6]

Lastly, there is the description of prophecy in 2 Peter 1 :21 : 'No prophecy ever came by the impulse of man, but men moved by the Holy Spirit spoke from God.' Prophecy is not something that proceeds from the human will, it comes from God, and men are carried when they prophesy to a destination of his choosing, not theirs.[7]

[5] For a full explanation of the word λόγιον see B. B. Warfield, *The Inspiration and Authority of the Bible*, pp. 351–407. This is an important study in view of the fact that scholars of repute have lent their names to the idea that a λόγιον is simply a 'saying' and that λόγιοι are merely 'discourses'. There is not yet full agreement as to the precise nuances of this word. For references to more recent literature, see E. E. Ellis, *Paul's Use of the Old Testament* (Edinburgh, 1957), p. 20 n.9. This is the standard work on the subject and gives an excellent introduction to both Pauline and contemporary methods of biblical interpretation.
[6] *The Inspiration and Authority of the Bible*, pp. 245–296. The Authorized Version translated : 'All Scripture is given by inspiration of God, and is profitable.' The Revised Version emended this to : 'Every scripture inspired of God is also profitable,' while reserving for the margin 'Every scripture is inspired of God, and profitable'. The Revised Standard Version relegated the RV meaning to the margin, and virtually restored the AV to the text, reading : 'All scripture is inspired by God and profitable.' Much unnecessary ink was wasted in arguing the pros and cons of the RV, for whether the text refers to the totality of Scripture or to the sum total of individual scriptures makes little odds. And certainly neither the RV nor NEB 'every inspired scripture' could be interpreted as 'every scripture that happens to be inspired'. It must mean 'since it is inspired'. So that, as far as the doctrine of inspiration is concerned, the two renderings imply the same.
[7] '(Being) moved' is the present participle passive of φέρω. In the Arndt-Gingrich *Lexicon*, the relevant entry (slightly abbreviated) reads : *'be moved, be driven, let oneself be driven* – a. lit., by wind and weather Ac. 27:15, 17. b. fig., of the Spirit of God, by whom men *are moved.'*

So then to the New Testament writers the Scriptures are true, authoritative, inspired, and may be appropriately described as being 'God-breathed', the work of men 'moved by the Spirit', the 'oracles of God'. As to Christ, so to them : What Scripture says, God says. But must we not go a stage further and say : To them, What Scripture says, God says, *because they had been so taught by Christ*? The teaching of Jesus on many points of traditional Judaism was profoundly disturbing, but on the matter of loyalty to Scripture, both he and his disciples stood firmly in the line of contemporary orthodoxy. There were three supreme tests of orthodoxy – loyalty to the Sabbath, loyalty to the Temple, loyalty to the Torah. Jesus was repeatedly in trouble on the first count and to some extent on the second, but his acknowledgment of the inspiration of Scripture was never questioned. Surely the unshaken adherence of the early church to the Jewish Scriptures, even at the height of the controversy over obedience to the Law, derives from the unshakable adherence of Christ himself? It is intrinsically probable that the main lines of biblical belief and interpretation in the early church should have come from Christ, seeing that he carefully instructed the disciples during his ministry and that he gave particular attention to the exposition of Scripture during his post-resurrection appearances.[8]

SOME PROBLEMS OF NEW TESTAMENT USAGE

References to non-canonical literature

This concept of oracular Scripture held by our Lord and the apostles has on the face of it (quite apart from any findings of modern research) certain difficulties. Some have seen a difficulty in the occasional New Testament reference to extra-canonical literature, as though this in some way lowered the authority of the canonical Scriptures. This difficulty is purely

---

The literal use in Acts refers to the storm in which, 'when the ship was caught and could not face the wind, we gave way to it and *were driven* . . . then, fearing that they should run on the Syrtis, they lowered the gear, and so *were driven*.' Thus the man inspired is laid hold of by the irresistible power of God's Wind and is carried to the place of God's choice.

[8] The coherence of NT exegesis and the likelihood of its derivation from Jesus is argued by C. H. Dodd, *According to the Scriptures*, pp. 109f.

imaginary. That a writer shows knowledge of, or even quotes,
material from the Apocrypha, pseudepigraphs or from secular
Greek authors, does not indicate that he has lowered his view
of Scripture to the level of his view of these other writings. Only
if he unequivocally quotes them *as Scripture* is there any problem. The statement of Jude 14 that Enoch 'prophesied' does
not amount to this.[9] What does constitute a more serious problem is the free way in which these supposedly verbally inspired
Scriptures are quoted in the New Testament.

Quotations from memory

Certain aspects of the problem are quite straightforward. We
have of course no right to demand of believers in verbal inspiration that they always quote Scripture verbatim, particularly
when the Scriptures are not written in the native language of
either writer or reader. As with the word preached, we have a
right to expect that quotations should be sufficiently accurate
not to misrepresent the passage quoted; but, unless the speaker
makes it clear that his quotation is meant to be verbatim, we
have no right to demand that it should be so. In the nature of
the case, the modern scholarly practice of meticulously accurate
citation, with the verification of all references, was out of the
question. There were no printed books, no chapter and verse
divisions, no marginal references, no concordances. There were
probably not even bound codices. The verification of references
required the laborious scrutiny of a lengthy parchment roll,

[9] See further, E. E. Ellis, *Paul's Use of the Old Testament*, p. 36 n. 7.
The *Book of Enoch* is not part of the Apocrypha, but is a composite
work, probably of the second and first centuries BC. It was certainly not
regarded as canonical by either Jews or Christians in the first century
AD, though it was highly esteemed in some circles. It is impossible to say
whether Jude regarded the quotation which he makes (which apparently
comes from the book, 1:9, though it might conceivably have circulated
as oral tradition) as literally from the antediluvian patriarch. He certainly regarded it as a true description of the judgment to come. It is
likely that the pseudepigraphic device was generally understood and that
intelligent Jews did not really believe that pre-Mosaic works had survived uncanonized. Having no access to modern typographical tech-
niques there was no unclumsy way of indicating that the name was
recognized as a *nom de plume*. Jude might well have approved of the
paraphrase: 'The prophetic words of "Enoch the Seventh from Adam"
applies to these people.' For the status of the Apocrypha in the early
church, see pp. 141ff.

which itself would not necessarily be ready to hand. Thus quotations were normally from memory and the writers did not pretend that they were anything else.[1]

This is not, however, to say that their memories were just like ours. Far from it. There is good reason to believe that the ordinary peasant Jew would have known his Bible far better than the ordinary devout Christian of today knows even his New Testament; better, that is, than the Christian who really loves his Bible and reads it carefully twice a day. I well remember Dr A. Lukyn Williams, a great authority on Judaism, uttering a warning against the facile acceptance of solutions to biblical problems based on the assumption that the writers did not know their Bibles properly. The devout Jew, schooled in the Scriptures from the cradle, would in fact have known much of his Bible by heart, and much more of it nearly by heart. As Josephus says, 'We take most pains of all with the instruction of children, and esteem the observation of the laws and the piety corresponding with them the most important affair of our whole life.'[2] Instruction began in the home. The Law took first place, but the Prophets and the Writings were also diligently taught. In 4 Maccabees 18:10ff. a widowed mother reminds her sons of the example of their martyred father : 'He used to teach you when yet with you the law and the prophets. And he read to us of Abel who was murdered by Cain; and of Isaac, who was sacrificed, and of Joseph, who was in prison. And he told us of the zealous Phineas; and taught us concerning Ananias, Azarias, and Misael in the fire. And he praised Daniel

---

[1] An eminent scholar once wrote to the author: 'If both Testaments were verbally inspired, I should have thought that God might be expected to remember what he had written in the OT, and to have quoted himself accurately. I can understand a man giving a loose quotation; I find it harder to attribute this to God.' This shows a complete failure to understand the humanity of the Scriptures, which is no more destroyed by inspiration than is the humanity of Christ by incarnation. Preservation from error does not involve the destruction of normal mental processes. Interestingly, in ordinary life, freedom of quotation is often a sign of mastery of one's material. The more sure a teacher is that he understands the writer the less is he afraid of expounding his ideas in terms that are not precisely those of the author. When he is not sure, he quotes exactly and then labours to expound what the quotation *seems* to mean.

[2] *Against Apion,* i. 12.

who was in the den of lions, and called him blessed. And he
reminded you of the scripture of Isaiah, which says : "If thou
pass through the fire it shall not burn thee." He chanted to you
David the Psalmist, saying, "Many are the troubles of the righteous." He recited to us proverbs, even Solomon.'[3]

This home teaching was supplemented by further instruction
in the synagogues, which in the time of Christ were to be found
in every town and village. Synagogues were schools even more
than they were places of worship, and a national system of
elementary education based on the village synagogue dates
from about 70 BC. The 'teachers of the Law' who came 'from
every village' to hear our Lord (Lk. 5 : 17) were evidently these
local school-masters. The only textbook used was the Bible,
and education consisted largely in learning the Bible by heart.
To quote E. C. S. Gibson (to whom I am considerably indebted
in this section) : 'The ideal school-boy was likened to "a plas-
tered cistern that loseth not a drop", and the result of this was
an extraordinary familiarity on the part of the Jews at large
with the letter of Scripture. "If anybody," says Josephus, "do
but ask one of our people about our laws, he will more readily
tell them than he will tell his own name, and this in consequence
of our having learnt them immediately as soon as ever we became sensible of anything, and of our having them, as it were,
engraven in our souls." To such an extent were the powers of
memory cultivated that St. Jerome (speaking, of course, at a
much later date) tells us of the Jews in his days, that "in childhood they acquire the complete vocabulary of their language,
and learn to recite all the generations from Adam to Zerubbabel
with as much accuracy and facility as if they were giving their
own names." '[4]

[3] A reflection of this interest in all three sections of the Canon is to be
seen in one of the favourite methods of exposition that came to be developed in the synagogue. It was known as 'the stringing together (of
pearls)'. The preacher would quote a passage from the Law, then string
on to it some related passages from the Prophets and the Writings. A.
Edersheim, *The Life and Times of Jesus the Messiah* (Glasgow, 1953),
vol. I, p. 449. For further reference, see K. Stendahl, *The School of St.
Matthew* (Uppsala, 1954), p. 216 n. 4. There is something very like this
in Rom. 11:8–10; 15:9–12.
[4] E. C. S. Gibson, *The Old Testament in the New* (London, 1907), pp.
9f., who gives references *Pirqe Aboth II*, 11; *Apion* 2. 19; *Comment. in
Epist. ad Titum* ch. 3 (Migne VII, p. 735).

J. R. Green said of the sixteenth and seventeenth centuries that 'England became the people of a book, and that book was the Bible'.[5] Yet it probably never approached the standard of first-century Jewry in its devotion to the one book. Amongst the more well-to-do other books were of course to some extent available, but amongst the common people their whole literary education consisted of Bible teaching. The entire society was built upon the foundation of this tiny collection of magnificent literature, which moulded the thought and language of the people. Thus it is rash to assume that divergences from the standard text which appear to involve a mis-statement of fact were due to memory lapse. But the ordinary limitations of memory provide the most obvious way of accounting for many of the minor differences of form between quotation and original source and as such cause no difficulty.

Use of the Septuagint

We should naturally expect quotations to approximate to the standard versions in use in the community. We should expect to find English authors of the eighteenth and nineteenth centuries approximating their quotations to the Authorized Version. Similarly in New Testament times we should expect to find, and we do in fact find, that the authors usually approximate their quotations to the Septuagint, the current Greek translation of the Old Testament.[6] (The Septuagint is often denoted by the abbreviation LXX.) Such a practice does not involve any doctrine of the inspiration of the LXX any more than it does of the AV. But no author is bound exclusively to the standard version; he is perfectly at liberty to substitute words from other versions, or from his knowledge of the original language, or even from extraneous sources of interpretation, in order to bring out the meaning of the scripture that he quotes. He may adapt syntax so as to weave his quotation tidily into

[5] J. R. Green, *A Short History of the English People* (London, 1874), ch. 8, sect. 1.
[6] Interestingly the quotations from the Septuagint agree mainly with the characteristically Palestinian form of the LXX, represented by MSS A, Q and Lucian.

his own writing.[7] And he may do this without specifying precisely what he is doing. Sometimes his sources will be recognized
at once, sometimes not. Such interpretative quotations account
for a large number of free quotations.[8]

Sometimes, however, it appears that not only is there a quotation from the Septuagint, but an argument is based upon a
quotation, at a point where the meaning of the Greek version
does not agree with the Hebrew. If the Hebrew is regarded as
the inspired text, it might seem that the writer has given to an
Old Testament passage a meaning which cannot be extracted
from the original by fair exegesis. In approaching this matter,
great caution is required, because a number of uncertain factors
enter in. We shall have occasion to discuss the reliability of the
text of the Bible later on.[9]

We shall see that, taking a broad view, the texts of both Old
and New Testaments have been remarkably preserved. When,
however, it comes down to the minutiae with which we have
to concern ourselves in comparing different versions of the same
text, a variety of uncertainties enter into the discussion. Sometimes there are variant readings in the New Testament text. It
is almost certain in any particular case that the original reading has been preserved in one of the variants, and it is possible
to form a rough judgment as to the relative merits of such
variants. But it is often far from certain that the reading ad-
judged the 'best' was in fact the original reading. With the
Septuagint the uncertainty is far greater. Like the New Testament, the Septuagint is represented by a considerable number

[7] E.g. E. D. Freed, *Old Testament Quotations in the Gospel of John*
(Leiden, 1965), p. 129, says: 'Torrey and others . . . begin with the false
assumption that each quotation is meant to be given literally. In reality,
however, the writer adapts each quotation to his context, to his literary
style, and to the whole scheme of composition.'
[8] It is worth recalling the words of B. Jowett, *Epistles of St. Paul to
Thessalonians, Galatians and Romans* (London, 1894), p. 190: 'Quotation, with ourselves, is an ingenious device for expressing our meaning
in a pointed or forcible manner; it implies also an appeal to an authority.
And its point frequently consists in a slight, or even great, deviation from
the sense in which the words quoted were uttered by their author.'
[9] See Chapter 7, where more will be said about the differences that exist
between the various manuscripts and early translations of the Bible, and
some explanation given of how their closeness to the original text may be
judged.

of manuscripts, but in the case of the Septuagint textual criticism is both more difficult and less advanced than in the case of the New Testament. Often there is a choice of texts, the relative merits of which are difficult to weigh. H. B. Swete's excellent edition of the Septuagint (1900–07) was based primarily on one manuscript (Codex B), and comparisons between the New Testament and Septuagint have usually been made on the basis of such a text. But later discoveries have increased the authority of the text of Codex A and other related manuscripts, which text is often nearer to the New Testament form of Old Testament quotations than B. In Stendahl's words, 'This considerably diminishes the gap between the OT quotations in the NT and the LXX.'[1]

The first-century Hebrew text

Again, there is uncertainty about the Hebrew text. The discoveries of the ancient scrolls at Qumran (and other places in the Dead Sea region) have in the main vindicated our traditional Hebrew text (the so-called Massoretic text), which dates from about the tenth century AD. In one fell swoop, these discoveries have pushed back our knowledge of the Hebrew text almost a thousand years, revealing a wonderful fidelity in scribal transmission during the intervening period. But the picture revealed is not one of an entirely uniform Hebrew text in the first century AD. Sometimes readings appear which had hitherto been known only in the Septuagint (this applies especially to the historical books), or in the form of the Pentateuch used by the Samaritans; occasionally a new reading appears. Generally speaking the Massoretic text is vindicated, but where we have first-century evidence of another reading (as in the case of a New Testament quotation) it is quite possible that this ancient reading itself comes from an exact use of a text not otherwise known to us.[2]

---

[1] K. Stendahl, *The School of St. Matthew*, p. 174.
[2] Eph. 4:8 'he *gave* gifts to men' looks like a reversal of the sense of Ps. 68:18 (RV) 'Thou hast *received* gifts among men'. The passage is discussed by M. McNamara, *The New Testament and the Palestinian Targum to the Pentateuch* (Rome, 1966), pp. 78ff., who calls Ps. 68 'probably the most difficult psalm of the entire Psalter'. The psalm contains a strong note of God's triumphant bounty to his people, and it

The Epistle to the Hebrews comes far ahead of all other New Testament books for examples of quotations which correspond to the Septuagint, and not to the Massoretic text. Some of these are striking. Yet on close examination it is surprising how trivial most of them are. Of eleven examples listed, six are of no great importance;[3] of the remaining five, four may well represent the original meaning better than the Massoretic text; and possibly the fifth.[4] But in fact we are probably wrong to think of this as a question of Septuagint versus Massoretic text. Hebrews is itself a very early witness to an important text-type, found in some of the Dead Sea Scrolls and akin to the Samaritan Pentateuch, which existed in the first century.[5] In the rest of the New Testament the other outstanding variants are in Acts. The most striking are 7:43 and 15:16f. Yet these[6] are not exact quotations from the Septuagint, but also show affinities to texts found in the Dead Sea Scrolls. Again it looks as though the New Testament may be using a text more primitive than the Massoretic. In any case, it should be observed that, as far as inspiration is concerned, not one of these quotations does anything to undermine the view that the writer regarded his Old Testament as verbally inspired. Rather the reverse. We see him pondering his texts and individual words in the texts in order to extract

---

could be that Paul altered 'received gifts' to 'gave gifts' as his own interpretative adaptation. But the sense of verse 18 as it stands both in the Massoretic and Septuagint texts is not altogether clear. It could well be that Paul had before him the verb *ḥlq* ('distribute') which was only later corrupted into *lqḥ* ('receive'). Paul's sense is supported by the Aramaic Targum, most mss of the Syriac Peshitta and the Old Latin Psalterium Romanum.

[3] 1:10; 3:10; 4:4; 8:2; 11:21; 12:26ff.

[4] 1:6; 8:9; 10:38; 12:6. 10:5. 'Let all God's angels worship him' (1:6) is an interpretative translation of the best text (found at Qumran) 'worship him all gods'. *Cf.* similar LXX translations in Pss. 8:5; 97:7 (Heb.), and see R. Meyer: 'Die Bedeutung von Dt. 32:8f. 43(4Q) für die Auslegung des Moseliedes' in *Verbannung und Heimkehr* (Festschrift W. Rudolph, Tübingen, 1961), p. 200.

[5] *Cf.* B. K. Waltke, *Prolegomena to the Samaritan Pentateuch* (Harvard Ph.D. thesis, 1965), p. 209: 'it seems likely that the writer of Hebrews had a *Vorlage* similar to the Samaritan Pentateuch and not the one familiar to most today.' For further discussion of this text-type, see pp. 167ff.

[6] Also 3:22f. and 13:41. See J. de Waard, *A Comparative Study of the OT Text in the Dead Sea Scrolls and in the NT* (Leiden, 1965) p. 78.

their fullest meaning. An interesting further fact, however, emerges : it so happens that, even though it may have been the Septuagint over which a writer pondered, no argument in the New Testament is actually made to turn on a demonstrably bad text. This suggests, either that the writers were also aware of the Hebrew text, or that the Holy Spirit was preserving the writers from hidden pitfalls.

Seemingly unnatural interpretation of texts

But, not only are there examples of New Testament quotations based on texts other than the Massoretic, there are also cases where the Hebrew text is given an interpretation which at first sight does not seem to be the natural meaning. The obvious examples are certain Matthean quotations, and Paul's argument in Galatians 3:16 about the use of the word 'seed'. This is a difficult and intricate subject. But the conviction grows that both Matthew and Paul are entirely innocent of the stupidity with which they are sometimes credited. They do not think that the Christian message may be proved by the one-to-one correspondence of plain predictions and clear fulfilments in a number of isolated proof-texts. Matthew knows as well as we do that Moses was speaking of the people of Israel when he said, 'Out of Egypt I called my son' (Mt. 2:15; Ho. 11:1); and that Jeremiah was speaking of the exile of his own days when he spoke of Rachel 'weeping for her children' (Mt. 2:18; Je. 31:15). Paul was not making a crass grammatical blunder when he argued from the singular form of the word 'seed'. Christian convictions about the Old Testament were formed in the first place from Christ's own teaching. But those who were outside the fold did not accept his interpretations uncritically. Rabbi Paul must have brought out every weapon from his powerful intellectual armoury in order to overthrow the Christian blasphemies. And after his conversion he must have pored over the Scriptures and turned over every argument again and again in his mind, till he was convinced that he had an unanswerable case to present to his fellow-countrymen. That case did not just require the checking up of a few proof-texts. It was not a question of text, it was a question of meaning. Earnest Jews

already knew the text of the Bible well. They needed to *search*
the Scriptures to discover if the whole thrust of the Old Testament agreed with what had been seen in Jesus. They in fact
had to do the very thing that we ourselves have to do. They
were confronted with writings that were supposed to be prophetic of Jesus. To decide whether they were really prophetic
of him required profound study.

Prefiguring

Alfred Edersheim, with his deep and sympathetic understanding of Rabbinical learning, shows that Matthew is often concerned rather with the fulfilment of what is prefigured, than
with the fulfilment of predictions. The Immanuel sign that the
land would be freed of its dangers in the days of Ahaz prefigured the saving of Israel from its ultimate dangers by the
advent of the true Immanuel. Israel's sojourn in Egypt prefigured the sojourn of Israel's Messiah in Egypt. 'Those who
have attentively followed the course of Jewish thinking, and
marked how the ancient Synagogue, and that rightly, read the
Old Testament in its unity, as ever pointing to the Messiah as
the fulfilment of Israel's history, will not wonder at, but fully
accord with, St. Matthew's retrospective view. The words of
Hosea were in the highest sense "fulfilled" in the flight to, and
return of, the Saviour from Egypt. To an inspired writer, nay,
to a true Jewish reader of the Old Testament, the question in
regard to any prophecy could not be : What did *the prophet* –
but, What did the *prophecy* – mean? And this could only be
unfolded in the course of Israel's history. Similarly, those who
ever saw in the past the prototype of the future, and recognized
in events, not only the principle, but the very features, of that
which was to come, could not fail to perceive, in the bitter wail
of the mothers of Bethlehem over their slaughtered children,
the full realization of the prophetic description of the scene
enacted in Jeremiah's days. Had not the prophet himself heard,
in the lament of the captives to Babylon, the echoes of Rachel's
voice in the past? In neither one nor the other had the utterances of the prophets (Hosea and Jeremiah) been *predictions* :
they were *prophetic.* In neither one nor the other was "the

fulfilment" literal: it was Scriptural, and that in the truest
Old Testament sense.'[7]

Verbal inspiration

It is difficult for us fully to make this thinking our own. But at
least it is crystal clear that such thinking presupposes a belief
in the inspiration of the very words of Scripture. The significant
thing to Matthew is that Hosea (and Moses before him: Ex.
4:22) was prompted to use the particular word 'son' – an unusual description for the nation of Israel. Had he been
prompted to say 'people', or 'sons' even, the message would
have lost half its relevance. But Mary had been told that her
child was to be called 'the Son of God' (Lk. 1:35). When the
disturbing and tumultuous experiences of these harassed
parents led finally to exile in Egypt, one could imagine the
words of Hosea coming to them with unspeakable comfort,
'Out of Egypt I called my son'. Or again, take the use of
Zechariah 9:9 in Matthew 21:5. It is often said[8] that Matthew's introduction of a second donkey 'must apparently have
been the work of someone who did not understand the nature
of Hebrew parallelism'. This seems absurd, in a book steeped in
Old Testament language. Surely Stendahl is much nearer the
mark. 'In breaking up the parallelism Matthew deviated from
the common messianic interpretation of the Rabbis. The only
reason for such a treatment of the OT text must be that Matthew knew a tradition, which spoke about two asses. That is
why he stresses the two asses more than does the LXX in the
rendering of the prophecy, which to him was fulfilled in a very
exact way.'[9] What interests Matthew is the surprising verbal
coincidence between prophecy and fulfilment. He notes that,
although the Hebrew poetical form need imply no more than
one animal, yet, strangely, there were in fact two animals,
corresponding exactly to the verbal form of the poetry. The
same is true of John's quotation of Psalm 22, with its reference

[7] *The Life and Times of Jesus the Messiah*, I, 156, 215f. Edersheim held
(and this has been argued by E. J. Young, *Studies in Isaiah*, London,
1954, pp. 143ff.) that in the case of the Immanuel prophecy there is not
only prefigurement, but also direct prediction.
[8] *E.g.* by C. H. Dodd, *According to the Scriptures*, p. 127 n.1.
[9] K. Stendahl, *The School of St. Matthew*, p. 200.

to 'garments' and 'clothing' (19:24). This is not a logical proof
from the fulfilment of prophecy; but to the believer, who
knows that the Scriptures are from God and that the events of
the Passion were ordered by God, it is a coincidence that can
scarcely be accidental. That Jesus should have had no bone
broken does not prove him to be the true Paschal Lamb, but it is
a striking confirmation of that belief (19:36).

Again, with Paul's comment on the singular form 'seed' in
Galatians 3:16, verbal inspiration is presupposed. It is scarcely
conceivable that Paul did not understand the collective use of
the word 'seed' to mean 'descendants', and that he was arguing
that 'seeds' (which in Hebrew and Greek means 'grain', not
'descendants') would have been used if God had meant to refer
to a plurality of descendants. Rather he is asking the question,
Why did the Holy Spirit use a collective singular when he might
well have used a plural word? And his answer is that the ultimate fulfilment of the promise was in fact in one Man. There
was of course in a limited sense a fulfilment of the Abrahamic
promise of blessing to the world through the instrumentality of
the scattered individuals of the Jewish nation. But ultimately it
all depended on the one Man, Israel's Messiah, the woman's
'Seed' by whom alone the serpent's sway would be overthrown.
The promise was not to Abraham's descendants after the flesh.
Only those could properly be regarded as Abraham's seed who
were in Christ (verses 28, 29). Thus the term 'seed' was admir-
ably suited to express both the individual and collective aspects
of Christ's person.

Yet, as we have seen already, the writers' *primary* concern is
not with verbal coincidences, but with meaning.[1] They are not

[1] We might add the comments of two scholars, one ancient and one
modern. Jerome said that wherever the evangelists and apostles quote
the Old Testament it should be noted that 'they have not followed the
wording, but the meaning' (Migne, *Patrologia Latina*, 22, col. 1011).
T. W. Manson says: 'For them the meaning of the text was of primary
importance; and they seem to have had greater confidence than we
moderns in their ability to find it. Once found it became a clear duty to
express it; and accurate reproduction of the traditional wording of the
Divine oracles took second place to publication of what was held to be
their essential meaning and immediate application. Odd as it may seem
to us, the freedom with which they handled the Biblical text is a direct
result of the supreme importance which they attached to it' ('The Argu-

concerned only with texts, but with passages. C. H. Dodd showed this in his book *According to the Scriptures*. Not only did the Christian church inherit the Jewish Scriptures, but it inherited (from Jesus) a particular interest in certain well-defined blocks of Scripture (mostly in the prophets and the psalms) which largely moulded its understanding of Jesus and of the church's mission. The Old Testament is not used merely as a quarry for proof-texts; attention is paid to context, without which allusions in the New Testament sometimes cannot be properly understood.

The Holy Spirit's foreknowledge in inspiration

But New Testament principles of interpretation do not end with a discovery of what the Old Testament writer meant. Each writer was author of a segment of Scripture, not comprehending the whole. But the inspiring Spirit who directed their pens was author of the whole and comprehended the whole. It is a truism in the secular realm that history cannot be written satisfactorily until sufficient time has elapsed to show which events were of long-term significance. In other words, history must be written *in the light of later events*. This presupposition underlies the New Testament approach to the Old. The Holy Spirit knew beforehand the course of history with its consummation in Christ, and so in guiding the writers he intended a deeper meaning than they understood. Not only was the ritual typical, but also the history. The first Adam was typical of the last Adam, the Flood typified the Last Judgment, Isaac and Hagar typified the church made free by the Spirit and Israel seeking justification by the law,[2] the Exodus typified redemption, the Red Sea baptism, the brazen serpent the cross. Therefore grammatico-historical exegesis of the Old Testament does not tell the whole story, nor even the main part of the story. The prophets 'were serving not themselves, but you' (1 Pet. 1:10–12). 'These things happened to them as a warning, but they were

---

ment from Prophecy', *Journal of Theological Studies*, 46 (1945), pp. 135f.).

[2] Though the term 'allegory' is used in Gal. 4:21–31, the historical truth of the Old Testament story is assumed. It too is thus properly a 'type', adumbrating the tensions in the New Testament church.

written down for our instruction, upon whom the end of the ages has come' (1 Cor. 10:11).

Scripture from beginning to end is prophetic; that is, it is forward-looking and it is Spirit-inspired. The ceremonies look forward and find their explanation in Christ, the history looks forward and finds its consummation in Christ, the experiences of the psalmists find their deepest fulfilment when Christ comes. The Old Testament, like the New, is also spiritual. The true understanding of the ceremonies is a spiritual one; the history of both Testaments is rightly understood as the dealings in grace and judgment of the one Covenant God with his chosen people;[3] their spiritual experiences in both dispensations are experiences of grace and judgment. The biblical revelation is an organism – the essential elements of the whole are to be found in every part.

The unity of the Divine Word

Few people have brought out the biblical understanding of Scripture more clearly than Adolph Saphir. He, like Alfred Edersheim, was a converted Jew, who came to see that Christ was the key to the understanding of the Old Testament, and that without Christ it could only be misunderstood. He draws a parallel from Schopenhauer. Schopenhauer, in the introduction to the 1,500 page exposition of his philosophy, says: 'I propose

---

[3] This comes out very clearly in 1 Cor. 10:1–13. The historical experiences were spiritual experiences. Christ, described as a 'spiritual following rock' in verse 4, was in their midst. In using his material provisions the Israelites were eating and drinking to themselves either salvation or condemnation. On the sources of Paul's thought and on the (dubious) connection between it and the amusing later Jewish legends about the movable well in the desert, see E. E. Ellis, *Paul's Use of the Old Testament*, pp. 66ff. Paul is sometimes held to have misused Dt. 25:4: 'You shall not muzzle an ox when it treads out the grain' in 1 Cor. 9:9f. and 1 Tim. 5:18, ignoring its literal meaning and applying it to the support of Christian workers. Dt. 25:4, however, comes in a passage concerned with human relations (24:19–22 gleanings for the needy; 25:1–3 restraint in corporal punishment; 25:5–10 duty of the near kinsman), and it may well have already been a proverbial saying indicating the wrongness of preventing anyone from gaining a livelihood. But if it was intended literally and was so taken by Paul, it is far better to take the πάντως of 1 Cor. 9:10 in the sense of 'clearly' (NEB) than of 'entirely' (RSV). It is then an *a fortiori* argument: if this is the rule for oxen, so much the more for men.

to point out here how this book must be read in order to be thoroughly understood. By means of it I only intend to impart a single thought. Yet, notwithstanding all my endeavours, I could find no shorter way of imparting it than this whole book . . . a *single thought,* however comprehensive it may be, must preserve the most perfect unity. If it admits of being broken up into parts to facilitate its communication, the connection of these parts must yet be organic, *i.e.,* it must be a connection in which every part supports the whole just as much as it is supported by it, a connection in which there is no first and no last, in which the whole thought gains distinctiveness through every part, and even the smallest part cannot be completely understood unless the whole has already been grasped . . . no other advice can be given as to how one may enter into the thought explained in this work than *to read the book twice,* and the first time with great patience, a patience which is only derived from the belief, voluntarily accorded, that the beginning presupposes the end almost as much as the end presupposes the beginning, and that all the earlier parts presuppose the later almost as much as the later presuppose the earlier.'[4] In other words the real meaning of Genesis 1 is better understood by the one who has mastered John 1 than by the person who has merely mastered the mind of the writer of Genesis; the meaning of the bruising of the serpent's head becomes clear only when the effect of the cross is understood (Col. 2:14, 15); the promises of blessing to the world through Abraham's seed are clearly seen only with the coming of Christ. Christ is to be found in all the Scriptures, not by discovering forced typological parallels at every point, but by understanding what the Bible in its various parts means. A Christian commentary should begin with exact grammatico-historical exegesis and then go on to show what fuller meaning a knowledge of the whole biblical revelation sheds upon the particular part.

To quote Saphir again: 'The New Testament exposition of the Old Testament is the only true exposition, for it

---

[4] A. Schopenhauer, *The World as Will and Idea,* E.T. (London, 1883) I, viif. A. Saphir, *The Divine Unity of Scripture* (London, 1894) 191ff.; *Christ and the Scriptures* (London, n.d.). Though popularly written, these two books are profoundly enlightening.

explains not merely what David and the prophets could understand, and tried to understand, but what the Holy Ghost understood, and deposited with them, distinctly, in this way. Supposing that there is a little plant before me. I can examine it. But supposing that I have a powerful microscope. I look at it, and now I can see a number of things which before were entirely non-existent to me. Have I put anything into that plant that was not there before? Have I changed the plant? Have I introduced my pet ideas into that plant? So, when we read Leviticus with the light of the epistle to the Hebrews; when we read the whole Old Testament with the light of the evangelists and the epistles, that is exposition, not imposition. We do not put anything into it. The Holy Spirit enlarges our vision to see what is there.'[5]

Jesus' use of typology

Jesus understood the Old Testament typologically, and it is to him that we owe the identification of himself (and of his disciples) with Israel. In the temptation narrative (Mt. 4:1–11; Lk. 4:1–13), where, if anywhere, we can see Jesus' own estimation of his status and calling, his answers are taken from Deuteronomy 6–8. In this passage Moses, at the end of the forty years' wandering in the wilderness, calls Israel to whole-hearted obedience to the Lord and to trust in his provision for them. It was a time of hunger and testing, preparatory to a special task, in which God disciplined his son Israel (8:5), to teach him to worship him alone. Jesus, at the end of the forty days, accepts afresh his status as God's Son; he sees himself as the new Israel, called to succeed where the old Israel had failed. His belief in his resurrection after three days seems to be inspired on the one hand by the promises of Israel's resurrection (Ho. 6:2) and on the other by seeing Jonah as a type of himself (Jon. 1:17; Mt. 12:40). He sees his own experience prefigured in psalms of suffering and vindication (Pss. 22, 41, 42 and 43, 118),[6] 'which were composed originally by an individual Israelite, but which were used corporately by the whole nation.

R. T. France sums up the evidence of the Synoptic Gospels

5 A. Saphir, *The Divine Unity of Scripture*, p. 64.
6 Mt. 27:46; Mk. 15:34. Mk. 14:18. Mt. 26:38; Mk. 14:34. Mt. 21:42; 23:39; Mk. 12:10f.; Lk. 20:17; 13:35.

in these words: 'He uses *persons* in the Old Testament as types of himself (David, Solomon, Elijah, Elisha, Isaiah, Jonah) or of John the Baptist (Elijah); he refers to Old Testament *institutions* as types of himself and his work (the priesthood and the covenant); he sees in the *experiences* of Israel foreshadowings of his own; he finds the *hopes* of Israel fulfilled in himself and his disciples, and sees his disciples as assuming the *status* of Israel; in Israel's *deliverance* by God he sees a type of the gathering of men into his church, while the *disasters* of Israel are foreshadowings of the imminent punishment of those who reject him, whose *unbelief* is prefigured in that of the wicked in Israel and even, in two instances, in the arrogance of the Gentile nations.

'In all these aspects of the Old Testament people of God Jesus sees foreshadowings of himself and his work, with its results in the opposition and consequent rejection of the majority of the Jews, while the true Israel is now to be found in the new Christian community. Thus in his coming the history of Israel has reached its decisive point. The whole of the Old Testament is gathered up in him. He himself embodies in his own person the status and destiny of Israel, and in the community of those who belong to him that status and destiny are to be fulfilled, no longer in the nation as such.'[7]

If a secular understanding of the Old Testament exhausts its meaning, this is of course arbitrary nonsense. If, however, Christ is the source, sustenance and goal of history, then the real meaning of everything in the experience of Israel and in the experience of mankind is found in him. It is because Jesus *is* the representative of Israel that words originally spoken of the nation can rightly be applied to him, and it is because Jesus *is* the representative of mankind that words originally spoken by a psalmist can be 'fulfilled' by him.[8] Christ is the key to the understanding of everything and everything points to Christ. For this reason the significance of the Old Testament is not exhausted even by the fulfilment of its predictions and prefigurations.

[7] *Jesus and the Old Testament*, pp. 75f. R. N. Longenecker, 'Can We Reproduce the Exegesis of the New Testament?' in *Tyndale Bulletin*, 21 (1970), pp. 3–38 has useful references to recent literature.
[8] *E.g.* Jn. 13:18; 15:25; 19:28.

Because it all points to the living Christ, Scripture does not belong to the past, it is the word of the living God here and now. This is often revealed in experience to the unsophisticated, even when it is hidden from the wise.

The conviction grows that the New Testament writers used the Scriptures with knowledge and spiritual understanding, fully knowing what they were doing. To them the Old Testament as a whole and in all its parts was a witness to Christ. It was God's Word written, to be studied with heart and mind, both as a comprehensive unity and in its minutest particulars. This earliest Christian view of Scripture derives from and underlines the view of Scripture taught by our Lord. In the New Testament Christ's view of Scripture is the Christian view of Scripture.

JESUS
AND THE
NEW TESTAMENT

5

Our argument thus far has been as follows. If we are prepared to accept the Gospels as giving, at least in a general sense, a substantially true account of the Jesus of history, we are led to two conclusions: (a) that he taught the divine authorship of the Old Testament scriptures, and (b) that he taught the entire truth of his own teaching. We have argued that it is a sound methodology to set out what the New Testament has to say without assuming that every sentence is true, and allowing each reader to make his own critical subtractions. The evidence is so strong on these two points that the conclusion can be denied only if the subtractions become so massive that the Gospels can no longer be held to be, even in a general sense, substantially true.

The same methodology will lead us to a third conclusion, namely, that Jesus in principle authenticated the New Testament. Some of the evidence will take us into other New Testament writings besides the Gospels, and many of these have had assaults upon their authenticity and historicity similar in kind to those upon the Gospels. For those who doubt the substantial truth of the Gospels, these assaults merit scholarly refutation in their proper place. But for those to whom our argument is directed the attempt to do so would be a side-track. For, once we have accepted as facts of revelation that God was incarnate in Jesus and that God is the author of the Old Testament, it is straining at a gnat to swallow the Old Testament *in toto*, while doubting even the substantial truth of the only documents left to us by Providence for an understanding of the central act of revelation. We shall therefore take the New Testament records as they stand.

The divine authentication of the New Testament was in two

stages, which are sharply different in character. In the first stage Jesus directly appointed and trained the apostles as the authorized teachers of the New Covenant, and they were recognized as such by the church. The evidence for this (which is the subject of this chapter) comes from the New Testament itself. In the second stage (the subject of the next chapter) the Holy Spirit guided the church in its recognition of certain 'apostolic' writings as being in fact additional scriptures. This was a gradual process, the evidence for which comes from a biblically based understanding of church history. The first stage may be considered under four headings: Christ's training of the apostles; the teaching of the Holy Spirit; the apostles' understanding of their commission; the church's attitude to the apostolic writings.

CHRIST'S TRAINING OF THE APOSTLES

In addition to the many references in the Gospels which speak of judgment and of the life to come, there are fully forty in which Jesus looks beyond the time of his death. Before his passion he repeatedly spoke of his resurrection.[1] Mark's statement that 'he said this plainly' (8:32) is confirmed by the fact that the rumour had gained currency that he was to build the temple in three days,[2] and by the fact that the chief priests should say to Pilate, 'We remember how that impostor said, while he was still alive, After three days I will rise again.'[3] He also envisaged a considerable programme of events before his coming in glory, including a world-wide preaching of the gospel, the destruction of Jerusalem and the treading down of the city until the fulfilment of the 'times of the Gentiles'. His disciples would have to face civil and religious charges and even excommunication (Mt. 10:19f.; Mk. 13:9; Lk. 12:11; Jn. 16:2). Peter would live to old age and then suffer martyrdom (Jn. 21:18). Meanwhile they were to observe the Lord's Supper in commemoration of him (Lk. 22:19; 1 Cor. 11:24).

He trained disciples, of whom twelve were given a place of

[1] Mt. 17:9, 23; 20:19; Mk. 8:31; 9:9; 10:34; 14:28; Lk. 18:33; 24:7, 46; Jn. 2:19.
[2] Mt. 26:61; 27:40; Mk. 14:58; 15:29; Jn. 2:19.
[3] Mt. 27:63.

special intimacy.[4] They believed themselves to be in training for a world-wide heralding of the kingdom of God, into which Gentile as well as Jew would eventually come.[5] They did not understand the teaching about the resurrection,[6] but they gained the impression that Jesus knew what was going to happen, and that he was preparing them for his eventual withdrawal from the world. This is particularly clear in the farewell discourses and the high priestly prayer of John 14–17. It is impossible to speak with certainty about the methods used by Christ in instructing his disciples, but there is great intrinsic probability that our Lord taught his disciples by methods similar to those used by the rabbis in teaching their disciples. He is called 'Rabbi' some fifteen times even in our Greek Gospels, and doubtless this word lies behind many of the passages where 'Teacher' is used, and perhaps even where 'Lord' is used.[7] The rabbis considered themselves to be the bearers of a 'tradition', which they had 'taken over' and which it was their task to 'hand over' to approved pupils who committed it to memory. Certainly the Twelve were conscious of a special commission, and they not only preached, but also gave themselves to intensive instruction. It was their task to give themselves to the Word of God and it was the church's task to continue steadfastly in the apostles' doctrine (Acts 6:2; 2:42).

Both before and after the resurrection, Jesus made known his intention of building a church in which the apostles were to have authority and which should have members from all nations. To Peter he said: 'On this rock I will build my church. ... I will give you the keys of the kingdom of heaven and whatever you bind on earth shall be bound in heaven, and whatever you loose on earth shall be loosed in heaven' (Mt. 16:18f.). He was to have authority to admit members to the church and to interpret to it the law of Christ. Speaking of discipline in the local congregation, he said that one who had been wronged was to 'tell it to the church'. Speaking presumably of the church's collective judgment he said: 'Whatever you bind on earth shall

[4] In Mark, for instance, see 1:17; 2:14; 3:14; 4:34; 5:37; 6:7.
[5] Mt. 10:18; 24:14; 26:13; Mk. 14:9; Mt. 8:11; Lk. 13:29.
[6] Mk. 9:10, 32; Lk. 18:34.
[7] Jn. 1:38; 20:16; and see the variant readings of Mk. 10:51 and the discussion in G. Dalman, *Words of Jesus* (Edinburgh, 1902), pp. 327f.

be bound in heaven, and whatever you loose on earth shall be loosed in heaven' (Mt. 18:17f.). Twice he spoke of the apostles judging the twelve tribes of Israel (Mt. 19:28; Lk. 22:30). After the resurrection he said, 'If you forgive the sins of any, they are forgiven; if you retain the sins of any, they are retained' (Jn. 20:23). 'As the Father has sent me, even so I send you' (Jn. 20:21). 'Go therefore and make disciples of all nations' (Mt. 28:19; cf. the Marcan appendix, 16:15). He said that 'repentance and forgiveness of sins should be preached in his name to all nations' and they were to be 'witnesses of these things' (Lk. 24:47f.). In this way his earlier saying was to be fulfilled in which he declared that he would draw all men to himself (Jn. 12:32).

THE TEACHING OF THE HOLY SPIRIT

The establishment and extension of this church is intimately bound up with the promises of the Holy Spirit, which were given both before and after the resurrection. 'Wait for the promise of the Father, which, he said, you heard from me.' 'You shall receive power when the Holy Spirit has come upon you; and you shall be my witnesses . . . to the end of the earth.' 'I remembered the word of the Lord, how he said, John baptized with water, but you shall be baptized with the Holy Spirit' (Acts. 1:4, 8; 11:16). The Spirit was to give them the words they needed: 'When they deliver you up, do not be anxious how you are to speak or what you are to say; for what you are to say will be given to you in that hour; for it is not you who speak, but the Spirit of your Father speaking through you' (Mt. 10:19f.; cf. Mk. 13:11). 'The Holy Spirit will teach you in that very hour what you ought to say' (Lk. 12:12). The Spirit was to recall his words to their minds: 'The Counsellor, the Holy Spirit, whom the Father will send in my name, he will teach you all things, and bring to your remembrance all that I have said to you' (Jn. 14:26). The Spirit was to lead them into new truth: 'I have yet many things to say to you, but you cannot bear them now. When the Spirit of truth comes, he will guide you into all the truth; for he will not speak on his own authority, but whatever he hears he will speak, and he will declare to you the things that are to come' (Jn. 16:12f.).

The last two promises quoted do not of course refer specifically or exclusively to the inspiration of a New Testament Canon,[8] but they provide in principle all that is required for the formation of such a Canon, should that be God's purpose. If God-given words are promised for the emergencies of persecution, how much more might they be expected for her abiding Scripture. If remembrance of the Lord's words was necessary for the proper instruction of the infant church when many eye-witnesses were still alive, how much more when they were dead. It would be most natural to believe that the promises of remembrance and of guidance into new truth found their most far-reaching fulfilment in a New Testament Canon.

It should be noted also that the teaching and guidance of the Spirit is not divorced from the historical testimony of those who had been trained by Jesus and who had been eye-witnesses of his life and deeds. There is a unique place given to these first-generation witnesses, which was not to be shared by any other generation. 'The Spirit . . . will bear witness to me; and you also are witnesses, because you have been with me from the beginning' (Jn. 15:26f.). Peter was conscious of this in Acts 5:32 : 'We (emphatic, the apostles) are witnesses to these things; and so is the Holy Spirit.' The mystery of Christ was 'revealed to his holy apostles . . . by the Spirit' (Eph. 3:4, 5). The Spirit is concerned with the handing on of the tradition as well as with its revelation, but in this process the chosen eye-witnesses have special authority. Luke, in setting forth the tradition that was most surely believed amongst them, stresses that it was handed on to them by those who were from the beginning eye-witnesses and ministers of the word (1:1–4). Their special status is illustrated by the way our Lord prayed separately for the apostles and for those who should believe in him through their word (Jn. 17:20).

THE APOSTLES' UNDERSTANDING OF THEIR COMMISSION

Our Lord's teaching compels us to listen with the closest attention to those whom he thus appointed as the accredited teachers of his church, and to ask how they themselves regarded their commission. In general it may be said that although the New

[8] Several of the New Testament writers were not in the Upper Room at the time.

Testament writers take the same high view of the Old Testament as does our Lord, they never for a moment consider that they, as ministers of the New Covenant, have less authority than the ministers of the Old Covenant. Rather does the ministration of the New exceed that of the Old in glory, resulting therefore in great boldness of speech (2 Cor. 3). The New Covenant was a 'better covenant', its message was 'declared at first by the Lord, and it was attested to us by those who heard him, while God also bore witness by signs and wonders and by various miracles and by gifts of the Holy Spirit' (Heb. 8:6; 2:3f.). They considered the Old Testament Scriptures to be 'God-inspired', never to have come 'by the impulse of man', but 'from God' (2 Tim. 3:16; 2 Pet. 1:21), yet in a sense they put their own authority above them. Though the Epistle to the Romans is steeped in Scripture and is in reality an exposition of Scripture, Paul tells them that 'my gospel' (16:25f.) is required for its full understanding. 'The gospel' is a declaration of the eternal purposes of God, hidden from other generations, but now 'revealed to his holy apostles and prophets by the Spirit' (Eph. 3:3–12; cf. 1:3–14; 2 Tim. 1:9–11; Tit. 1:1–3; 1 Pet. 1:18–23).

The meaning of 'apostle'

It is true that the term 'apostle' has certain ambiguities. The Greek word may represent the Aramaic *shaliach*, a legal term for one who had a commission to act on behalf of his principal.[9] Much play has been made of the idea that a *shaliach* is a plenipotentiary. There is a rabbinic saying, repeated nine times in the Talmud, to the effect that 'a man's *shaliach* is as it were himself'. But it is an unsound inference to argue from this that the words of the apostle of God are therefore invariably the words of God, or that the acts of the apostle necessarily and unalterably commit the One who sent him.[1] The authority of the *shaliach* is of course strictly limited by the terms of his commission. Simply to appeal to the fact of apostleship is of little

[9] So K. H. Rengstorf, *Apostleship* (London, 1952). With equal learning the identification of ἀπόστολος with *shaliach* is firmly discarded by A. Ehrhardt, *The Apostolic Succession* (London, 1953), pp. 15ff.
[1] Dom Gregory Dix, *Apostolic Ministry*, ed. K. E. Kirk (London, 1946), p. 230, for instance, writes thus: 'Whosoever sins they remit or retain are remitted or retained (John 20:23). The *shaliach's* action irrevocably commits even his divine principal.'

significance until the terms of the apostolic commission are precisely known.

There is real difficulty here, because the word 'apostle' is used in at least two senses in the New Testament. It is used of the delegates sent by the churches to take the collection to Jerusalem.[2] It is also used of the Twelve, whom our Lord called and upon whom, as foundations, the New Jerusalem was built.[3] In the one case the apostle is just a representative of his local church, with a temporary commission. In the other case his commission is to the church universal, of which he is a foundation stone. But in between these two uses there are other references to apostles, not so easily defined. Pre-eminent is Paul, who without question regarded himself as an apostle in the fullest sense, equal in authority to the Twelve, prepared if necessary publicly to resist even Peter (2 Cor. 12:11; Gal. 2:6–14). Once Barnabas is called an apostle (Acts 14:14), probably also James, the Lord's brother (Gal. 1:19; 1 Cor. 15:7); possibly Silvanus and possibly even Timothy.[4] Adronicus and Junias (or perhaps Junia – feminine) are said to be 'of note among the apostles' (Rom. 16:7), which could mean either that they were note-worthy apostles or, perhaps rather less naturally, that they had a note-worthy reputation as Christians in the apostolic circle. In addition we have 'false apostles' (2 Cor. 11:13; Rev. 2:2), which suggests that either the number of apostles had grown so much that it was possible for some to claim the title without the fraud being generally obvious; or that the general understanding of the term 'apostle' lacked the precision readily to distinguish the authority of a (supposed) delegate of the Jerusalem church from the authority of an 'apostle of Christ'.

It is possible to take the view, as Dix does, 'that during the first generation there is an increase in the numbers of the apostolate proper',[5] and that Timothy and Titus, though not called apostles, fulfilled certain specifically apostolic functions.

[2] 2 Cor. 8:23; cf. Phil. 2:25.
[3] Lk. 6:13; Rev. 21:14. 'The Twelve' and 'the apostles' seem to be used interchangeably in Acts. The choosing of Matthias emphasizes the strictly defined nature of the apostolic body.
[4] Pace K. H. Rengstorf, Apostleship, pp. 28f. See 1 Thes. 2:6; cf. 1:1 and Acts 16:1–4; 17:14.
[5] Apostolic Ministry, p. 231.

It is possible to take the view, as Rengstorf does, that there are
only two grounds for apostleship, an encounter with the risen
Lord,[6] and a personal commission from him. Apostles so defined must have been fairly numerous, and they included Paul,
James and a good many others in addition to the Twelve. Or it
is possible to maintain, as Geldenhuys does, that the apostolate
'in the highest sense'[7] was confined, and known to be confined,
to the Twelve and Paul (and possibly James, who had a personal
encounter with Jesus after the resurrection and later became
president of the Jerusalem church). They, and they alone, were
'apostles of Christ', and the use of the term 'apostle' elsewhere
is not intended to carry theological significance. This view can
scarcely claim to be capable of demonstrative proof, yet it
corresponds closely with the over-all impression given by the
New Testament. There is no authority quite on a level with that
of the Jerusalem apostolate and of the apostle of the Gentiles.
The church is founded on these men, and in their claims we can
certainly see what true apostolic authority means.

The claims of Paul

Paul's claims to authority, both in matters of discipline and
doctrine, are far-reaching. He has a right to issue commands to
the churches, and that right he exercises with every assurance.
It was an 'authority which the Lord gave', as he twice says in
the Second Epistle to the Corinthians (10:8; 13:10). If necessary he can come 'with a rod'; he can deliver a transgressor to
Satan (1 Cor. 4:21 – 5:5); he warns, 'If I come again, I will
not spare' (2 Cor. 13:2). 'We command you in the name of our
Lord Jesus Christ'; 'we command and exhort in the Lord Jesus
Christ'; 'we gave you this command'; 'we have confidence in
the Lord about you, that you are doing and will do the things
which we command'; 'if any one refuses to obey what we say in
this letter, note that man, and have nothing to do with him' (2
Thes. 3:4–14); 'you know what instructions we gave you
through the Lord Jesus'; 'work with your hands, as we charged
you' (1 Thes. 4:2, 11); 'I adjure you by the Lord' (1 Thes. 5:27);

---

[6] *Apostleship*, p. 43. See 1 Cor. 9:1: 'Am I not an apostle? Have I not
seen Jesus?'
[7] J. N. Geldenhuys, *Supreme Authority* (London, 1953), pp. 70f.

'This is my rule in all the churches' (1 Cor. 7:17); 'About the
other things I will give directions when I come' (1 Cor. 11:34).
Paul could issue such commands because he was the bearer of
an authoritative tradition: 'I delivered to you as of first importance what I also received' (1 Cor. 15:3). They were therefore to hold the traditions which they had been taught, under
pain of censure if they transgressed, and with the assurance of
commendation if they were faithful (2 Thes. 2:15; 3:6; 1 Cor.
11:2). Yet he was far more than the transmitter of a tradition;
he was the recipient of revelation.

He speaks of 'the abundance of revelations' which he had
from the Lord, and of how he 'was caught up into Paradise, and
he heard things that cannot be told' (2 Cor. 12:1–7). Paul's
gospel was 'according to the revelation of the mystery, which
was kept secret for long ages, but is now disclosed ... according
to the commandment of the eternal God' (Rom. 16:25f.).
'The mystery was made known to me by revelation ... of Christ;
which was not made known unto the sons of men in other
generations as it has now been revealed to his holy apostles and
prophets by the Spirit' (Eph. 3:3–5). Eternal life was manifes-
ted 'through the preaching with which I have been trusted by
command of God our Saviour' (Tit. 1:3). 'The depths of God'
have been revealed to us through the Spirit (1 Cor. 2:10). He
received his gospel, not from man, but by 'revelation of Jesus
Christ' (Gal. 1:12). So sure is he of this, that he invokes a curse
on anyone who preaches a different gospel (Gal. 1:8). Hence it
is that he can claim for his message that it is 'God's gospel' (2
Cor. 11:7), 'a command of the Lord' (1 Cor. 14:37), 'the word
of God' (1 Cor. 14:36; 1 Thes. 2:13); he can claim to have 'a
secret and hidden wisdom of God', 'the mind of Christ' (1 Cor.
2:7, 16); he can say, 'The truth of Christ is in me', 'Christ ...
speaking in me' (2 Cor. 11:10; 13:3).[8]

[8] It has been argued (*e.g.* R. R. Williams, *Authority in the Apostolic Age*,
London, 1950, p. 22) that Paul's language in 1 Cor. 7:25, 26, 40 contra-
dicts all this. 'Paul is markedly tentative – it is all "after my judgment",
"I *think* that I have the Spirit of God".' It is true that Paul here claims
neither direct tradition nor revelation from the Lord, and that he gives
his own judgment. But to make his judgment, and consequently his
authority, in this matter merely tentative, is to misunderstand the meiosis
in 'I think'. This is an understatement, gently ironical, recalling his well-
known spiritual discernment and authority.

Paul is conscious of speaking the word of God, not merely according to the best of his limited human ability, but in language that is given by God: 'But we impart this in words not taught by human wisdom but taught by the Spirit' (1 Cor. 2:13).[9] The authority pertaining to his spoken words and to his written words are the same: 'Hold to the traditions which you were taught by us, either by word of mouth or by letter' (2 Thes. 2:15); 'what we say by letter when absent, we do when present'; 'I write this while I am away from you, in order that when I come I may not have to be severe in my use of the authority which the Lord has given me' (2 Cor. 10:11; 13:10). Disobedience to the epistle demands a man's ejection from fellowship : 'If any one refuses to obey what we say in this letter, note that man, and have nothing to do with him' (2 Thes. 3:14). Recognition of the authority of what Paul writes is a criterion of spiritual understanding: 'If any one thinks that he is a prophet, or spiritual, he should acknowledge that what I am writing to you is a command of the Lord' (1 Cor. 14:37). Paul's epistles were intended to be read in the Christian assemblies: 'I adjure you by the Lord that this letter be read to all the brethren' (1 Thes. 5:27); 'When this letter has been read among you, have it read also in the church of the Laodiceans: and see that you read also the letter from Laodicea' (Col. 4:16).

Though Paul had to face bitter opposition from heretical groups, believers generally received his message like the Thessalonians – as the word of God (1 Thes. 2:13). There is certainly no adequate ground for the old Tübingen view (still cherished by some[1]) that there was a permanent feud between Peter and Paul. In 1 Corinthians 15:5-11, Paul places himself at the bottom of the apostolic list, with Cephas at the top. He is 'the least of the apostles', but whether 'it was I or they' they all preach the same gospel. The apostles are God's first gift to the church (1 Cor. 12:28; Eph. 4:11). The Jerusalem leaders, Paul

---

[9] λόγοι can mean 'propositions' or even 'treatises', so that this text must be used with reserve when discussing verbal inspiration.

[1] E.g. H. Lietzmann, *Beginnings of the Christian Church* (London, 1949), p. 110: 'Reading between the lines of his letters, we perceive behind the "servants of Satan", the "false apostles", and the "spurious brethren", the shadows of the great figures in Jerusalem.' See J. N. Geldenhuys, *Supreme Authority*, pp. 86f.

says, 'gave to me and Barnabas the right hand of fellowship, that we should go to the Gentiles and they to the circumcised' (Gal. 2:9). Peter speaks of 'our beloved brother Paul' and of 'the wisdom given him' (2 Pet. 3:15). Paul accepted Peter's authority, and Peter accepted Paul's.

Other New Testament claims

Peter likewise claims to declare the word of God. His converts have been begotten again 'through the living and abiding word of God ... that word is the good news which was preached to you' (1 Pet. 1:23ff.). His readers are bidden to 'remember the predictions of the holy prophets and the commandment of the Lord and Saviour through your apostles' (2 Pet. 3:2). He links closely the word of God spoken direct to the three apostles on the Mount of Transfiguration with the divinely given word of prophecy; and the divinely given word of prophecy he links closely with the divinely given word of the gospel. The preaching of the gospel in the power of 'the Holy Spirit sent from heaven' was a further stage in the process of divine revelation, which had been given only in part to the prophets, but which was of the deepest interest to the angelic hosts (2 Pet. 1:17–21; 1 Pet. 1:10ff.). In the Johannine Epistles, the message is one 'which we have heard'; it bears witness to the life 'which was with the Father, and was made manifest to us' (1 Jn. 1:1ff.). Failure to hold this 'teaching of Christ' must be met with refusal of hospitality and fellowship : 'If any one comes to you, and does not bring this doctrine, do not receive him into the house or give him any greeting' (2 Jn. 10). Jude 17 stresses the authority of apostolic teaching : 'You must remember ... the predictions of the apostles.'

The Apocalypse claims to be prophecy, and it concludes with a most solemn warning echoing the words of Moses with regard to the commandments of the Lord : 'I warn every one who hears the words of the prophecy of this book; if any one adds to them, God will add to him the plagues described in this book; and if any one takes away from the words of the book of this prophecy, God will take away his share in the tree of life and in the holy city, which are described in this book' (Dt. 4:2; Rev. 1:3; 22:18ff.).

Two of the Gospels claim truth for their contents : 'We know that his testimony is true' (Jn. 21 :24); 'it seemed good to me ... to write ... that you may know the truth concerning the things of which you have been informed' (Lk. 1 :1–4).

The apostles and elders, writing to the Gentile churches from Jerusalem, imply that they have authority to issue commands, and over the matter of obedience to the Mosaic law they declare their united judgment to be also that of the Holy Spirit (Acts 15 :24–28).

THE CHURCH'S ATTITUDE TO THE APOSTOLIC WRITINGS

In spite of what has been often said, there are no grounds for thinking that the New Testament books were either written or received in the consciousness that they were actually Scripture. Yet the conditions were present – reliable sources, accredited teachers, Spirit-given utterances – which normally characterize the writing of Scripture, and at an extremely early date parts of the New Testament were being spoken of as Scripture. Within the New Testament itself we have two possible examples – from 2 Peter and 1 Timothy. If these letters were written by the apostles whose names they bear,[2] we have Epistles and perhaps a Gospel being spoken of as Scripture in the sixties of the first century.

The context of 2 Peter 3:16 is one of great solemnity. The writer is talking about the end of the world, and is answering sceptics who question the promise of Christ's coming. His whole argument depends on God's faithfulness to his promise spoken by the prophets and given to his readers by the apostles. The argument is clinched by an appeal to the God-given wisdom of Paul and to the 'scriptures' that he has written. He says : 'So also our beloved brother Paul wrote to you according to the wisdom given him; speaking of this as he does in all his letters. There are some things in them hard to understand, which the ignorant and unstable twist to their own destruction as they do the other scriptures.' This turn of phrase can hardly be accidental. He has already spoken of the 'prophecy of scripture' and

[2] They are commonly dated long after the deaths of Peter and Paul. Their apostolic authorship is argued by E. M. B. Green, *2 Peter and Jude* (London, 1968), pp. 13ff. and D. Guthrie, *New Testament Introduction*, 3rd ed. (London, 1970), pp. 584ff., 814ff.

defined the mode of prophetic inspiration : 'no prophecy ever
came by the impulse of man : but men moved by the Holy
Spirit spoke from God' (1 :21). In using the word 'scripture' for
Paul's letters, he seems to be deliberately ascribing to them the
same inspiration that he ascribes to the prophetic scriptures of
the Old Testament.

1 Timothy 5:18 has a quotation from Deuteronomy 25:4,
which is bracketed with a saying of the Lord, known elsewhere
only in Luke 10:7,[3] under the common heading of 'scripture',
thus : 'The scripture says, "You shall not muzzle an ox when
it is treading out the grain," and, "The labourer deserves his
wages."' If, as may well be, Luke's Gospel had already been
in regular use in the Pauline churches for reading at public
worship for some years,[4] such a juxtaposition of Torah and
Gospel must almost certainly have been deliberate.

[3] Mt. 10:10 gives a saying only slightly different.
[4] It is hoped to discuss the dating of the Synoptic Gospels in a later
volume. C. Spicq (*Les Epîtres Pastorales*, Etudes Bibliques, Paris, 1947,
p. 186), sees a reference to Luke's Gospel also at 1 Tim. 6:3, where he
quotes Schlatter : 'It is difficult to believe that Paul could so speak of the
words of Jesus if no Gospel existed in the community.' There is a vicious
circle in New Testament criticism, which begins by denying (on in-
adequate grounds) the traditional date and author to one book, which
weakens the evidence for a second book, which weakens the evidence for
a third, and so on – till the New Testament turns out to be something
altogether different from what the unsophisticated reader in the early
church (or today) ever imagined. E. J. Goodspeed (*Introduction to the
New Testament*, Chicago, 1937, p. 213) has drawn up a very interesting
table in order to demonstrate that the Pauline Epistles were virtually
unknown till about AD 90, at which date they suddenly begin to be widely
quoted. The relevant part of it is given below. An 'x' indicates that Goodspeed believes the writer clearly to show knowledge of that particular
Epistle.

Knowledge of the Pauline Letters

	Rev.	Heb.	1 Pet.	John	James	Pastl.	2 Pet.
Eph	x	x	x	x	x	x	x
1 Cor.	x	x		x	x	x	x
2 Cor.		x	x	x		x	x
Gal.	x	x	x	x	x	x	x
Phil.	x	x		x	x	x	x
Col.	x	x		x		x	x
1 Thes.	x	x	x	x	x	x	x
2 Thes.			x	x		x	x
Phm.	x			x		x	x

Now of course Goodspeed's whole argument is bound up with the dating

Thus we see within the New Testament itself, not only an immense authority given to the apostles as the God-sent founders of the Christian church, but we see also that the church of the New Covenant is to have Scriptures of the New Covenant. There is no definition of the limits of the New Testament Canon, but the beginning of a canon is there, duly attested, apparently by Peter and Paul themselves.

Recognition of New Testament Scriptures was confirmed and extended in the days immediately following the apostolic era. Four things characterize the writers of the sub-apostolic period : 1. For them the words of the Lord possess unconditional authority. 2. They assume that the dominical and apostolic doctrine is the only norm of Christian belief. 3. They show considerable knowledge of apostolic writings and there is at least one instance (Barnabas 4:14) of a quotation from a New Testament book introduced by 'as it is written', and there are probable instances of the use of the terms 'Scriptures' (Polycarp 12) and 'Oracles' (Papias – Eusebius, *Ecc. Hist.* X iii. 39) in reference to New Testament books. 4. They show no knowledge, however, of a formal establishment of a new Canon of Scripture by the apostles during their lifetime. By AD 170 (at the latest) not only was the concept of New Testament Scripture firmly established, but the main contents of the new Canon were undisputed : four Gospels, Acts, thirteen letters of Paul, 1 Peter, 1 John. Complete unanimity had not yet been reached about the other books, but there was no doubt as to the existence and main contents of an extended Canon.

It did not, however, settle the precise limits of the Canon. The fringe of uncertainty presented by the disputed books of the Canon (and by variations in the biblical text) takes us out

---

of the non-Pauline documents. If Hebrews and 1 and 2 Peter (to mention no others) are dated in the sixties, a completely new complexion is put upon the whole matter. We have 'something like mutual attestation' of one living writer by another (this is a phrase of W. H. Griffith Thomas, *The Principles of Theology*, London, 1930, p. 111). It is of course difficult to know whether it is mutual attestation or the use of common liturgical or catechetical material, which might itself have originated with Jesus. 2 Peter at any rate would indicate that a considerable body of Pauline writings was known to Peter's constituency during the lifetime of Paul, and that Peter himself saw no incongruity in calling them Scriptures.

of the limited field of biblical study into the wide field of church history; out of the realm of the direct teaching of Christ into areas which can be explored only in a less direct way. It is important to stress the peripheral nature of this 'fringe' discussion. The heart of the matter has been established on the direct authority of Christ : the truth of Old Testament, of Christ's teaching and of the teaching of the apostles. Herein without question lies the divine revelation, the Word of the living God, by which the church should be taught and ruled. But there is good reason to believe that God has guided his church to identify precisely the inspired books. With revelation as our guide, it should be possible to discern his activity within his church.

We seem justified in saying :

To Christ his own teaching and the teaching of his Spirit-taught apostles was true, authoritative, inspired.

To him, what he and they said under the direction of the Spirit, God said.

To him the God of the New Testament was the living God, and in principle the teaching of the New Testament was the teaching of the living God.

THE EXTENT
OF THE
CANON

6

THE PROBLEM

In discussing the question of canonicity, it is best to deal with the two Testaments together, as the one sheds light upon the other. At first sight the Bible appears to be an arbitrary collection of books. We have Esther, in which the name of God is not mentioned; Canticles, a love song; Ecclesiastes, with its apparent blend of Epicureanism and Pessimism. We have pages of incomplete genealogies, as in 1 Chronicles 1–8; duplication, as in 2 Kings 18–20 and Isaiah 36–39; over-lapping, as in Kings and Chronicles and in the Gospels; repetition, as in the twelve-fold reiteration of the offerings of Numbers 7:12–83; strange symbolism, as in the apocalypses of Old and New Testaments.

Furthermore there has never been complete unanimity amongst Christians as to the limits of the Canon. Traces of uncertainty about the book of Esther persist in the Eastern church till at least as late as the fourteenth century.[1] From early times there has been difference of opinion amongst Christians of both East and West as to whether the books of the Old Testament Apocrypha should be regarded as Scripture. In the West it was not till the Council of Hippo in 393 that something like unanimity was reached as to the limits of the New Testament Canon. In the churches of the East uncertainties about some books persisted far longer, notably with regard to the Apocalypse; so much so that Westcott could say that, during the middle ages, 'in no one of the Eastern Churches was there any fixed judgment or consistent tradition'[2] as to the contents of the Canon.

[1] B. F. Westcott, *The Bible in the Church*, 3rd ed. (London, 1870), p. 227.
[2] *Ibid.*, p. 243.

Luther's strictures on the Epistle of James are well known. Most modern New Testament critics confidently affirm that the Second Epistle of Peter does not come from the apostolic circle. Part of the process of canonization appears to have been from the human standpoint more or less undesigned, and in any case, the early definers of the Canon do not always command our confidence as trustworthy authorities. Are there reliable criteria of canonicity?

Criteria of canonicity are neither obvious nor neatly simple. Subjective assessment of the spiritual value of the various books is not by itself adequate. No two people acting independently would agree in their selection. Certainly they would not have identified the (at first sight) strange selection that we find in our Bible. The inner witness of the Holy Spirit gives an important measure of general guidance. To countless thousands the Bible has become a new and living book after an experience of re-birth by the Spirit, and, as the Westminster Confession says (1:5), 'our full persuasion and assurance of the infallible truth, and divine authority' of the Bible, 'is from the inward work of the Holy Spirit, bearing witness by and with the word in our hearts.

But the Spirit does not by a subjective process give a clear witness to the believer that the genealogies are God-given oracles. Many a devout reader has on occasion been known to skip the early chapters of Chronicles! The Spirit does not give unanimity as to the authenticity of Mark 16:9–20 – devout and well-informed readers have come to opposite conclusions. John 7:53 – 8:11, which was not an original part of the Fourth Gospel, and which even so conservative a scholar as A. Edersheim did not regard as strictly historical,[3] has none the less been treasured by multitudes of Christians down the centuries. And this lack of unanimity, as we shall see later, goes beyond these minor divergences to some questions of considerably greater importance.

Conversely, I can clearly recall the zest with which I read and underlined the book of Ecclesiasticus not long after my own

[3] A. Edersheim, *The Life and Times of Jesus the Messiah* (London, 1901), Vol. II, p. 163, n. 1. For further discussion of these passages, see pp. 181f.

conversion, in a way quite indistinguishable from that which I had used for the Old and New Testaments.

John Bunyan recounts in his autobiography, *Grace Abounding*,[4] how after many weeks of the deepest depression, a 'sentence fell with weight upon my spirit, "Look at the generations of old and see; did ever any trust in the Lord, and was confounded?" At which I was greatly lightened and encouraged in my soul ... I presently went to my Bible to see if I could find that saying, not doubting but to find it presently; for it was so fresh, and with such strength and comfort on my spirit, that I was as if it talked with me.' After more than a year of fruitless search and enquiry, he says : 'At last, casting my eye into the Apocrypha books, I found it in Ecclesiasticus 2:10. This, at the first, did somewhat daunt me; but ... when I considered, that though it was not in those texts that we call holy and canonical, yet forasmuch as this sentence was the sum and substance of many of the promises, it was my duty to take the comfort of it; and I bless God for that word, for it was of God to me : that word doth still, at times, shine before my face.' He thankfully acknowledged that a verse from the Apocrypha played a major part in his conversion.

But if subjective tests can give no simple answer, neither can any simple objective test be found. The criterion of prophetic or apostolic authorship (taken in its simple and natural sense) does not cover all cases. We have no good reason for regarding the judgment of Jewish Synods as authoritative. Councils of the Christian church have on occasions been conducted in a disgraceful manner, and quite certainly at times 'have erred'. No attempt was made during the discussion of the Canon in the early centuries to look to the Pope for an infallible *ex cathedra* ruling. There are objective criteria, but they are not in themselves neat and decisive.

It seems that we may best enunciate the grounds of canonicity in some such terms as this : *Grounds of canonicity are to be found in an interplay of subjective and objective factors over-ruled by Divine Providence.*

---

[4] John Bunyan, *Works*, Vol. 1 (1860), para. 62ff., pp. 13f.

THE HISTORY OF THE OLD TESTAMENT CANON

Biblical evidence

Taking the Old Testament at its face value,[5] the first stage in the formation of the Canon is plain enough. It was through the agency of Moses that the Israelite theocracy was established. God spoke to Moses face to face (Ex. 33:11) and Moses wrote down the words of the Lord (Ex. 24:4; Dt. 31:9). Then, 'when Moses had made an end of writing the words of this law in a book, until they were finished, he commanded, saying, "Take this book of the law, and put it by the side of the ark of the covenant of the Lord your God, that it may be there for a witness against you"' (Dt. 31:24ff.). The Mosaic documents, edited probably by Eleazar or some other early Israelite leader, constitute thenceforth the authoritative Law of Israel.

Joshua was bidden to meditate continually in the book of the law, and it was said of him that he 'left nothing undone of all that the Lord commanded Moses' (Jos. 1:8; 11:15). The survival of the heathen nations in and around Canaan during the period of the judges was 'to prove Israel ... to know whether they would hearken unto the commandments of the Lord which he commanded their fathers by the hand of Moses' (Jdg. 3:4). God had commanded that in the event of the appointment of a king a copy of the Law should be provided for him (Dt. 17:18). Throughout the monarchy the fate of the kings is bound up with their attitude to the Law. Saul (1 Sa. 15), David (1 Ki. 3:14; 9:4; 11:34, 38), Solomon (1 Ki. 2:3; 8:56ff.; 2 Ch. 8:13), Jeroboam (1 Ki. 14:7ff.), Asa (2 Ch. 14:4), Jehoshaphat (2 Ch. 17:9), Joash (2 Ch. 23:18; 24:6), Amaziah (2 Ki. 14:6; 2 Ch. 25:4), Hezekiah (2 Ki. 18:6; 2 Ch. 30:16), Manasseh (2 Ki. 21:2ff.), Josiah (2 Ki. 23:3ff.; 2 Ch. 34:14ff.) all have their actions weighed by this standard. The Captivity results from disobedience to the Law (2 Ki. 17:7ff.; 2 Ch. 33:8; Dn. 9:11; Ne. 1:7–9; 9:14–30). The restored exiles return to its obedience (Ezr. 3:2; 6:16; Ne. 8:1–8; 10:28; 13:1).

[5] A later volume is to be given to a consideration of the critical issues concerning the historical value of the Old Testament, arguing the essentially Mosaic authorship of the Pentateuch and a sixth-century date for the book of Daniel.

Thus, according to the Bible's own witness, the authority of
the Law of Moses pervades the whole history of Israel. But of
the composition and preservation of other writings, we get only
an occasional glimpse. Joshua at the end of his life wrote the
words of the covenant at Shechem in the book of the law of
God (Jos. 24:26). Samuel 'told the people the manner of the
kingdom, and wrote it in a book, and laid it up before the
Lord' (1 Sa. 10:25). This shows that Israel had the practice,
common to many of the nations of antiquity, of depositing
sacred records in the sanctuary. This is borne out by the discovery of Josiah's book of the law in the Temple (2 Ki. 22 and
23). We have a glimpse of the collection of prophetical writings in Jeremiah 36 :4; 45 :1, and of proverbs in Proverbs 25 :1,
but otherwise we gain very little information from within the
Old Testament itself. The one thing that stands out clearly is
the central place occupied by the Law of Moses, which place it
has occupied in all the subsequent history of Jewry.

But revelation did not end with Moses. After a long period
of political disunity and spiritual degradation, new life came to
Israel through a succession of prophets, who had been foreseen
in measure by Moses (Dt. 18:18–22). Beginning with Samuel,
Elijah and Elisha, and continuing with the so-called writing
prophets from Amos and Hosea to Malachi, they played a part
in the history of revelation almost as important as that of Moses.
The God-fearing in Israel recognized their utterance (prefaced
by 'Thus says the Lord') as divine oracles, and collections of
some of their messages were made while they were still alive.
Jeremiah himself (chapter 36) directed that his oracles should
be written down, and others may have done the same (Is. 8:16),
and there is no reason to doubt that the written message would
have carried the same authority as the spoken word. We have
an instance of a later prophet quoting an earlier prophet in
Daniel 9:2, where Jeremiah is quoted; references to the former
prophets collectively by Zechariah (1:4–6; 7:7, 12); and an
instance of earlier prophets being quoted as authoritative by
the elders of the land in Jeremiah 26:17. During the Prophetic Era were also produced – if we take the Old Testament
at its face value – many of the psalms, the book of Proverbs and
Canticles.

These and some other books found their way into our Old Testament, yet a large number of books that were regarded as in some degree authoritative and valuable were excluded. The Old Testament mentions the following by name, and we have no reason to think that the list is exhaustive :

The Book of the Wars of the Lord (Nu. 21:14).

The Book of Jashar (Jos. 10:13).

The book concerning the manner of the kingdom (1 Sa. 10:25).

Presumably there had been a collection of Solomon's three thousand proverbs, his thousand and five songs and his works on natural history (1 Ki. 4:32f.).

The Book of the Acts of Solomon (1 Ki. 11:41).

The Book of the Chronicles of the Kings of Israel (1 Ki. 14:19).

The Book of the Chronicles of the Kings of Judah (1 Ki. 15:7).

The History of Samuel the Seer;

The History of Nathan the Prophet;

The History of Gad the Seer (1 Ch. 29:29).

The Prophecy of Ahijah the Shilonite;

The Visions of Iddo the Seer (2 Ch. 9:29).

The History of Shemaiah the Prophet (2 Ch. 12:15).

The History of Jehu (2 Ch. 20:34).

The Acts of Uzziah by Isaiah the Prophet (2 Ch. 26:22).

The Lamentations (by Jeremiah over Josiah – Josiah is not mentioned in our Lamentations) (2 Ch. 35:25).

Is it possible to discover why these books were not included in the Canon?

We shall look in vain for a direct answer to this question from the Bible. It has often been said that Scripture, because it is the Word of God, is self-authenticating, and that therefore all Scripture is immediately received as the Word of God by believers from the time of its first promulgation. No doubt there is an important element of truth in this. Yet it is palpably untrue that the Word of God is always recognized as such immediately by all true believers. If it were so, why should Peter have said, 'God forbid, Lord! This shall never happen to you' (Mt. 16:22)? Why should there have been a need for the

Council of Jerusalem in Acts 15? Why should Luther have underrated the Epistle of James?

It is surely impossible to prove that the tiny, personal Epistles of the New Testament were self-authenticating from the first and immediately received by the church at large. It is plain rather that the early church felt in need of objective, historical tests to establish their apostolicity, before accepting them as canonical. Similarly, in the case of the Old Testament, it is rash to suppose that all inspired psalms were immediately distinguishable from uninspired psalms, or that Esther, Ecclesiastes and Canticles were immediately accepted as soon as they were written. Nor can it be proved that all the books pass the test enunciated by W. H. Green: 'Those books, and those only, were accepted as the divine standards of their faith and regulative of their conduct *which were written for this definite purpose* by those whom they believed to be inspired of God.'[6] Nor can it be said that R. Laird Harris,[7] for all his vigorous argumentation, has proved that prophetic authorship is the one determining principle of canonicity. That the authors of Joshua, Judges, Ruth, Chronicles, Ezra, Nehemiah, Esther, Job, Proverbs, Ecclesiastes and Canticles were prophets, takes some proving!

Extra-biblical evidence

There is an interesting passage in Josephus on this subject. Josephus, born about AD 37, was perhaps the most distinguished and most learned Jew of his day. His father was a priest and his mother was descended from the Maccabean kings. Given the best possible education, he proved to be something of a prodigy. At the age of sixteen he began a careful investigation of the Jewish sects, and actually spent three years in solitude with the Essenes. At nineteen he joined the Pharisees. After desperate fighting in the Jewish War against the Romans, he was taken prisoner, and used by the Romans as a means of communication with his countrymen. After the conquest of

[6] W. H. Green, *General Introduction to the Old Testament: the Canon* (London, 1899), pp. 35f. (Italics mine.)
[7] R. L. Harris, *Inspiration and Canonicity of the Bible* (Grand Rapids, 1957), chapter 7.

Judea he wrote his great works, the *Antiquities of the Jews* and the *History of the Jewish War*. It was towards the end of the century, at his most mature, that he composed his reply to the violent attack that had been made upon the Jewish people by the Alexandrian grammarian, Apion. Such a man was pre-eminently qualified to report on Jewish beliefs, and in the circumstances he would have had special incentives to avoid mis-statements that his opponents could have refuted. He is defending the Jewish Scriptures, and writes :

'We have not tens of thousands of books, discordant and conflicting, but only twenty-two, containing the record of all time, which have been justly believed (to be divine). And of these, five are the books of Moses, which embrace the laws and the tradition from the creation of man until his (Moses') death. This period is a little short of three thousand years. From the death of Moses to the reign of Artaxerxes, the successor of Xerxes, king of Persia, the prophets who succeeded Moses wrote what was done in thirteen books. The remaining four books embrace hymns to God and counsels for men for the conduct of life. From Artaxerxes until our time everything has been recorded, but has not been deemed worthy of like credit with what preceded, because the exact succession of the prophets ceased. But what faith we have placed in our own writings is evident by our conduct; for though so long a time has now passed, no one has dared either to add anything to them, or to take anything from them, or to alter anything in them. But it is instinctive in all Jews at once from their very birth to regard them as commands of God, and to abide by them, and, if need be, cheerfully to die for them.'[8] Philo, who wrote in the first half of the first century AD, and whose eminence rivalled that of Josephus, spoke in similar terms. Like Josephus he was a man of letters, deeply versed in Hebrew learning. His reputation in Alexandria was such that he was chosen for an embassy that went to Caligula in Rome to defend the Jews against the accusations of Apion and others. Philo, as quoted by Eusebius, says that the Jews 'have not altered even a single word of what had been written by him (Moses), but would rather endure to

[8] *Against Apion* i. 8. 41, 42.

die ten thousand times, than yield to any persuasion contrary
to his laws and customs'.[9]

What is particularly interesting about the statement of Josephus is the clear distinction between the canonical books which
were completed in the time of Artaxerxes, and those written
later which were not considered worthy of like credit 'because
the exact succession of the prophets ceased'. The idea evidently
is that the canonical books were either written (or accredited)
by the prophets, but that when the prophetical era was over, no
more books suitable for the Canon were written. This notion
of the long period without prophecy, coupled sometimes with
a looking forward to the coming of a Faithful Prophet, has a
considerable place in inter-testamental times and among the
rabbis and the early fathers.[1]

The second point of interest is that Josephus commits himself to a fairly precise date for the closing of the Canon. Artaxerxes Longimanus reigned for forty years, 465 to 425 BC.
Ezra came to Jesusalem in the seventh, and Nehemiah in the
twentieth, year of his reign (Ezr. 7 : 1, 8; Ne. 2 : 1). In addition
to Josephus there are several other witnesses who point to the
time of Ezra and Nehemiah, with occasionally a reference to
the ministries of Haggai, Zechariah and Malachi, as the time
of the collection, completion and recognition of the Old Testament Canon. Though there is an absence of historical sense
among the Talmudic rabbis, there can be no warrant for dis-
regarding their persistent elevation of Ezra to a position second
only to Moses. It is to Ezra and the men of the Great Synagogue
that appeal is continually made.[2]

In one of the minor tractates of the Talmud, *Aboth of Rabbi
Nathan* (1.3), it is said of the Mosaic tradition, 'Haggai,
Zechariah and Malachi received it from the prophets. The men
of the Great Synagogue received it from Haggai, Zechariah

[9] Eusebius, *De Pref. Evang.* viii. 6, Gifford's translation.
[1] 1 Macc. 4 :46; 9 :27; 14 :41. Jerome, *Comm. on Isaiah* chap. 49, verse
21; Augustine, *City of God* xvii. 24. For references in the Jewish chronicles *Seder Olam Rabba* and *Seder Olam Zuta*, see articles in *Jewish Encyclopaedia*; R. H. Pfeiffer, *Introduction to the Old Testament*, p. 63;
M. Stuart, *The Old Testament Canon* (London, 1849), p. 205.
[2] See G. F. Moore, *Judaism* (Cambridge, Mass., 1927), I, ch. 2, 'Ezra
and the Great Synagogue', and the excursuses in C. H. H. Wright,
Ecclesiastes (London, 1883), pp. 451ff.

and Malachi.' In the book of the Apocrypha, 2 Esdras 14, to be dated probably about AD 100, is found the Ezra Legend, which tells how in forty days, under the inspiration of the Most High, Ezra dictated all the books of the Old Testament (and seventy more which were not for publication), to five scribes. 2 Maccabees 2 : 13, to be dated somewhere between BC 120 and 50 AD, records how Nehemiah 'collected the chronicles of the kings, the writings of the prophets, the works of David'. These traditions are of little value for establishing the details of the history, but the traditions need accounting for. It seems gratuitous to reject the obvious explanation and deny them a historical root.

Normally it requires a period of great upheaval and decisive leadership to make a community adopt a body of authoritative documents as normative for its life. In the history of Judaism, only three periods stand out as times when the people as a whole would welcome such authoritative guidance. The first was after the deliverance from slavery in Egypt when the children of Israel found themselves defenceless in a terrifying wilderness. Their inescapable dependence upon Moses made them ready to accept his word as law. The last was after the destruction of Jerusalem in AD 70 when Jewry had to face a complete re-modelling of its life, and when, under the leadership of Rabbi Johanan ben Zakkai, the rabbis of Jamnia established the norms of Jewish orthodoxy which have governed its life ever since. In between came the no less decisive upheaval of the restoration from Babylon. Here was a people, battered almost beyond endurance by the successive terrors of its history, back in a land of desolation, weighed down with poverty, surrounded by enemies, facing a future inscrutable yet ominous. Their only hope lay in the God of their fathers, who had redeemed them and chastened them and visited them and restored them. They needed leaders who would enable them to re-establish Jerusalem and its Temple, and who would teach them afresh the glories of their faith. Delays and frustrations seemed interminable—it was some ninety years after the return under Zerubbabel before the walls of Jerusalem were rebuilt – yet God sent them prophets and leaders to sustain and encourage them.

There is no reason to doubt that the decisive role was played by Ezra the scribe towards the end of the period. One can picture him preparing accurate, clearly-written copies of the Law of Moses; collecting and setting in order and bringing up to date the narrative of the Lord's dealings with Israel; collecting the works of the prophets and the wise men; authorizing the psalter of the Second Temple. There is no reason to doubt that the Canon of the Old Testament is substantially Ezra's canon, just as the Pentateuch was substantially Moses' canon. The work of Ezra's successors, as of those of Moses, would have been no more than a rounding off of a task already almost complete. The establishment of such a clearly-defined canon under the influence of one outstanding man provides the best explanation of the great tenacity of the Jews throughout their history in adhering to this particular collection of books as alone inspired. As far as I know, there is no external evidence against this view. Its rejection seems to be based entirely on internal considerations. Yet once the essentially Mosaic origin of the Pentateuch is accepted and the Maccabean date of Daniel is abandoned, the remaining reasons for giving late dates to the other books seem to be quite flimsy.

ARGUMENTS AGAINST THE TRADITIONAL VIEW
Theory of three successive canons

It may be argued that the threefold form of the Hebrew Canon is best explained by positing a successive authoritative recognition of three different groups of sacred books. H. E. Ryle,[3] for instance, calls them respectively the First, Second and Third Canons. He dates the conclusion of the First Canon sometime before 432 BC, and says (p. 93) that 'at that time, no other writing was regarded by the Jews as sacred and authoritative'. With regard to the Second Canon : 'we arrive at the probable conclusion that the formation of the group of "the Prophets", having been commenced not earlier than the year 300 BC, was brought to a completion by the end of the same century' (p.

---

[3] H. E. Ryle, *The Canon of the Old Testament* (London, 1892). The order of the present Hebrew Canon is : *Law* – Gn., Ex., Lv., Nu., Dt. *Prophets* – Jos., Jdg., 1 and 2 Sa., 1 and 2 Ki.; Is., Je., Ezk., minor prophets. *Writings* – Pss., Pr., Jb., Ct., Ru., La., Ec., Est., Dn., Ezr., Ne., 1 and 2 Ch.

113). Of the Third Canon (known to the Jews as 'The Writings', but sometimes called the Hagiographa) he says : 'We believe (there) to have been some sort of an official declaration by the Jewish Rabbis, that finally determined the limits of the Hebrew Canon,' 'which cannot be placed much later than the end of the first cent. AD' (p. 171). This explanation has one obvious merit at first sight. It would explain the grouping of certain historical books – Joshua, Judges, Samuel, Kings (the so-called Former Prophets) – with the great body of written prophecies – Isaiah, Jeremiah, Ezekiel and the Twelve (the so-called Latter Prophets); and the jumbling of poetry, history and wisdom literature with the noteworthy prophecy of Daniel under the general heading of the Writings. But the theory is pure conjecture. Other principles of arrangement are possible.

W. H. Green held that the Former Prophets were in fact drawn up by men holding the prophetic office, whereas the writers of the third group, the Hagiographa, were inspired men who did not hold the prophetic office.[4] It is true that the historical books of the Hagiographa can be attributed to Ezra and Nehemiah with some show of reason, and the Wisdom books largely to David and Solomon, and it is true that Daniel, though temporarily endowed with the prophetic gift, was not a prophet by office. But that the Former Prophets were written, or given their present form, by prophets is capable of neither proof nor disproof. That such was a widespread Jewish belief when this arrangement was first made (and it certainly was at a later date) is altogether possible. The fact, however, that Amos could say, 'I was (or even, I am) no prophet' (7:14), makes the distinction between his position and that of Daniel somewhat precarious.

R. T. Beckwith, in a forthcoming book on the Old Testament Canon in first-century thought, sees the matter differently. He argues thus : Although many of the books do not fall into neat categories, each of the three divisions has a historical section. The Torah covers the history to the death of Moses; the Prophets to the Captivity; the Writings carry it on through the Captivity to the Restoration. The main part of this final section

[4] W. H. Green, *General Introduction to the Old Testament: the Canon*, pp. 8off.

of history is given in Ezra-Nehemiah, but noteworthy episodes
of Captivity history are also given in Daniel and Esther. Finally,
Chronicles recapitulates the whole history from Adam to the
Restoration. So we find that : linked with the Mosaic history
is Mosaic law; linked with the 'prophetical' history are the
writings of the prophets; linked with the captivity and restoration history are the devotional and sapiential books. Daniel of
course has large sections of prophecy, just as the major prophets have large sections of history; Daniel also has its wisdom
element; but it is at least not irrational to put Daniel with
Esther, Ezra-Nehemiah and the sapiential books.

   It is probably true, though far from obvious, that the order
of the books mentioned in the Baba Bathra (14b, 15a) in the
Talmud was a standardized order in the first century AD. R. D.
Wilson[5] detailed the forty-three ancient lists of Old Testament
books known to him, and showed that 'no two ancient sources
agree as to the order of the books', and he declared that 'Daniel
... is found ... always in the ancient sources among the
Prophets, except in the list found in the Baba Bathra'. But these
ancient sources are Christian, and Christians clearly felt no
obligation to follow Jewish practice. At first sight Josephus
might seem to confirm the view of Wilson that Daniel was
originally placed among the prophets. We have already seen
that Josephus speaks of twenty-two books – five books of Moses,
thirteen written by the prophets and the remaining four 'hymns
to God and counsels for men for the conduct of life'. The four
are almost certainly Psalms, Proverbs, Ecclesiastes, Canticles;
the thirteen are Joshua, Judges-with-Ruth, Samuel, Kings,
Chronicles, Ezra-with-Nehemiah, Esther, Job, Isaiah, Jeremiah-
with-Lamentations, Ezekiel, Daniel, the Minor Prophets. This
arrangement, however, seems (like those adopted by most
Christian groups later) to have been an attempted simplification
and rationalization designed for Gentile consumption.

   Strange to say, Jerome is the most ancient direct witness to
Jewish practice and he (*pace* Wilson) confirms the Talmud's
grouping. Furthermore, the Talmud's own witness is more
primitive than might at first appear. Although the Talmud was

---

[5] 'The Book of Daniel and the Canon', *Princeton Theological Review*,
13 (1915), pp. 405f.

written down probably in the fifth century, the statement about
the order of the books is itself a *baraita*, a quotation from an
earlier source, and the Talmud says expressly that it was the
traditional order. The fact is that all Jewish authorities, apart
from Josephus, distribute the books between the Prophets and
the Writings in the same way as the Talmud, even though the
actual order of the books varies. It would seem, therefore, that
Wilson's scepticism about the tradition is excessive, and that we
are justified in taking our Lord's reference to the blood shed
from Abel to Zechariah (Mt. 23:35; *cf*. Lk. 11:51) as meaning
'all murders recorded in the Bible, from the first book of the
canon to the last' – making the Zechariah in question the
Zechariah mentioned in 2 Chronicles 24:20f.

Thus the view that the threefold structure of the Hebrew
Bible demands the successive acknowledgment of three separate
canons is unproved. The words of C. H. H. Wright[6] are not too
strong: 'There is nothing worthy to be regarded as real "evidence" concerning the settlement of the so-called Canon of the
Old Testament Scriptures. No one can prove when or by what
authority the books of the Old Testament were arranged into
three distinct divisions. It is vain to speak of three distinct
canons, and to assign . . . a date for the closing up of each
division. Those attempts rest upon unhistorical conjectures.'
That the number of the canonical books was both fixed and
believed to be of long-standing in the time of Josephus seems
clear. That there was a threefold classification of the recognized
books is evident in our Lord's day (Lk. 24:44) and in the time
of Ben Sira (say about 180 BC[7]), but one is not justified in being

[6] C. H. H. Wright, *Daniel and His Prophecies* (London, 1906), p. 50.
[7] See Prologue to *Ecclesiasticus*. This is the commonly accepted date of
Ben Sira, though it should be noted that a number of excellent scholars
would put the date a century earlier. See H. A. C. Hävernick, *Introduction to the Old Testament* (Edinburgh, 1852), p. 28; A. Edersheim,
Life and Times (London, 1901), I, p. 26; J. H. A. Hart, *Ecclesiasticus*
(Cambridge, 1909), p. 271. Edersheim says: 'To my mind at least, the
historical evidence, apart from critical considerations, seems very strong.
Modern writers on the other side have confessedly been influenced by
the consideration that the earlier date of the Book of Sirach would also
involve a much earlier date for the close of the OT Canon than they
are disposed to admit.' It behoves those who are not impressed by the
critical considerations advanced by the regnant schools of criticism to
re-examine the whole matter carefully. Of Hart's detailed arguments

completely dogmatic as to the limits of 'the prophecies' and 'the
rest of the books'. That the great re-organization of Jewish life
under Ezra and Nehemiah included a careful collection of the
prophetical, historical, liturgical and didactic literature upon
which the resurrected nation had been nourished seems altogether likely. One can imagine these works, together with the
official records of the Return and the words of the prophets who
helped in the work of restoration, being carefully stored as a
sacred library in the Second Temple. These would be copied
and made available for use elsewhere as need dictated. Increas-
ingly Judaism became a book religion. Till the voice of John the
Baptist was heard crying in the wilderness, no prophet arose to
utter the word of the Lord. This at least gives a picture agree-
able to the Old Testament itself and in line with the best Jewish
tradition.

Debates at Jamnia

If we take this traditional view as a working hypothesis, what
are we to make of the later debates concerning the canonicity
of certain books? Among the rabbis of Jamnia Ezekiel came in
for question, because of its apparent departures from the Law.
In Proverbs the flat (formal) contradiction between 26:4 and
26:5 caused some trouble. Ecclesiastes was thought by some not
to be ethically sound. Canticles came into disrepute through
being used as a secular song and sung in taverns. Esther introduced a non-Mosaic festival.

Does this mean that in fact the Canon at this date was still
fluid? The truth appears to be, in the words of A. Bentzen:
The discussions of the so-called Synod of Jamnia 'have not so
much dealt with acceptance of certain writings into the Canon,
but rather with their *right to remain there*. That Ezekiel is
mentioned in this connection is a proof of this. For the Canon of
Prophets had then long been finished. If we study the discussion in the *Mishna* and the *Talmud* we see that it is always
presupposed that the disputed books are canonical ... The synod
of Jamnia did not define the Canon, but it undertook a *revi-*

R. H. Pfeiffer (*History of New Testament Times*, New York, 1949, p.
365) says that they are 'utterly unconvincing'. Unfortunately, however,
he finds no space to answer them.

sion.'[8] Or, if 'revision' suggests to English ears some measure of alteration, it might be better expressed: 'The academy at Jamnia did not define the Canon, it re-examined it.' This judgment agrees with an earlier statement of H. L. Strack: 'Seriously meant contradictions against the canon of the twenty-four sacred books were never raised in ancient Jewry; books once received were neither seriously contested, nor was any book, that is spoken of in the preceding discussion as not received, ever subsequently admitted, or attempts made to admit it. In all the Talmudic disputations the question was not of the reception of new books, nor of the enlargement of the canon, nor of the exclusion of a book on the ground of any critical doubts, but only that individual scholars adduced reasons taken from the contents for the exclusion of one book or another long since received, without in a single instance practical effect being given to these discussions. The debates often make the impression that the doubts were only raised in order to be contradicted; in other words, on the one hand as an exercise of acuteness, and on the other to demonstrate the authority of the sacred books as absolutely assured. There is no passage from which it follows that there was any wavering in the religious consciousness of the people as to the canonicity of any one of the twenty-four books.'[9]

The Qumran use

Owing, it would seem, to some rather loose thinking, the Dead Sea sect has been called in as evidence of the existence of a wider canon than the later official Jewish canon. B. J. Roberts,[1] for instance, says: They 'did not limit themselves to the tripartite Hebrew canon as we know it, nor to the slightly larger

[8] A. Bentzen, *Introduction to the Old Testament* (Copenhagen, 1948), I, p.31. J. P. Lewis, 'What do we mean by Jabneh?' (*Journal of Bible and Religion*, 32, 1964) has shown that there was an academy, rather than a synod, at Jamnia (or Jabneh), and that it had no perceptible effect on Jewish discussions about the Canon. On one occasion the canonicity of Canticles and Ecclesiastes was officially upheld, but 'the frequently made assertion that a binding decision was made at Jabneh covering all scripture is conjectural at best' (p. 132).
[9] *Herzog-Plitt Real-Encyklopädie*, Art. 'Kanon des Alten Testaments', 1880, VII, 429, as translated by W. H. Green, *General Introduction to the Old Testament: The Canon*, pp. 134f., n. 1.
[1] 'The Dead Sea Scrolls', *Trans. Victoria Inst.*, 1952, p. 167.

collection which Rabbinic Judaism discussed in the Mishnah.
They did submit to the Torah, and interpreted it; likewise they
were exponents of the Prophets and Writings; they included
also one or two of the books of the Apocrypha, for we find in the
scrolls quotations from 1 and 2 (*sic*) Esdras and Ecclesiasticus.
But they also accepted books which go far beyond this compass,
and include books in the Pseudepigrapha. Actually, the scrolls
have more in common with the apocalyptic ideas and interpretations found in the Pseudepigrapha than with most of the
Rabbinic teaching in the Mishnah and Talmuds.' It is clear that
the sect was intensely preoccupied with the Law and the
Prophets, which they studied and on which they wrote commentaries. It is clear, too, that they were steeped in the Psalms;
Proverbs is specifically cited as Scripture and is often (like Job)
echoed in the hymns; Daniel, Ecclesiastes and Lamentations all
seem to be known. In the words of T. H. Gaster, 'An interesting
feature of the Old Testament parallels is that there is no quotation from the Book of Esther, the one book of Scripture that has
not yet turned up among the Qumran fragments.'[2] An occasional quotation from other books does not make them canonical, and mere parallels have no bearing on the question at all.
The strictly canonical status of Law and Prophets and some of
the Writings is fully confirmed, but for some of the Writings the
evidence is insufficient to provide either confirmation or contradiction of the explicit teaching of Josephus and Philo.

The Sadducean use

And what are we to make of the Sadducees, who, according to
Acts 23:8, denied the resurrection and the existence of angels?
Many of the Fathers believed that the Sadducees, like the

---

[2] T. H. Gaster, *Scripture of the Dead Sea Sect* (London, 1957), p. 319.
It is perhaps unfortunate that Gaster incorporates the term 'Scriptures'
in his title. Commentaries, hymn-books and manuals of discipline are not
Scripture in the proper sense. Although no copy of Esther has been
found, there is reason for thinking that the Qumran community recognized its canonicity. For if they shared the rabbinical doubts about
Esther, it is curious that they did not share the rabbinical doubts about
the other books. Ezekiel and Proverbs they certainly regarded as inspired. Moreover, they seem to have had a twenty-two book canon (see
the best text of Jubilees 2:23), and it is clear from Josephus that the
twenty-two book canon included Esther.

Samaritans, acknowledged only the Pentateuch as Scripture. According to E. Schürer, however, this 'is not confirmed by documentary authority, and has therefore been given up as erroneous by modern scholars'.[3] Disbelief in the resurrection is perfectly understandable on the basis of an appeal to the Pentateuch alone; but disbelief in angels is as difficult to understand in one who believes only in the Pentateuch[4] as in one who accepts the whole Old Testament. It seems that Luke was not speaking in an absolute sense. The Sadducees presumably believed the very restrained biblical account of the angel of the Lord and of the other heavenly messengers that are mentioned from time to time in the Old Testament, but they repudiated the elaborate system of angelic hierarchies taught by the Pharisees. The same may reasonably be supposed to be true with regard to Old Testament teaching about the resurrection. It was not so much a case of absolute denial, as of a denial of crude popular representations of a kind that could lead to the picture of a man in heaven with seven wives. The Law would obviously be the one part of the total Jewish tradition which no rationalizer could reject and still call himself a Jew. It would not be fatal to the traditional view of the Canon if it were proved that the rationalistic approach of the Sadducees led to a rejection, not only of the traditions of the elders, but also of the Prophets and the Writings, for the Sadducees were an unrepresentative, aristocratic clique. But, as it stands, the evidence does not point this way, and we must presume that the Sadducees had methods of interpretation which enabled them to square their views with the teaching of the Old Testament.

The Alexandrian Use: The role of the Apocrypha

Further, what are we to make of the apparent aberrations of Alexandria? It is generally held that it was the existence of a wider collection of Jewish books in Alexandria, the home of the Septuagint translation of the Old Testament, than in Jerusalem

[3] E. Schürer, *History of the Jewish People* (Edinburgh, 1898), Division 2, Vol. 2, p. 35. He gives references to Origen, Jerome and others who held this view. See also A. Bentzen, *Introduction to the Old Testament*, 1, p. 35, for a possible explanation for this patristic misunderstanding.
[4] 'Angel' is used in the Law nearly thirty times, in the Prophets about sixty times, and in the Writings about sixteen times.

that caused the Greek-speaking early church to use and to revere
the books of the Apocrypha in addition to those of the Palestinian canon. This is a matter of considerable importance, because
of the serious differences of view that have arisen in Christen-
dom over it. The relevant decree of the Council of Trent runs as
follows: 'The holy, ecumenical, and general Council of Trent
... follows the example of the orthodox Fathers and with the
same sense of loyalty and reverence with which it accepts and
venerates all the books both of the Old and the New Testament,
since one God is the author of both ... as having been received
orally from Christ or inspired (dictated) by the Holy Spirit and
continuously preserved in the Catholic Church. . . . The Old
Testament: five books of Moses ... Josue, Judges, Ruth, four
books of Kings, two of Paralipomenon; the first book of Esdras,
and the second, which is called Nehemias; *Tobias, Judith,*
Esther, Job, David's Psalter of 150 psalms, Proverbs, Ecclesiastes, the Canticle of Canticles, *Wisdom, Ecclesiasticus,* Isaias,
Jeremias with *Baruch,* Ezechiel, Daniel; the twelve minor
prophets ... two books of *Machabees* ... If anyone does not
accept these books as sacred and canonical in their entirety,
with all their parts, according to the text usually read in the
Catholic Church and as they are in the ancient Latin Vulgate
... let him be anathema.'[5]

The Vulgate treats the Story of Susanna, the Song of the
Three Children (the Benedicite) and the Story of Bel and the
Dragon as integral parts of the Book of Daniel, and the so-
called Additions to the Book of Esther as an integral part of the
Book of Esther. The First and Second Books of Esdras[6] and the
Prayer of Manasses, which are included in the Apocrypha in
Article 6 of the Thirty-Nine Articles and in the *New English
Bible,* but are not included in the Tridentine list, are sometimes

[5] Fourth Session, Decree Concerning the Canonical Scriptures, as translated in J. F. Clarkson and others, *The Church Teaches* (St. Louis,
1955), pp. 44ff. *Cf.* H. Denzinger, *Enchiridion Symbolorum,* 30th ed.,
E. T. *The Sources of Catholic Dogma* (St. Louis, 1957), pp. 244f. For
Latin text, see Mansi 33.22A.
[6] The nomenclature of these books is confusing. Actually the Thirty-
Nine Articles calls them the Third and Fourth Books, following the LXX
usage, which gives Ezra and Nehemiah the titles 1 and 2 Esdras. We
shall reserve the Greek name, Esdras, for the two Apocryphal books, and
call them 1 and 2 Esdras respectively, as in AV and RV.

printed as an appendix to the Roman Bible, standing after the
New Testament, and sometimes they are omitted. Indeed, at
least one edition of the Douay Bible couples with these the
Third and Fourth Books of Maccabees, concluding the Old
Testament with this note : 'N.B. The Third and Fourth book
of Maccabees, as also the Third and Fourth book of Esdras,
(which some call the First and Second of Esdras), and the Prayer
of Manasses, are here omitted; because they have never been
received by the Church.'[7] 1 and 2 Esdras and the Prayer of
Manasses are found in most Latin MSS of the Bible and appear
in the Authorized Version of James I, when it is printed in full.
The official standard of the Church of England since the
Reformation is set out in Article 6 : 'The other Books (as
Hierome saith) the Church doth read for example of life and
instruction of manners; but yet doth it not apply them to establish any doctrine.' In this the Church of England follows the
lead of Luther, who took Jerome's hint and in his German
Bible for the first time separated the books of the Apocrypha
from what he regarded as the Old Testament proper. The books
had been mingled hitherto; now they were printed in two
distinct sections. The churches that took their lead from
Geneva went a stage further. The Westminster Confession (1:3)
says: 'The Books commonly called Apocrypha . . . (are not) to
be any otherwise approved, or made use of, than other human
writings.' It was a logical step from this, and one of profound
importance for the world-wide development of the Christian
church, when in 1827 the British and Foreign Bible Society
(and later the American Bible Society) decided to regard the
Bible as being complete without the Apocrypha. It would take
us too far afield to discuss the attitude of the various Eastern
churches to this question. With their help we could enumerate
a considerable number of other possible claimants to canonicity.
Suffice it to say that their doctrinal formulations do not seem to
be of such a type as to bind them irrevocably to the view that
any apocryphal books are canonical.

In order to assess fairly the merits of the case, it will be well
to outline the main points in the history of the recognition of
the apocryphal books. The instrument through which these

[7] *The Holy Catholic Bible* with Dr Challoner's Notes (London, 1829).

books found their way into the Christian church was the Septuagint, for, in a general sense at least, the Septuagint was the Old
Testament of the early church. More than that, the Septuagint
was undoubtedly a divinely-provided instrument to prepare the
world for the gospel. The knowledge of Hebrew had greatly
declined amongst the Jews; Greek had become the lingua
franca of the Roman world; the Jews translated their scriptures
into Greek, thus unwittingly preparing the way for the gospel
to spread throughout the whole Roman Empire.

What did this first-century Septuagint contain? Unfortunately that is a question to which we have no precise answer.
The large codices on which we depend come at best from the
fourth and fifth centuries. In these codices apocryphal books
appear, but with no consistency as to the books contained or
their order; they are mixed up with the undisputed books of the
canon. This is the order of these books in the three most notable
codices. Vaticanus: Wisdom, Ecclesiasticus, Judith, Tobit,
Baruch, Epistle of Jeremiah. Sinaiticus (which has some gaps):
Tobit, Judith, First Maccabees and Fourth Maccabees, Wisdom,
Ecclesiasticus. Alexandrinus: Tobit, Judith, First, Second,
Third and Fourth Maccabees, Wisdom, Ecclesiasticus, Psalms
of Solomon. Many of these books were known in the first
century, but to suggest that there was at that date a clearly-
defined deutero-canon included as part of the Septuagint, seems
to be entirely contrary to the evidence.[8]

The truth appears to be that the Jews were perfectly clear as
to the limits of the Canon[9] in spite of the fact that they read
and esteemed highly a number of other books. The apocalyptic
writings had particular popularity in a Palestine seething with
Messianic hope, and the apocryphal books that sought to effect
a reconciliation between Judaism and Greek philosophy had a
particular popularity in Hellenistic Judaism, especially in such
cultural centres as Alexandria. But, as Josephus and Philo show
by their quotations as well as by their direct comments on the

---

[8] For further details, see H. B. Swete, *Introduction to the Old Testament in Greek* (Cambridge, 1900), pp. 201ff.
[9] Against the view that the Talmud occasionally gives canonical status
to Baruch and Ecclesiasticus, see W. H. Green, *General Introduction to
the Old Testament: The Canon*, pp. 137f.; C. H. H. Wright, *Ecclesiastes*, pp. 46ff.

subject, knowledge and use of the Septuagint translation of
Law, Prophets and Hagiographa does not imply the recognition
of the canonicity of the apocryphal books that were incorporated in the later codices.[1]

The later practice seems to be a Christian innovation brought
about by three causes. In the first place, the books of the
Apocrypha that had been created for a Hellenistic environment had an obvious relevance for Gentile Christians who
wished to adjust themselves to their new Jewish-derived religion. Secondly, the rapid separation between church and synagogue after AD 70 meant that knowledge of Hebrew and of
things Jewish soon almost disappeared in the church, leaving
Christians with little means of assessing critically the status of
their Jewish writings. Thirdly, the physical fact of the separate
existence of the individual rolls made it easy for the various
treasured volumes to get inter-mingled.

We can see a progression in Christian practice. In the New
Testament there are allusions[2] to the Apocrypha, but no quotations. To infer canonical authority from allusions is absurd.
On such grounds allusions in modern religious literature would
canonize *Hymns Ancient and Modern*. In any case, even quotation does not canonize a book. Otherwise Paul would have
canonized the works of Aratus, Menander and Epimenides.[3]
Even a quotation formally introduced, as in Jude 14, does not
canonize a book. The Book of Enoch here quoted (1:9) gained
a sort of canonical status in the isolated outpost of Christianity
in Ethiopia, but it never approached canonical status in the
church as a whole.

[1] The fact that Josephus used I Esdras and the Additions to Esther and
knew the Greek of I Maccabees justifies the view that he regards their
history as authentic. It does not justify Pfeiffer's generalization (*Introduction to the Old Testament*, pp. 67f.): 'Josephus apparently regards
(the apocryphal material) as equally authentic with the canonical books.'
[2] L. Dennefeld (*Introduction à l'Ancien Testament* (Paris, 1934), p.
208) sees undeniable allusions to Wisdom in Mt. 27:39–42 (presumably
2:18), Rom. 1:20–32 (ch. 12 and 13), Rom. 9:21 (15:17), Eph. 6:13–17
(5:17–20), Heb. 1:3 (7:26), 1 Pet. 1:6, 7 (3:5f.); to Ecclesiasticus in
Mt. 6:14 (28:2) and Jas. 1:19 (5:13f., ch. 20); to 2 Macc. in Heb. 11:34f.
(6:18ff.; 7:9); to Judith in 1 Cor. 2:10 (8:14). E. E. Ellis, however,
says: 'Paul's use of non-canonical Jewish literature is very doubtful at
best' (*Paul's Use of the Old Testament*, p. 77).
[3] Acts 17:28; 1 Cor. 15:33; Tit. 1:12.

With the early Christian Fathers a second stage was reached. The books of the Apocrypha, especially Wisdom and Ecclesiasticus, were frequently quoted by them often in just the same way as the canonical books. In the East the theoretical distinction between Old Testament and Apocrypha was well known, though often not observed in practice. In the West the distinction was less clear, though even Augustine, whose influence largely established the position of the Apocrypha in the Western church, was aware of the difference.[4] It was Jerome, with his knowledge of Hebrew and of Jewish practice, who laboured to keep the distinction clear. But by this time miraculous tales were believed concerning the origin of the Septuagint, and the apocryphal books were found mingled with the books of the Old Testament in the codices. Although there was a succession of learned men throughout the subsequent centuries who argued Jerome's view, it was not till the Reformation that it was effectually established once more; but at the cost of a major section of the church binding itself to the other view. The Reformers believed that they were correcting a false trail begun in patristic times. The doctors of Trent believed that they were pursuing the course followed by the Fathers to its logical conclusions. Even in the period since Trent, however, a number of Roman Catholics have continued to show unwillingness to grant the Apocrypha full canonical status.[5] And with reason.

There seems to be no justification for the view that the Septuagint with Apocrypha had been from the first the clearly-recognized Canon of the church, and that it was owing to malign Jewish influence that Melito and Origen produced lists of Scriptures without the Apocrypha, that the Syriac Peshitta was originally translated without it, and that Jerome took his

---

[4] See *City of God* xvii. 24; xviii. 36, 38, 42–45 for Augustine's views concerning canonicity, Septuagint, *etc.* E. B. Pusey (*Is Healthful Reunion Impossible?* (Oxford, 1870), pp. 129f.) sums up an interesting discussion thus: 'Both (S. Jerome and S. Augustine) agree as to what books are read in the Church; both have a distinction within that larger Canon of books which are to be read; and both, I think, use the title "Canonical Scriptures" in a more limited sense, including therein those books only upon which our Lord set His seal.'

[5] See L. Dennefeld, *Introduction à l'Ancien Testament*, pp. 208ff.

stand against the traditional teaching of the church. The statement in the Introduction to the *New English Bible* Apocrypha
is thus so loose as to be seriously misleading: '(The books of the
Apocrypha are) in the Greek version of the Old Testament made
for the Greek-speaking Jews in Egypt. As such they were
accepted as biblical by the early Church.' To be exact: they
came to be accepted in post-apostolic times by many Christians.

We have tended to speak of the Apocrypha as though it were
a well-defined unit. R. H. Malden[6] once compared the border-
land between the canonical and non-canonical books with the
English-Welsh border: once fluid, now fixed, in detail arbitrary.
As far as the Old Testament is concerned, this is (on our view)
quite untrue. But with regard to the Apocrypha as defined by
the Roman Church, it is an admirable description. As we have
seen, the codices differ remarkably in their selection, such books
as 3 and 4 Maccabees and the Psalms of Solomon being sometimes included; and the Fathers do not restrict themselves to the
books of the Tridentine canon for their quotations. As L.
Dennefeld says, authors such as Justin, Tertullian and Clement
of Alexandria occasionally use books outside this canon,
especially Enoch and 2 Esdras. It is hard to escape the conclusion that the Tridentine definition is arbitrary. The Council of
Trent unfortunately seems to have had no Hebraists and few
good Greek scholars, with the result that the church appears to
have been saddled with the task of defending books which are
scarcely defensible.

It ill becomes those who are prepared to exercise great
patience and diligence in defending the inerrancy of the Jewish
canon against modern criticism, to make ill-considered attacks
upon the books of the Tridentine canon in order to rend them
with the same sort of arguments. It is probably not true to say
that a decisive argument against the Tridentine canon can be
based on the demonstration of errors of history and geography
in such books as Tobit and Judith. The ultimate possibility of
defending these books depends on the truth or otherwise of the
whole Roman *Weltanschauung*. None the less the difficulty of
defending these books seems to be much greater than with any

[6] R. H. Malden, *The Apocrypha* (Oxford, 1936), pp. 6f.

of the books of the Jewish Canon.[7] The moral difficulties are also considerable, though at first sight perhaps no more insurmountable than some in the agreed canon. Doctrinal issues are of some importance. In the Apocrypha can be found proof texts to support the Roman doctrine of justification (Tobit 12:9; 14:10f.; Ecclus. 3:30; 1 Macc. 2:52), and of purgatory (2 Macc. 12:41ff.). These alone are likely to encourage Rome to hold to the apocryphal books tenaciously. The book of Wisdom seems to countenance doctrines of pantheistic origin, difficult to reconcile with pure biblical theism: emanation (7:25), pre-existence of souls (8:19, 20), creation out of pre-existent matter (11:17), the body as a weight upon the soul (9:15). If these books are not demonstrably inspired, they should certainly not be used to establish any doctrine.

We conclude, then, that orthodox Jewry, Jerome, the Reformers and the founders of the great Bible Societies were right in their view of the Old Testament Canon, and that the attempt by either Rome or liberalism to put the Jewish Canon and the Apocrypha on a level is misguided. Since the Apocrypha cannot be brought up to the level of the Old Testament, it tends to bring the authority of the Old Testament down to the level of the Apocrypha. The books of the Apocrypha are valuable, and should be given a leading place in anthologies of the inter-testamental period. We should not tie ourselves to some artificial rule that forbids their public reading, but they are not Scripture, and (however venerable the practice) it is seriously misleading to have them bound with the Scriptures in a single volume.

---

[7] For a short statement of the conventional Protestant position, see W. H. Green, *Introduction to the Old Testament: The Canon*, pp. 195ff. For a defence of the historical truth of Tobit and Judith, see J. E. Steinmueller, *Companion to Scripture Studies* (New York, 1942), Vol. 2, pp. 123ff. F. F. Bruce says, 'It is possible for scholars, armed with the most up-to-date archaeological and philological knowledge, to defend the historicity of Daniel and Esther'; but it is 'very difficult indeed to argue for the historical inerrancy of Tobit and Judith' (*Evangelical Quarterly*, 42 (1970), p. 55).

THE HISTORY OF THE NEW TESTAMENT CANON

The history of the New Testament Canon, as of the Old, is in part obscure.[8] We know that from the first the Christian church regarded the words of Christ as of equal authority with the words of the Old Testament. We know, too, that the doctrine committed to the apostles was regarded as divine revelation. We know, further, that in the sixteenth century the Council of Trent enumerated the twenty-seven books of our New Testament, receiving them with 'an affection of piety' equal to that rendered to the Old Testament, declaring them to have God as their author. These same books were acknowledged by the Confession of Würtemberg, the Thirty-Nine Articles and the Westminster Confession. This Western tradition stretches back to the end of the fourth century with scarcely a break.

At the time of the Reformation all theological questions, including that of the Canon, were thrown open for debate. Luther was among those who questioned the status of certain New Testament books. He approached the Canon with a subjective criterion, and seemed to wish to deny full canonical status to those books which did not clearly set forth the doctrine of justification by faith. In the first edition of his preface to his translation of the New Testament, plainly set forth for all the world to see, he called James an 'epistle of straw' compared with the 'best' books. In addition he relegated it, along with Hebrews, Jude and the Apocalypse, to the end of the Bible; and in the list of books, he gave these four no number, leaving a blank line between them and the other books. But this was a vagary of which Luther himself apparently soon thought better, seeing he omitted the offending sentence from subsequent editions. Luther's influence was so great that at least certain elements in his unusual views had powerful advocates in the Lutheran churches till after the time of the making of the great Lutheran Confessions. The result is that there is no list of the New Testament books in the Confession of Augsburg

[8] B. F. Westcott, *A General Survey of the History of the Canon of the New Testament* (Cambridge, 1855 and later editions); A. Souter, *The Text and Canon of the New Testament*, 2nd ed. revised by C. S. C. Williams (London, 1954); R. M. Grant, *The Formation of the New Testament* (London, 1965) may be consulted.

or the Formula of Concord; and even to the present day there is a Lutheran minority that shows some reserve as to the limits of the Canon. In the Reformation ferment, there were some others who made judgments adverse to the full canonical status of certain ·New Testament books. Zwingli, for instance, said that the Apocalypse was 'not a book of the Bible'.[9] But such views were rejected by the reformed churches as a whole. Apart from this there is scarcely a dissentient voice between the fourth and sixteenth centuries.[1]

The position in the Eastern churches was much more confused, due probably to the fact that the course of history and the Eastern temperament never produced circumstances where clear-cut, agreed formulations became an urgent requirement. The Western canon was sometimes clearly followed – for example, at the beginning of the sixth century, 2 and 3 John, 2 Peter, Jude and Revelation, which were not in the Peshitta, the authorized version of the Syriac-speaking church, were included in the new Syriac translation of Philoxenus, bringing it into line with the Western list.[2] At other times one or more books were added or omitted or reckoned doubtful. No less than six different lists of the Scriptures were received more or less widely in the tenth century in the Greek church alone.[3] It is not that the East had a different canon – after all, the famous Festal Letter of Athanasius, which for the first time enumerated precisely the twenty-seven books of our Canon, was an Eastern product; rather, in the East neither the concept of the Canon nor its limits found consistent expression. It is evident that, if there is a qualitative difference between Scripture and all other writing, and if it was the will of God that the church should come to recognize clearly the difference between the one and the other, then it is to the West that we must look for the elucidating of this part of her theology. The Letter of Athanasius was a local and individual ruling. It was written in AD 367 for the purpose of excluding from use in the regular services of the

[9] Zwingli, *Werke*, II. 1, p. 169 (ed. Schuler). Calvin, in the Argument which introduces his commentary and in his comments on 3:15, was guardedly non-committal concerning 2 Peter.
[1] For minor exceptions, see B. F. Westcott, *op. cit.*, 5th ed., pp. 451ff.
[2] A. Souter, *Text and Canon of the New Testament,* pp. 55f.
[3] B. F. Westcott, *The Bible in the Church,* p. 227.

church the large number of apocryphal books which were very popular amongst Egyptian Christians. But it was in the West that the twenty-seven books first received conciliar recognition, at Hippo in 393 and again shortly after at Carthage in 397. The earliest known confirmation of this list by a Bishop of Rome comes from Pope Innocent in 405.

Stretching back from the end of the fourth century to at least AD 170, there is a period in which the church as a whole had a well-established concept of a New Testament Canon. Just as the revelation of the Old Covenant contained in the Jewish Scriptures was read and revered as the Word of God in the church, so also a number of Christian books were regarded as Scriptures of the New Covenant, inspired by God equally with the Old and read alongside them in the Christian assemblies. But during this period there was not complete unanimity as to which books were to be regarded as Scripture. The statements of Eusebius of Caesarea at the beginning of the fourth century and of Origen at the beginning of the third give a good picture of the situation, since both were men of great learning who deliberately tried to discover the position in all parts of the church. Eusebius divided the books that were in circulation into three classes, the Acknowledged, the Disputed and the Spurious (*i.e.* heretical). The Acknowledged were the Gospels, Acts, Pauline Epistles, 1 Peter, 1 John and Revelation (with reserve). The Disputed he sub-divided into those 'well known and recognized by most' : James, 2 Peter, 2 and 3 John and Jude; and the 'Spurious' : the Acts of Paul, Hermas, Apocalypse of Peter, Barnabas, Teaching of the Apostles, Gospel to the Hebrews, and perhaps Revelation. It is thus clear that the weight of his testimony is precisely upon the books of our New Testament (though with some serious doubt concerning the last book), but in the church as a whole there are differences of opinion.

The views of Origen, gleaned from a number of sources, are summarized by Souter thus : Amongst the books everywhere recognized 'he gives the four Gospels, thirteen letters of Paul, First Peter, First John, Acts, and the Apocalypse ... The disputed works according to him were Hebrews (which he himself, especially in his earlier works, cites as Pauline and canoni-

cal); Second Peter (which he himself, if we may trust the Latin
translations of his commentaries, regarded as genuine and as
Holy Scripture); Second and Third John (here he expresses
real doubts as to their genuineness); James (often cited by him,
but he admitted its want of general recognition); Jude (nearly
always cited as Holy Scripture and highly valued, but he once
mentions that doubts were entertained about it); ... Barnabas
... Hermas ... the Teaching of the Twelve Apostles ... The
Gospel according to the Hebrews. ...' [5] Thus in Origen's time
the great bulk of our New Testament was known and recognized throughout the whole church, but there was a fringe of
uncertainty concerning some books which were either too small
or too personal to attract universal attention, or whose apostolicity was doubtful. And in addition there were some books in
use in the church which were found edifying, which were not
as yet universally distinguished from the books which were
later regarded as exclusively canonical. In broad principle this
situation can be traced back at least to the third quarter of the
second century. But before that time the evidence is more
scanty and the picture becomes less clear.

How did this concept of a New Testament Canon emerge?
As examples of the more extreme attempts to answer this question we might consider the views of Harnack and Warfield.
Harnack was a brilliant Liberal, who believed that the development of Catholic orthodoxy was a perversion of the religion of
Jesus. The religion of Judaism was a religion of a book, the
religion of Jesus (and of the very earliest church) was a religion
of the spirit. The church of course inherited the Old Testament, but its very existence was a formidable obstacle to any
idea of a New Testament Canon. Its creation of a New Testament was a retrograde step, concerning which Harnack was
happy to echo the words of Tertullian and say that thereby the
Spirit was chased into a book. He regarded the notion of a
Canon of the New Covenant as being a direct result of the rise
of heresy. The Gnostics and Marcion, having thrown away the
Old Testament, needed an authoritative source of doctrine.
Marcion drew up his list of sacred Christian writings, and his
example, perhaps partly unconsciously, prompted the leaders

[5] Souter, *The Text and Canon of the New Testament*, pp. 167f.

of the great churches to do likewise. In addition, the rise of Montanism, claiming new and dubious revelations, drove the church back to the apostolic period. 'It was in opposition to this position that the leaders of the Church first thought out and developed the idea of a covenant established and finally sealed in the manifestations of Christ and in the work of His Apostles, so that they were able to consistently reject *every* work which did not belong to this primitive epoch.'[6] It is to Marcion that we owe the idea of a new Canon, and to the Montanists, by opposition, that we owe the idea of a closed Canon.

At the opposite extreme is Warfield. Warfield held that not only were the New Testament books inspired at the moment of writing, but that they were known to be inspired from the first. Ministers of the new covenant had at least as great authority as ministers of the old. They spoke and wrote with words given by the Holy Spirit (1 Cor. 2:13). Their commands were of divine authority and their writings were the depository of these commands (1 Thes. 4:2; 2 Thes. 2:15). These writings were to be read in their meetings (1 Thes. 5:27; Col. 4:16; Rev. 1:3) alongside the Old Testament Scriptures. Such new writings (whether written by apostles or authorized by them) were imposed upon the infant churches as their authoritative rule of faith and practice: 'The principle of canonicity was not apostolic authorship, but *imposition by the apostles as "law"*.' There is no evidence of a gradually-heightening estimate of the New Testament; they are received as Scripture from the very beginning.

'This immediate placing of the new books – given the church under the seal of apostolic authority – among the Scriptures already established as such, was inevitable. It is also historically evinced from the very beginning. Thus the apostle Peter, writing in AD 68, speaks of Paul's numerous letters not in contrast with the Scriptures, but as among the Scriptures and in contrast with "the *other* Scriptures" (2 Pet. 3:16) – that is, of course, those of the Old Testament. In like manner the apostle Paul combines, as if it were the most natural thing in the world, the book of Deuteronomy and the Gospel of Luke under the

6 A. Harnack, *The Origin of the New Testament* (London, 1925), p. 35.

common head of "Scripture" (1 Tim. 5:18) : "For the Scripture saith, 'Thou shalt not muzzle the ox when he treadeth out the corn' (Deut. 25:4); and, 'The labourer is worthy of his hire'" (Luke 10:7). The line of such quotations is never broken in Christian literature. Polycarp (c.12) in AD 115 unites the Psalms and Ephesians in exactly similar manner : "In the sacred books, ... as it is said in these Scriptures, 'Be ye angry and sin not,' and 'Let not the sun go down upon your wrath.'" So, a few years later, the so-called second letter of Clement, after quoting Isaiah, adds (2:4): "And another Scripture, however, says, 'I come not to call the righteous, but sinners'" – quoting from Matthew, a book which Barnabas (c. 97–106 AD) had already adduced as Scripture. After this such quotations are common.'[7]

It is unnecessary to attempt a historical reconstruction of the process whereby the church at large came to a belief that the New Testament books were inspired Scriptures like the books of the Old Testament. Since the discovery of the Jung Codex, it seems clear that on any view Harnack makes the emergence of the New Testament too late and too sudden. W. C. van Unnik dates the *Gospel of Truth* round about AD 140–145. It is a Valentinian Gnostic work, written in Rome, probably by Valentinus himself. The writer is acquainted with the Gospels, Pauline Epistles, Hebrews and Revelation, and shows traces of Acts, 1 John, 1 Peter and perhaps other New Testament books. His language is permeated by them, because for him the language of these books is the language of the church. This shows that before the middle of the second century a collection of writings was known at Rome and was accepted as authoritative, which was virtually identical with our New Testament. To quote van Unnik : 'Before the Books could be used in the way they are used in the *Gospel of Truth*, they must have already enjoyed authority for a considerable time. To treat them as a collection was not a discovery of a few months before. Moreover, we should notice that this all took place before the condemnation of Marcion.'[8] This evidence alone gives us the New

[7] B. B. Warfield, *The Inspiration and Authority of the Bible* (London, 1959), pp. 415, 412.
[8] *The Jung Codex*, edited by F. L. Cross (London, 1955), p. 125.

Testament in the middle of the first half rather than in the middle of the second half of the second century.

But if Harnack places the emergence of the New Testament too late, Warfield places it too early. That the Synoptic Gospels were known to Paul before the end of his life and that they were already regarded as the authoritative records of the life and teaching of Christ is, as we hope to show in a later volume, perfectly possible.[9] The four Gospels were circulating as a collection within a very few years of the latest date normally given to St John's Gospel. 2 Peter 3:16 suggests that Paul's letters were collected, and regarded as authoritative over a considerable area, while he was still alive. There was, therefore, written material of the highest authority in use in the churches alongside the Old Testament Scriptures in apostolic times. But that is not quite to say that our New Testament had apostolic sanction and that it was regarded actually as Scripture from the very beginning. Loyal recipients of an apostolic writing would certainly have regarded it as of God-given authority *for them*, but the evidence does not suggest that every apostolic writing was immediately recognized as Scripture, that is to say as part of a new Canon by which the whole church was to be governed. The step from apostolic authority in a local church to recognition as part of the Canon of Scripture of the universal church was a small one, and easily made, but it was an important one which necessarily took time. There is no evidence that the twenty-seven books of the New Testament were imposed on the church in this sense. That a New Testament Canon could have been built up in stages with apostolic approval no-one can deny. With traditional authorships and dating, there could have been a considerable Jerusalem corpus, which was combined (with Peter's approval) with the Pauline works, and finally completed and ratified by the apostle John.

[9] A. Souter (*The Text and Canon of the New Testament*, 1st ed., p. 151) says: 'Whencesoever derived, his knowledge of his Lord's teaching was complete and exact ... that he knew the teaching of Jesus thoroughly is beyond cavil. Even close students of the Gospels and Epistles would probably be surprised at the stupendous list of parallels between the two which Alfred Resch has provided in his *Der Paulinismus und die Logia Jesu* ... the conviction deepens in the present writer that Paul had a written compendium of Jesus' teaching.'

But proof of this there is none. The evidence suggests that there was a very early, widespread recognition of the Gospels, Acts, Paul, 1 Peter and 1 John, but that the other books had a somewhat more independent existence and lacked the cohesive influences of definite collections of books.

Even the theory that the various books were imposed piecemeal upon the individual people and churches that first received them, though more plausible, is devoid of proof in many instances. It seems clear that if this criterion operated in the first century, it had been forgotten by the end of the second, since no attempt was made to appeal to it. Discussions turned upon whether the books in use were apostolic, not upon whether they had been imposed by the apostles as law. Papias is an early example of one who was determined to test the apostolicity of everything he heard and prove the pedigree of every saying. Matthew and Mark are acceptable to him because he is convinced that an apostle stands behind each.[1] The apostles occupied a unique place as authorized teachers of the revelation of Jesus Christ. After the threatened breach between Paul and the Jerusalem authorities had been averted, the apostolic circle was to most people a readily recognizable entity, and it was a fair assumption that books proceeding from the apostolic circle, whether actually written by apostles or not, were true to that revelation. It is indeed extremely likely that Mark and Luke and Acts and Hebrews (to mention no others) had the warmest apostolic approval, but that there was direct historical proof of that fact a hundred years later is quite uncertain. A book had in practice to pass two tests before gaining canonical recognition. It had to pass the test of continuous and widespread approval amongst Christians, otherwise its candidature would have automatically disappeared. It is possible that many writings of the apostolic circle never survived.[2] There is no reason to think that such letters, if they existed, had less apostolic imposition than the others. But the collective judgment of the Christian community was continually experiencing the inner witness of the Spirit, predisposing it to accept some books and reject others, thereby retaining only those books which were in

[1] Eusebius, *Ecc. Hist.* iii. 39.
[2] 1 Cor. 5 : 9 may refer to one such letter.

general accord with the received revelation and which had permanent value for the edification of the church as a whole. But edification is not a prerogative of apostolic books exclusively, and mere helpfulness was not considered to be an adequate ground for canonicity. Providentially, through the rise of novel teachings, the church had to ask herself afresh where the revelation of the New Covenant was to be found unadulterated. She knew only one answer – the apostolic church. And that answer was firmly grounded in the teaching of the books already received as being of the highest authority in the church. The calling, training and commissioning of the twelve apostles was plain for all to see in the four Gospels, and the apostleship of Paul was clearly set out in his Epistles. Thus the criterion of apostolicity became paramount. But the ambiguities of the term 'apostolicity' contributed significantly to the hesitation with which some books were received. There was a persistent tendency to try to equate apostolicity with the writing of a book by an actual apostle – hence the uncertainties about Hebrews. It looks as though Hebrews was accepted at an early date in Rome, although known not to be Pauline; it was later doubted because its apostolic authorship was in doubt; later still it was accepted again because it was believed to be Pauline ! Serious doubts were felt about 2 Peter and the Apocalypse because their style seemed to indicate different authorship from the undoubted works of Peter and John. This (together with the growing unpopularity of chiliasm, which these books might appear to legitimatize) probably accounts for the apparent deterioration in status of the Apocalypse between Origen and Eusebius. The true understanding of the term apostolicity was probably : apostolic authorship or approval (perhaps only tacit approval) by one or more of the apostles.

THE HAND OF PROVIDENCE

a. In the recognition of the Old Testament Canon

This sketch of the history of Old and New Testament Canons justifies, we believe, our proposition that the grounds of canonicity are to be found in an interplay of objective and subjective factors overruled by divine Providence. In Old Testament times the objective fact was God's sending of his messengers to address and to mould the nation of Israel. Moses, David, Solomon, the succession of prophets, and finally Ezra and Nehemiah were recognized unmistakably as the teachers and instruments of the Lord. They were not all in the literal sense prophets – men whose primary mode of utterance was the divine oracle; but they were men singled out by God and authenticated to the nation by him, and so they were his spokesmen. Their writings, and other writings emanating from the Prophetic Era, spoke to the hearts of the faithful in Israel, and their teaching was recognized as the word of the Lord. So much so that Moses and David could be called prophets (Dt. 18:18; Acts 2:30) and the unknown authors of Joshua, Judges, Samuel and Kings came in due course to be known collectively as the Former Prophets. Then, if the traditional view is to be accepted, in the providence of God, there was a cessation of prophecy for more than four hundred years. Though there were wise and gifted teachers like Ben Sira, no-one impressed himself upon the nation as a prophet of God until John the Baptist appeared upon the scene. During this period the canonical books, without (as far as we know) any external pressure or any official decree, so established themselves in the life of the nation, that no books were in danger of ejection from the Canon, and no books, however greatly respected, could find an entrance.

As far as the Old Testament is concerned there is the further objective fact of our Lord's attestation of 'the law, the prophets and the psalms' (Lk. 24:44). There is no reason to think that his threefold collection of scriptures is anything but our present Old Testament.[3] Even if an attempt is made to question their exact equivalence in matters of detail, on any critical theory the great bulk of the Old Testament is independently attested by Christ and the New Testament writers. There are quotations from the Law and the Prophets, and from at least

[3] For a long time there was no agreed title for the third group of books. (Ben Sira's introduction describes it in three different ways.) The earliest known use of the term 'Writings' comes from Gamaliel II (c. AD 80–117) (Sanh 90b; see J. P. Lewis, 'What do we mean by Jabneh?', *Journal of Bible and Religion*, 32, 1964, p. 126). Philo speaks once of 'psalms and the other things (=writings?) by which knowledge and piety are increased', and 'Psalms' was apparently in use among the Jews as late as the tenth century (Philo, *De Vita Contemplativa* 25 (Loeb, Vol. 9); P. E. Kahle, *The Cairo Geniza*, 2nd ed., Oxford, 1959, pp. 88f.).

the main books of the third division of the modern Hebrew Bible. The Psalms, Proverbs and Daniel are quoted often, Job a number of times, and there are occasional references to Chronicles. Only Ruth, Ezra, Nehemiah, Esther, Ecclesiastes, Canticles and Lamentations are without clear quotation.

b. In the recognition of the New Testament Canon

In like manner the New Testament. There was the objective fact of the divinely-given teaching of Christ and the apostles which was committed to writing in the apostolic age, much of it with direct apostolic authority, almost all of it probably with apostolic approval. There was the subjective fact of the establishment of a large section of these writings in the life of the church. Our Lord had laid down the principle that his sheep would recognize his voice (Jn. 10:3–16). These writings were not at once consciously received as Scripture. But the New Covenant from the very first meant more to believers than the Old Covenant and in these books from the apostolic circle believers recognized the voice of the Good Shepherd. They were read in assembly alongside the Old Testament Scriptures, and in a very short time, with no authoritative imposition or theological deduction, they formed a de facto New Testament. It simply required the impact of heresy to evoke the explicit statement of what was implicit in the irrevocably established practice of the church. By this process the bulk of the New Testament found unquestioned recognition in the whole church. The remaining books had to run the gauntlet of severe critical scrutiny. Their apostolicity was tested by the strength of the historical tradition that supported them and by the evidence of their reception as Scripture by the people of God. By this process the church came to a remarkable, though not an absolutely complete, unanimity on the subject round about the fifth century, and that unanimity has remained sufficiently complete to the present day to make any revision of the Canon appear most improbable.

c. Problems raised by the doctrine of Providence

Are we right to see here the hand of God and confidently to receive these twenty-seven books, neither more nor less, as his

New Testament? Such a doctrine of Providence can be a dangerous thing, and it raises questions.

1. *Is it not a magic carpet that transports one to any destination desired?* Newman's doctrine of development was criticized in these terms. He could argue that the situation now existing, though very different from that of the primitive church, was a development brought about by the Holy Spirit. But to say that because a thing is, it is therefore right, is to deprive oneself of the power of self-criticism and self-reformation.

In the case of the New Testament Canon, however, Providence is not being used to explain some anomaly in the Christian revelation. The existence of a New Testament Canon is congruous with the existence of the Old, and a knowledge of its limits is a practical need of the church. Furthermore, it is not being used as a short cut to decide an issue that divides Christians. The issue is not between one or more rival canons, but between a definite canon and an indefinite one. There is no reasonable alternative to our twenty-seven books. No significant body of opinion wishes to see the Canon either enlarged [4] or reduced. There is no likelihood that individual strictures on particular books will commend themselves to the church as a whole. They will die a natural death as did Luther's views on the Epistle of James.

2. *Cannot the unanimity of the church be explained by mundane circumstances?* It is argued that the desire for uniformity, combined with the great influence of Augustine and Jerome, is sufficient to explain the position in the fifth century; the relative stagnation of the next thousand years explains the rest.

This is probably true, but the specific result of a general providence may be such that theological deductions can be made from it. There was nothing manifestly supernatural about the Babylonian Captivity, but it was rightly seen as an act of God. There was nothing manifestly supernatural about the

---

[4] Adolf Schlatter remarked: 'All other oral traditions . . . are surprisingly meagre both in quality and quantity, which only goes to show the Church's dependence on the canonical writings even in the second and third generations' (*The Church in the New Testament Period*, London, 1955, p. 315). It suggests that God did not intend to preserve rivals to the canonical writings.

formation of the Canon, but by the way it came about and by its results it too can reasonably be seen as an act of God.

3. *Does not the doctrine of Providence justify the Apocrypha?* It is true that in the providence of God various apocryphal books had a long and honoured history in the Christian church. They were bound up with the Scriptures and were widely quoted by Christian writers. But the significant thing is that, despite the enormous influence both of Augustine and the Vulgate, they never did succeed in establishing themselves as fully canonical. As we have seen, there was a succession of learned men down the centuries who held Jerome's view, and in no sense did Providence shut up the church to the acceptance of the Apocrypha. On the contrary, enough weighty evidence was preserved to make a decisive case against them in spite of the prestige of Augustine and the influence of the Latin Bible.

4. *Was not Luther right in considering the Canon's limits not finally decided?* If stress is laid on the word *finally*, the answer is, Yes. Prior to the Council of Trent there had been no pronouncement on the Canon by any council that purported to be ecumenical. Luther knew that his doubts about certain books had been shared by some leaders of the early church. Thus in principle Luther was perfectly justified, even on the basis of mediaeval theology, in re-opening the question.[5] Where he went wrong was in failing to see the full value of the books that he underrated, and their harmony with the rest of Scripture. Since Luther's day the twenty-seven books have re-asserted their unique authority in both wings of the sundered church, and we have less grounds than he for questioning their canonicity. But the question is not so finally and absolutely closed that future generations are absolved from examining their credentials afresh. Nevertheless it does mean that Providence has given

---

[5] At a date subsequent to his contact with Luther, the staunch Romanist Cardinal Cajetan, who was generally considered to be the leading Thomist of his day, expressed doubts about Hebrews, evidently without any thought of being heretical. He considered that Paul could not confidently be held to be the author of Hebrews, and he argued that doubt as to authorship involved doubt as to authority. After his unsuccessful conference with Luther he said: 'I do not want to have any further parley with that beast; for he has sharp eyes and wonderful speculations in his head!' B. F. Westcott, *Hebrews* (London, 1892), p. lxxv; *Schaff-Herzog Encyclopaedia* (New York, 1894), art. 'Cajetan', I, 358.

each generation a great presumption against change, and it would require proof of error in a book to effect its ejection.

5. *Does not the appeal to this intangible criterion of Providence introduce such an element of doubt into the whole procedure as to rob the infallible guide of its infallibility?* In an academic sense, perhaps Yes. In practical reality, No. This is not the place for an extended discussion of the doctrine of infallibility; a few comments must suffice. To follow a guide-book infallibly requires three things : the infallibility of the book, an infallibility of understanding, and an infallibility of obedience to its directions. Such infallibility is not for mortal man. Rome offers a collection of infallible books, but it is doubtful whether she has made any infallible pronouncement as to which they are. The Pope has never declared which papal utterances have been spoken *ex cathedra* and which have not. In consequence there is difference of opinion within the church on the matter, and we have nothing better to go on than 'the common view of theologians'. When it comes to interpretation of the Bible, not even the Pontifical Biblical Commission would make any claim to infallibility. This in itself shows how precarious is the argument that an infallible book is useless without an infallible teacher. Rome can get along satisfactorily on a very modest amount of infallible teaching. It is useless and dangerous to argue that because a thing seems desirable, it therefore exists. Our reason for believing in the infallibility of Scripture is not that it seems necessary for our Christian lives, but that Christ taught it. It is for God to say, not us, whether infallible interpretation of the Bible, infallible understanding of it and infallible obedience to it are necessary for the working out of his purposes in us. On our view, none of these things are promised in the Bible. But he has given us all the teaching and understanding and powers of obedience that are necessary for our salvation and growth in holiness and for the spiritual well-being of the church.

God has given to us the divine oracles which he entrusted to the Jews (Rom. 3:2). God has given to us his only-begotten Son, who spoke as the Father taught him, and who solemnly confirmed the Jewish Scriptures. God has given to us the apostles whom Christ chose and commissioned to teach his word to all nations. God has given to us the Holy Spirit, who was sent to teach them and to establish the church. God intended this Spirit-taught church to have a function transcending that of its individual members. As 'the pillar and bulwark of the truth' (1 Tim. 3:15) its collective witness and judgment is stronger and more dependable than that of its constituent members. From this apostolic church emerged, as a further gift of God, another collection of divine oracles, and to this the church has borne a virtually consistent witness down the centuries. It is surely right to see both the collection of these books and the consistency of this testimony as the providential ordering of the exalted Head of the church. This was not a collection of books blown together by chance;[6] nor was it a collection that 'forced itself' upon the church. In the gentlest way it quietly and unhurriedly established itself in the church's life. There was no crisis of official decision. There was no noticeable change of attitude before and after the Festal Letter of Athanasius, no flourish of trumpets at Hippo or Carthage. They were not infallible pronouncements; they were weighty confirmations of views already held with more or less firmness throughout the church at large. Neither the decree of Carthage[7] nor that of Trent, nor the Thirty-nine Articles, nor the Westminster Confession is infallible, but in the case of the New Testament Canon they unite in testifying to the collective witness given by the Spirit to the church, thereby giving an immense presumption in favour of the New Testament Canon as we have it. We have not here a proof of mathematical precision, but we have evidence of weight and authority, more than sufficient to justify us in humbly taking up the books that God has put into our hands and receiving their teaching as his truth.

[6] This phrase is from H. A. C. Hävernick, *Introduction to the Old Testament*, p. 36.
[7] The Carthaginian list, incidentally, apparently includes five books (only) of the Apocrypha, which disqualifies it from use by either Roman Catholics or Protestants as an infallible witness to the true Canon! (B. F. Westcott, *A General Survey of the History of the Canon of the New Testament*, pp. 440, 541f.)

THE RELIABILITY
OF THE
BIBLE TEXT

7

The Scriptures as we now possess them are separated by a gap from the Scriptures 'as originally given'. The oldest manuscripts that we possess vary amongst themselves, showing that the text has suffered considerable corruption in the course of transmission. Two questions are often asked: 1. Is not the text so seriously corrupt, and therefore unreliable, as to make the doctrine of inerrancy valueless? 2. If God took the trouble to secure the entire accuracy of the original text, why did he allow it to be corrupted in transmission?

The answer to the first question requires quite distinct treatment as between Old and New Testament. In the case of the Old Testament we have the authority of Christ and the apostles for regarding the text of the first century AD as being a wholly adequate representation of the divine Word. The phenomenon of textual variants must have been well known to them. (Before the printing press gave readers identical copies, the presence of variants was probably more apparent to the layman than it is now.) Yet our Lord raised no question as to the adequacy of the Scriptures as he knew them. Therefore, since the preservation of the text from the first century to the present day can be proved to have been of a very high order indeed, the charge of wholesale corruption of the Old Testament would be a challenge to Christ's authority. We are not, however, dependent on authority only; there is independent confirmation of the general soundness of the Old Testament text. In the case of the New Testament we have no direct authorization by Christ. The church has always believed, as the Westminster Confession says, that the Scriptures have been 'by his singular care and providence kept pure in all ages' (1:8). This belief in Providence was never misplaced but (as we shall see) we now have for the New Testament a wealth of detailed confirmation for this belief which was quite unknown to the seventeenth-century divines.

THE OLD TESTAMENT TEXT

Its transmission since the time of Christ

The Preface to the Revised Version in 1884 said of the Old Testament: 'The earliest MS. of which the age is certainly known bears date AD 916.' At that time there seemed to be no grounds for daring to hope for anything much earlier. But the indirect evidence was good. It was well known that the copying of the Scriptures had been carried out with almost unimaginable care and reverence,[1] with the result that the differences between existing Hebrew manuscripts were small. There was good reason to think that this careful tradition dated back at least as far as the first century AD. There was the evidence of Jerome's Vulgate, translated direct from the Hebrew about AD 400. There were biblical quotations in the Gemaras of Babylonia (c. AD 500) and of Palestine (c. 350) and in the Mishna (c. 200). There were fragments of the absurdly literal (and therefore most valuable) Greek translation of Aquila (c. 130). Going right back into the first century AD, there were the biblical quotations in the New Testament, in Josephus and Philo. There were quotations in the Zadokite fragments. The Aramaic Targums originated probably earlier still. Vowel pointing was not in use during the early centuries of our era, and these sources do not always corroborate the vowels that were later adopted and standardized by the Massoretes, but all the sources show a remarkable constancy in the transmission of the consonantal text.

But this dependence on indirect evidence to establish the fidelity of the transmission of the text gave place to direct proof with the amazing discoveries at Qumran. First to be published were the complete manuscripts of Isaiah of probably the first or second century BC, showing only very small differences from the Massoretic text. Indeed, they appeared if anything to be

[1] For an account of the Talmudic rules for this work, see F. G. Kenyon, *Our Bible and the Ancient Manuscripts* (London, 1958), p. 79.

slightly inferior in text to the Massoretic manuscripts that were
written a thousand years later. Fragments of Leviticus were
found which may be as early as the fifth century BC. It seems
that Rabbi Akiba, who played a large part in determining the
text which was to be used by Judaism from the second century
onwards, did his work with great skill. There was considerably
more diversity of text in the first century than there was later,
and it seems that the scholarly work of the second century,
from which the whole later tradition derived, was soundly conceived. Thus by evidence direct and indirect the gap is spanned
from our Lord's day to the present. As regards the gap between
the time of writing and his day we have the authority implicit
in his attitude to the Scriptures *as he knew them* for believing
in their adequate transmission. But there is confirmatory evidence from other sources as well.

Its transmission before the time of Christ

We have indirect evidence, notably from the Greek Septuagint,
which takes us to the third century BC,[2] and the Samaritan
Pentateuch, which takes us back probably to at least the fourth.
Septuagint studies are themselves extremely intricate, and there
is often considerable uncertainty as to the Septuagint's original
text; furthermore, even when the Greek is not in doubt, it is
not always possible to be certain what Hebrew text the translators had before them. Sometimes, however, it can be used to
restore defects in the Hebrew text. There are major variants in
Job, Jeremiah, Samuel and Kings. In Job it seems that the
original text of the Septuagint omitted nearly a sixth of the
whole. In Jeremiah the order of sections differs greatly from
that of the Hebrew text, and considerable passages are omitted.
In Samuel there are a number of omissions – for instance, parts
of the story of David and Goliath are omitted by the best manuscripts (1 Sa. 17 :12–31, 41, 50, 55–58). Kings has considerable
additions. Nevertheless where the two texts cover the same

---

[2] This applies at least to the Pentateuch. Some of the other books were
translated in the second century. For a full account of the LXX, see S.
Jellicoe, *The Septuagint and Modern Study* (Oxford, 1968); for a short
one, see D. W. Gooding, art. 'Text and Versions: The Septuagint' in
The New Bible Dictionary, pp. 1258ff. We discussed the use of the
Septuagint in the New Testament on pp. 95ff.

ground, the Septuagint confirms the general reliability of the Hebrew text.

The Samaritan Pentateuch provides a form of direct evidence, though its precise value is a matter for debate. It is the Bible of the Samaritans, Hebrew in language, but written in an earlier type of script, and transmitted quite independently of the Palestine tradition. The schism between the Jews and the Samaritans became almost complete shortly after the return from the Babylonian exile, but the breach between North and South had been far-reaching from the time of Rehoboam in the tenth century. If our view of Pentateuchal criticism is right, the Samaritan text, like the Samaritan script, might have its roots in a remote past. The importance of this text seems to have been seriously underrated, due probably to the adverse report of the great Hebraist Gesenius, who early in the nineteenth century declared against its importance. It contains in all about 6,000 variations from the Massoretic text. But these are mostly trifling, showing that the area of general agreement is great. Where there is a difference unconfirmed either by other versions or by intrinsic probability, the Massoretic text is to be preferred, because in many cases the Samaritan version is demonstrably inferior and because the transmission of the Massoretic text from at least the second century AD is known to have been meticulous. It needs to be remembered, however, that AD 70 was a critical point in the history of the Old Testament text, because few manuscripts seem to have survived the sack of Jerusalem, with the result that the Massoretic text was based on a handful of manuscripts which happened to escape destruction. It is unlikely that the Septuagint and Samaritan versions ever influenced one another, therefore the existence of a reading common to both versions proves the widespread use of that reading five hundred years before the present Hebrew text began to become the exclusive text of Judaism. Therefore whenever there is agreement of the Septuagint and Samaritan texts against the Massoretic, there is perhaps a presumption that the Massoretic text is the later. At least the Septuagint-Samaritan readings are demonstrably ancient and must be considered with seriousness. More than a quarter of the Samaritan variants have this Septuagint support. In the *New English Bible* appeal is made to the

Septuagint about a hundred times and to the Samaritan version about sixty times for establishing the text of the Pentateuch.

In Stephen's speech in Acts 7 there are two cases where Acts seems to bear witness to a first-century text which differed from and which may be superior to the Massoretic text from which our current versions are translated. Stephen says in Acts 7:4 of Abraham: '*After his father died*, God removed him from there (Haran) into this land.' The Massoretic text of Genesis, however, seems to be self-contradictory in this matter, for according to Genesis 11:26 and 12:4, his father Terah would have been 145 years old when Abraham left Haran, whereas Genesis 11:32 says that he died in Haran at the age of 205. The Samaritan version, however, says that Terah died at the age of 145. Apparently Luke had the same reading in his text. If this was in fact the original reading, there was no self-contradiction in Genesis and no inconsistency between Genesis and Acts.

In Acts 7:6 Stephen says : 'his posterity would be aliens in a land belonging to others, who would enslave them and ill-treat them four hundred years.' This agrees precisely with Genesis 15:13 and approximately with Exodus 12:40, which says: 'The time that the people of Israel dwelt in Egypt was four hundred and thirty years.' This is usually taken to refer to the period from Joseph to the Exodus. Paul, however, in Galatians 3:17 says that the law 'came four hundred and thirty years' after the covenant with Abraham (which was given three generations before the time of Joseph). Paul here is in line with rabbinical exegesis which dates the covenant with Abraham thirty years before Isaac's birth,[3] and includes in the 430 years the patriarchal sojournings in Canaan and Egypt.[4] Again the Samaritan Pentateuch, this time supported (though not quite solidly) by the Septuagint and the Book of Jubilees (second century BC), comes to the rescue, stating specifically that Israel sojourned in Canaan and Egypt 430 years.[5] If this was deliberate harmoniza-

[3] D. Daube, *New Testament and Rabbinic Judaism* (London, 1956), pp. 409f., 440. This is presumably a round figure – Gn. 12:4 and 21:5 suggest roughly twenty-five years.
[4] The mention of Abraham's own sojourn in Egypt follows immediately after his original migration to Canaan: Gn. 12:10.
[5] Ex. 12:40. (Most LXX MSS say 435 years.) I am indebted to unpublished research by R. T. Beckwith for the information on the chronology of Jubilees. Josephus (*Antiquities* 2.15.2) also supports these authorities.

tion, it must antedate the sharp separation between Samaritans and Jews – in other words its authority is as ancient as the Massoretic text. That 'and Canaan' was accidentally omitted from the Hebrew text is at least as easy to believe as this. It shows a serious defect in the textual principles of RV, RSV and NEB that this variant is not even mentioned in the margin.[6]

Confirmation from philology

Another line of confirmation of the soundness of the Old Testament has come from the progress of comparative Semitic philology.[7] H. H. Rowley, confessedly over-stating, described the common view of the Old Testament text in the period before the First World War thus: 'Towards the text of the Old Testament, as represented by the Massoretic Hebrew, there was a rooted suspicion, and commentators vied with one another in the ingenuity with which it was emended. Where any version could be invoked in favour of a change its support was welcomed, but where no version could be laid under contribution it mattered little. Any guess was to be preferred to a text which was assumed to be untrustworthy.'[8] The *International Critical Commentaries* serve as a distinguished monument to this period. Now the atmosphere has completely changed. Conjectural emendation is regarded with great disfavour, and the Massoretic text with great respect. This is due largely to the strides that have been made in the study of Hebrew. Classical Hebrew literature, other than the Old Testament, is almost non-existent, and many rare words and constructions have therefore been unintelligible to Hebrew students. But study of other Semitic languages, especially Arabic, Accadian and Ugaritic, has been

[6] B. K. Waltke, *Prolegomena to the Samaritan Pentateuch* (Harvard PhD thesis, 1965), p. 210, comes to this conclusion: 'The readings peculiar to the Samaritan Pentateuch are not necessarily the product of . . . Samaritan recensional activity but derive from a recension once shared by the Jews. After the Samaritan schism this recension, or at least one of its collateral witnesses, maintained its identity even into NT times. The evidence of the Dead Sea scrolls certifies this.'
[7] For short statements, see D. Winton Thomas, *Recovery of the Ancient Hebrew Language* (Cambridge, 1939); H. Wheeler Robinson (editor), *Record and Revelation* (Oxford, 1938), pp. 374ff.
[8] H. H. Rowley (editor), *Old Testament and Modern Study* (Oxford, 1951), p. xv.

throwing light upon passage after passage. Many Septuagint variations, once thought to be due to a different Hebrew text, are seen to be correct interpretations of the existing text. Many obscure passages are now capable of reliable translation. A typical example is provided by H. S. Nyberg's *Studien zum Hoseabuche*, published in Uppsala in 1935. The text of the book of Hosea had been generally regarded as in a state of 'hopeless dilapidation'. Nyberg has shown that, on the contrary, the text is intelligible and that its peculiarities can be consistently explained as Northern dialectical variations. Nyberg has argued with great force the essential soundness of the Massoretic text, and the modern outlook has been concisely stated by J. P. Hyatt thus: 'The first duty of the modern translator should be to give a faithful rendering of the M.T., whenever that can be made to yield good sense; if not, he may then resort to emendation on the basis of the ancient versions; conjectural emendation should be a last resort, and is seldom necessary.'[9]

Confirmation from the correct transmission of names

Another line of confirmation, of a peculiarly powerful kind, is set out in some detail in a little known work of R. D. Wilson.[1] He first examines the names of the foreign kings that are mentioned in the Old Testament, and then the names of the kings of Israel and Judah that are mentioned on the monuments, and compares the biblical spelling with the spelling of the contemporary extra-biblical records. There are twenty-six foreign kings mentioned in the Old Testament, and ten kings of Israel or Judah mentioned in the Assyrian records. Now the correct transmission of names is notoriously difficult, as Wilson shows

[9] *Journal of Biblical Literature*, 69 (1950), p. 186. See also the judicious treatment of A. Bentzen, *Old Testament Introduction*, I (Copenhagen, 1958), p. 97: 'Pure conjecture is not justified until all witnesses are seen to have failed.' 'And then, too, it is best not to use it.' 'Correction of a text is an art which presupposes profound knowledge of textual history, and the language in which the text is written. Against dilettantism in emending the text too strong a warning cannot be given.'

[1] R. D. Wilson, *A Scientific Investigation of the Old Testament* (London, n.d.), chapter 2. The studies 'originally appeared in *The Princeton Theological Review* for 1919, and after thorough revision, with the addition of much new material, are now published in this permanent form'.

by concrete examples. For instance, in Manetho's work on the
dynasties of the Egyptian Kings there are 140 names. 'Of these,
49 appear on the monuments in a form in which every consonant of Manetho's spelling may possibly be recognised, and 28
more may be recognised in part. *The other 63 are unrecognis-
able in any single syllable.*' But of the biblical names, made up
of 183 consonants in all, 'we find that in 143 cases of transliteration from Egyptian, Assyrian, Babylonian and Moabite
into Hebrew and in 40 cases of the opposite . . . the text of the
proper names in the Hebrew Bible has been transmitted with
the most minute accuracy.' Wilson considers that the rules of
transliteration from one language to another are not transgressed for a single consonant. Even if a measure of doubt be
conceded in a few cases, his words are still true: 'That the
original scribes should have written them with such close con-
formity to correct philological principles is a wonderful proof of
their thorough care and scholarship; further, that the Hebrew
text should have been transmitted by copyists through so many
centuries is a phenomenon unequalled in the history of literature.'[2]

The present position in Old Testament textual studies

These conclusions were valid before the Dead Sea discoveries.
The latter confirm the general superiority of the Massoretic
text, but they also show that Hebrew texts lying closer to the
Septuagint and to the Samaritan Pentateuch than to the Massoretic text were in existence at the time of the Qumran sect.
There are, for instance, very large sections of a scroll of Samuel
standing directly in the Septuagint tradition, with a text evidently very like that used by the writer of Chronicles. There are
also fragments of Exodus very like the Samaritan version. It
looks as though there were three types of text current before
the reforms of Akiba: the Septuagint type, current particularly
in Egypt; the Massoretic type, which preserved the text used
and brought back by the Babylonian exiles; and the Samaritan
type, a Palestinian text. The Qumran discoveries forcibly confirm the impression that the Samaritan version is on the whole
inferior and secondary and in general they show that the Mas-

[2] *Ibid.*, pp. 81ff. The italics are mine.

soretic text is better than the Septuagint. But it confirms the
view that where the readings of the Samaritan text are intrinsically probable, or where they agree with the Septuagint
against the Massoretic text, they must be given full weight.

Other discoveries include copies of Jeremiah which show a
mixed text – partly Septuagint and partly Massoretic. A vast
field for exploration has been opened up, full of exciting pos-
sibilities; and no-one knows what may yet turn up. The Hebrew
University in Jerusalem is engaged in the publication, under the
title *Textus*, of a series of studies in preparation for a new
critical text of the Old Testament. There is no doubt that it will
be a text substantially nearer the original than any of its pre-
decessors. But in the meantime we have a number of converging
lines of evidence to show that the preservation of the text, even
in the centuries BC, was of a very high order, and that for practical purposes our present text is a dependable guide.[3]

THE NEW TESTAMENT TEXT

Comparison with classical texts

In the case of the New Testament it seems at first sight very
serious that we have no manuscript of the complete New Testament earlier than the fourth century. Much could have happened to the church's documents in the first three hundred
storm-tossed years of its history. Yet, relatively, even this interval is a short one. To quote F. G. Kenyon: 'For all the words of
classical antiquity we have to depend on manuscripts written
long after their original composition. The author who is in best
case in this respect is Virgil; yet the earliest manuscript of Virgil
that we now possess was written some 350 years after his death.
For all other classical writers, the interval between the date of
the author and the earliest extant manuscript of his works is
much greater. For Livy it is about 500 years, for Horace 900,
for most of Plato 1,300, for Euripides 1,600. On the other hand,
the great vellum uncials of the New Testament were written

---

[3] The statement in the Introduction to NEB: 'The Hebrew text . . . is full
of errors of every kind' is somewhat misleading. It would be true to say
that the Old Testament literature 'contains textual corruptions of every
kind, in aggregate a very large number'. But, as the general reader of
NEB will testify, these corruptions are like specks on a canvas, scarcely
affecting the impression conveyed by any part of the picture.

perhaps some 250 years after the date when the Gospels were actually composed.'[4] In addition, we now have papyri of considerable portions of the New Testament which reduce the interval by a further hundred years. For instance, two of the Bodmer Papyri (P66 and P75) are dated about AD 200.[5] P66 preserves 94 per cent of John's Gospel, and it is clear from its corrections that it was itself a copy of two yet earlier manuscripts – how much earlier, no-one can say.

It may seem cold comfort to answer the charge that the state of the New Testament text is bad by saying that the state of the classical texts is much worse. But the truth is that the state of the classical texts is not bad. The philosophers feel justified in laying great weight even upon minute turns of phrase in Plato in spite of the 1,300 year gap. In the case of the New Testament, with its gap of 100 to 150 years, the text is not merely not bad, it is very good.

The progress of textual criticism

The existence of more than 100,000 small variants is not in reality an embarrassment, except in the sense that it is an embarrassment of riches. The multitude of variants is simply the result of the multitude of manuscripts, of which there are several thousand still in existence which ante-date the printing-press.[6] The problem of New Testament textual criticism arises from the gigantic scale of the task, if all the materials are to be used to the full. But textual criticism has made, and is making, great strides. The medieval church in the West was almost wholly dependent on the Vulgate, a fine Latin translation made by Jerome from a good text round about AD 400, but which had itself suffered the usual chances of the process of copying. The Renaissance brought back the New Testament in Greek to its rightful place as the only proper text for use in scholarly dis-

[4] F. G. Kenyon, *The Story of the Bible* (London, 1936), pp. 33f.
[5] B. M. Metzger, *The Text of the New Testament: Its Transmission, Corruption and Restoration*, 2nd ed. (Oxford, 1968) gives the basic information and bibliography on the subject. For these papyri, see pp. 39ff. H. Hunger puts P66 mid-second century or even earlier (p. 40, n. 1).
[6] In 1968 5,255 Greek manuscripts (in various states of completeness) were listed, besides many in other languages (K. Aland, 'The Greek New Testament: Its Present and Future Editions', *Journal of Biblical Literature*, 87 (1968), p. 184).

cussion. The Greek Testament of Erasmus, which was based mainly on three manuscripts of a late type, was the foundation of the Textus Receptus, which is the text of the Authorized Version of 1611.

In the eighteenth and nineteenth centuries the collection and study of manuscripts proceeded apace, and progress was made in classifying them according to their general type of text. The Revised Version of 1881 was based primarily upon the text of the two great manuscripts of the fourth century, Codex Vaticanus and Codex Sinaiticus, to which the textual theory of F. J. A. Hort gave great weight. Since Hort's day, further manuscripts (including scores of papyrus fragments, many of them older than any manuscripts that he knew) have been found, and further intensive study of the already existing material has been carried out, with the result that a fairly clear picture of the state of the New Testament text in the latter part of the second century is beginning to emerge. The Revised Standard Version of 1946 and the New English Bible of 1961–70 attempted to incorporate the results of these studies. It is thus roughly true to say that in the fifteenth century we had no Greek text in use; in the seventeenth century we had a late medieval Greek text; by the end of the nineteenth century we were firmly established upon a good fourth-century Greek text; now we are finding our way about the early third-century (some would even say late-second-century) texts with growing confidence. AV, RV and RSV differ greatly as far as English rendering is concerned, but as far as text is concerned the differences are comparatively small. The small differences in text between AV and RV represent very fairly the difference between a late medieval and a fourth-century text; the tiny differences in the text between RV and RSV represent pretty well the difference between a mid-fourth and an early-third-century text.[7]

The theory of textual criticism

These conclusions are the result of a vast amount of scientific work. It is not easy to give an impression of the state of modern

---

[7] Each of these stages marks a real advance, yet the absolute differences in text are very small. R. A. Knox based his translation upon *the Vulgate* (though with an eye on critical texts of the original languages) and was still able to produce a result tolerable in the mid-twentieth century!

textual studies that will do justice both to its astronomical extent and to its microscopic subject-matter. It may be well to look a little more closely at the theory of textual criticism first. In its simplest form the history of a text is like the growth of a tree. The stem of the tree is the original manuscript. When this is transcribed certain mistakes are made, which are normally incorporated in all copies that are derived from it. Thus a branch of the tree grows, consisting of manuscripts that have certain characteristics in common. This sub-divides again and again, forming new branches and twigs and shoots. Now if the manuscripts are arranged according to their greater and lesser common characteristics, it should theoretically be quite easy to sort out the family tree, and get back nearer and nearer to the common stem. A manuscript's importance will depend, not upon its date, but upon its place in the tree. Conceivably a fourteenth-century manuscript might have been carefully copied direct from a second-century one, which would give it an importance out of all proportion to its date. Another helpful line of study is provided by 'Versions' – that is to say, by translations into other languages. The versions undergo their own processes of textual corruption, yet independently of the changes taking place in the manuscripts in the original language. The family tree of the version can be constructed, and this gives valuable evidence of the original text at the date when it was translated. A third line of study is provided by quotations in Christian writers. If the family tree of the manuscripts of the works of each 'Father' is constructed, it may give valuable evidence as to the text in existence when he wrote.

But, unfortunately, the textual tree does not grow so simply. While new variations are continually being created, old variations are frequently being eliminated by deliberate revision, whether by individual or official action; similarly quotations in the Fathers may become assimilated to a later contemporary form. The interacting forces are extremely complex. As E. C. Colwell says, 'We are dealing not with ordinary trees but with a thicket or jungle composed of banyans and mangroves, trees growing upside down, dropping roots from branches.'[8] Hort,

---

[8] E. C. Colwell, 'The Significance of Grouping of New Testament MSS', *New Testament Studies*, 4 (1958), p. 88.

developing the work of Griesbach and Lachmann, believed the
genealogical tree principle to be workable. He eliminated from
practical consideration the great majority of Greek manuscripts, because they bore the stamp of official revisions in the
Eastern church. This 'Syrian' type of text, as he called it, was
found in the Textus Receptus and could be traced back to the
time of Chrysostom in the latter part of the fourth century.
Behind this type of text he discerned three more primitive
branches, which he designated 'Western', 'Alexandrian' and
'Neutral', out of which he believed the Syrian text to have been
carefully constructed, in an attempt to supersede the chaos of
rival texts. As his choice of terms indicates, he considered both
the Western and the Alexandrian texts to diverge from the
earliest forms, and he regarded Vaticanus (pre-eminently) and
Sanaiticus as being least affected by divergent tendencies, and
therefore 'Neutral'. He reckoned that he had established objective criteria for the evaluation of readings, thus reducing the
element of subjective judgment in the evaluation of individual
readings to a minimum.

Modern developments

Hort's work was epoch-making. By the enunciation of a clear-
cut theory he gave some sort of order to the confused mass of
evidence, and he provided a new starting-point for further
detailed research. Since his day, however, many hundreds of
scholars have toiled away at the manuscripts and the versions
and the Fathers, with the result that many of Hort's positions
must now be modified. It is no longer possible to be so cavalier
with the Syrian text. The idea that it held unrivalled dominance
from the sixth to the sixteenth century is now known to be untrue. It is in any case a highly complex collection of texts, and
these, though they are generally speaking secondary, contain
valuable primitive readings.[9] The Neutral text is not now regarded as neutral. It is an Alexandrian revision, albeit a
scholarly and excellent one. The Western text has largely disin-

---

[9] In fact, the United Bible Societies' text of 1966 is reckoned by the
editors to be 80 per cent Westcott and Hort, *15 per cent Textus Receptus*
and 5 per cent other sources. I am indebted to the Rev. H. K. Moulton
for this information.

tegrated with the emergence of new and early groupings. A new line of advance was provided by the identification of a Caesarean text-type. This text was already known in Egypt round about AD 250, was at times used by Origen, and was influential well into the Middle Ages, and seems frequently to preserve the original text. Hardly had this text-type been identified than it began to disintegrate, for all these text-types themselves represent a lengthy process of revision and assimilation. We can distinguish earlier and later elements within them, with the result that it is possible to talk of proto-Alexandrian and proto-Caesarean readings. An Italian scholar, P. Sacchi, identifies what he calls the Pre-recensional Family.[1] O. Linton believes that he can show the existence of a revision of Mark 'probably at least some decades before 200', and that this reviser had a text before him 'which stood very near the original'.[2]

Immense labour is being spent on the critical editions of the ancient versions and the Fathers. Merely to give an incomplete list of the versions considered to have relevance, shows how monumental the task is: Old Latin (Italian, African and Spanish forms), Vulgate, Syriac (six varieties), Coptic (five varieties), Gothic, Armenian, Georgian, Ethiopic, Arabic, Sogdian, Old Slavonic. The study of Tatian's *Diatessaron*, a Syriac harmony of the Gospels, first published about AD 170, and eventually translated into many languages, forms an independent segment of the field, highly complex, but promising valuable results.[3] If Tatian's text could be established with certainty it would be invaluable. An illustration of the importance of the Fathers is to be seen in the minute examination to which the biblical quotations of Origen, Eusebius and Cyril of Jerusalem have been subjected in the quest of the Caesarean text.

[1] P. Sacchi, 'Θ, W in Mark, 565, 700, D'. (*Alle origini del Nuovo Testamento*, 1956, reviewed by B. M. Metzger, *Journal of Biblical Literature*, 77 (1958), pp. 93f.).
[2] O. Linton, 'Evidences of a Second-century Revised Edition of St. Mark's Gospel', *New Testament Studies*, 14 (1967), pp. 354, 351.
[3] To illustrate the ramifications of this study: in 1951 an edition of a sixteenth-century Persian harmony of the Gospels was published 'that contained hundreds of typically Tatianic readings.' (B. M. Metzger, 'Ancient Versions of the New Testament', *New Testament Studies*, 2 (1955), p. 5.)

All this effort is being directed to one end: the tracing of patterns of text. In evaluating a reading there are basically two procedures, one largely subjective, and the other largely objective. On the one hand rival readings can be judged on their individual merits: intrinsic probabilities can be weighed, and the likelihood of one reading being changed for another can be assessed. This is a subjective process and precarious unless tested by similar variants in other parts of the document. On the other hand when a reading is considered in relation to the characteristics of the document as a whole, and in relation to other documents of a similar type, a more objective check is possible. It may then be possible to determine with considerable probability whether it is due to the slip or quirk of an individual scribe, or whether it derives from a primitive and valuable textual ancestor. If a reading can be shown to belong to a proto-Caesarean or a proto-Alexandrian pattern, its objective authority is immensely enhanced. But what exactly is Caesarean or proto-Caesarean? It is impossible to say, exactly. Therefore research is being concentrated on Greek manuscripts and versions and Fathers with variants that conform more or less to these early types. Detailed knowledge of a text-type is the pre-requisite of any precise and meaningful answer to the question, and therefore of this sort of objective assessment of a reading's authority. It is research of this kind that has given us solid knowledge of the state of the early-third-century text, and a growing knowledge of the second-century text.

The text of the first and second centuries

The interesting and important thing about the late-second-century text is this: at that early date there was already a wide diversity of variants. These variants were of course mostly quite minor in character, but they show that there had been no recent systematic editing of the documents to make them conform to some standard version. G. D. Kilpatrick[4] considers it to be proved that our tradition reaches back before the time when the four Gospels circulated as a single Canon; before, that is, about AD 140. Similarly there is reason to believe that the variations

[4] G. D. Kilpatrick, 'Transmission of the New Testament and its Reliability', *Trans. of Victoria Inst.*, 89 (1957), p. 97.

in the Epistles go back into the first century, before the formation of the Pauline Canon. Thus the very existence of variants
is itself powerful evidence against a systematic, tendentious
alteration of the manuscripts in the very early stages of the
history of the text.[5] Kilpatrick also declares that, in spite of our
detailed knowledge of first- and second-century Greek, 'no one
has so far shown that the New Testament is contaminated with
the grammar or orthography of a later period.'[6]

A remarkable growth in the conviction of the integrity of the
text may be seen by comparing the attitude of Kilpatrick in
1957 with that of Westcott and Hort in 1885 with regard to
supposed primitive errors that are suspected of having affected
all existing documents. Westcott and Hort give a 'List of Suspected Readings', containing about forty-five such items. Over
a good many of them the two editors did not agree, but more
than a score carried their joint authority. Papyri discoveries,
however, have disposed of some of them,[7] and more careful
criticism has disposed of others. So that in 1957, when Kilpatrick comes to discuss the substitution of 'javelin' for 'hyssop'[8]
at John 19:29, of which he says, 'No other conjecture in the
New Testament has had the same plausibility', he rejects it
decisively. He believes that we are fully justified in assuming 'as
a rule of thumb that at each point the true text has survived
somewhere or other among our manuscripts'.[9] (Such an assumption would not be justified with some of the classical authors, or
even with the Septuagint.) Kilpatrick even feels it necessary to
give a warning of the danger of 'correcting' our authors: 'The
authors' copies cannot be assumed to be flawless' and 'if we set
out to correct and improve everything which seems faulty, we
soon find ourselves correcting our authors and doing what the

[5] This is not to deny the presence of some variants that seem to have
had doctrinal inspiration. See C. S. C. Williams, *Alterations to the Text
of the Synoptic Gospels and Acts* (Oxford, 1951).
[6] *Art. cit.*, p. 98.
[7] *E.g.* δοκίμιον in 1 Pet. 1:7.
[8] υσσωπω(π) for υσσω(π). This 'conjecture' is adopted by NEB, *Bible in
Basic English*, Moffatt, Goodspeed, Rieu, Phillips and Williams. Even
this is not strictly a conjecture as it appears in one Greek MS and is
confirmed by some Old Latin MSS.
[9] *Art. cit.*, p. 101.

second-century scribes did.'[1] We have our own reasons for believing the author's copies to have been flawless in the sense that
they taught no error, but that they were flawless according to
conventional standards of 'good' writing is quite unlikely.

To sum up. It is clear that most of the important variants
were already in existence before the end of the second century,
and that we cannot classify them into good and bad families as
simply as Hort did. This forces us to rely on what Lagrange
called 'rational criticism' and to construct an 'eclectic' text, with
readings taken from several text-types. But as this contains a
dangerous element of subjectivity, the labour of elucidating the
patterns of the second-century text, and then eliminating the
inferior elements in those patterns, is still essential. Amongst
others, the scholars of the Institut für neutestamentliche Text-
forschung at Münster under the direction of K. Aland are
tackling this in a massive way. The accomplishing of the task
will prove long and arduous, yet to those who are gripped by
the fascination of the quest, it is very much worth while. The
search for the original New Testament is a worthy task, provided always that it is seen in its true proportions.

The scale of textual corruption

It is easy to forget these proportions, because in the quest for
patterns of text minute variants are very important. Therefore
much textual criticism is concerned with microscopic matters
that have no bearing on the meaning of what is written. Technical commentaries rightly devote much space to matters of
text, because it is their function to concentrate on the problems
which require knowledge. But it might well come as a surprise
to many who are much immersed in such commentaries, to
realize how very small is the amount of significant variation
upon which this devoted toil is being expended. Hort said in
1885: 'If comparative trivialities, such as changes of order, the
insertion or omission of the article with proper names, and the
like, are set aside, the words in our opinion still subject to doubt
can hardly amount to more than a thousandth part of the whole
New Testament.'[2] One word in a thousand is about one word

[1] *Ibid.*, p. 101.
[2] F. J. A. Hort, *The New Testament in the Original Greek* (Cambridge,
1891), p. 565.

per three pages of the Westcott and Hort text. Possibly Hort was a trifle too confident as to the soundness of his text, and we might desire liberty to doubt a little more extensively than he, yet fundamentally his estimate is sound.

It is a good exercise to run through the references to text in the margin of, *e.g.*, the RSV and see how few and (often) how trivial they are. There are roughly 235 points which the translators consider of sufficient importance to mention. More than half of these are really quite trivial, the spelling of a name, the interchange of 'our' and 'your' (which in Greek were pronounced almost identically) in contexts where either are appropriate, and other matters of little significance. Proportionately the greatest number of variants of more significance are found in the Synoptic Gospels. This is partly due to the tendency for one Gospel to borrow phrases from parallel passages in another. Amazing though it sounds, the Herculean labours of the textual critics are virtually concerned with discovering the true reading at about a hundred points where there are variants of some significance to the ordinary reader.[3] About sixty of these are in the Synoptic Gospels and about forty in the rest of the New Testament. Of these one hundred readings the balance of evidence is in most cases already weighted more or less heavily in favour of the variant that has been chosen for the text, rather than the one that has been relegated to the margin. In most cases the variants are not contradictory, and could well both be true to fact.[4]

Important variant readings

The number of variants upon which much seems to hang are a mere handful. Perhaps five stand out. The two lengthy passages omitted from the critical text, the appendix to Mark (16:9–20) and John 7:53 – 8:11 (the woman taken in adultery),

[3] Of course 'significance' is a relative word. The editorial committee of the United Bible Societies of 1966 examined some 5,100 sets of variant readings, from which it selected 1,440 as being of some significance to the translator. But they are significant only for detailed work.
[4] Some good scholars set a high value on the remarkable variants in Acts to be found in Codex Bezae (D), which in places suggest a first-hand acquaintance with the events recorded. If they are right, this would not mean that the D-text is the true text, but it would mean that it records true facts otherwise unknown.

were certainly no part of the original text and should not presumably be regarded as Scripture. They are tradition; they
are certainly very early tradition, and are probably largely good
tradition.[5] For Christians to have treated them as Scripture is
not likely to have caused harm, and to regard them now as
tradition can cause a jar only to sentiment. The status of three
others is of great interest and uncertainty : the giving of the cup
after supper (Lk. 22:20); the appearance of the angel and the
bloody sweat of Luke 22:43, 44; and our Lord's prayer of forgiveness for his crucifiers in Luke 23:34. Though these were
not regarded as original by Hort, 'rational criticism' is seriously
reconsidering them.[6] These are events and words that have
taken deep root in the Christian imagination, and we should
like to be relieved of uncertainty as to their status. It seems
right that important variant readings (including 'noteworthy
rejected readings') should be recorded with appropriate comment in the margin of modern Bibles. There *is* a penumbra of
doubt which should be recognized as a God-given phenomenon.
History and tradition *are* important, even though Scripture
alone has final authority.

After these five notable cases, the importance of the variants
rapidly diminishes. Occasionally the critical text removes a
small difficulty. It does not now seem likely that John taught
that the periodical troubling of the water (Jn. 5:4) was due to
an angel. The Christmas message was probably not a message
of peace and goodwill to all men regardless of their state of
grace. It was peace to men of God's good pleasure (Lk. 2:14).[7]
Occasionally a harmonizing reading is removed, restoring an

[5] The Marcan Appendix seems, however, to overdo the theme of apostolic unbelief. The canonical Gospels suggest an initial incredulity followed
by a wondering half-belief, which culminated in complete assurance
when they had seen the risen Lord for themselves. That the Emmaus
road disciples were greeted by 'they did not believe them' (Mk. 16:13)
seems to be contradicted by Lk. 24:34 : 'The Lord has risen indeed, and
has appeared to Simon !' J. D. M. Derrett, *Law in the New Testament*
(London, 1970), ch. 7, 'The Story of the Woman Taken in Adultery' is
a brilliant treatment of the other passage.
[6] See C. S. C. Williams, *Alterations to the Text of the Synoptic Gospels*,
pp. 6ff.
[7] See especially K. Stendahl (editor), *The Scrolls and the New Testament* (London, 1958), ch. 7, 'Peace among Men of God's Good Pleasure'
by E. Vogt.

old difficulty. Mark 1:2 prefaces two quotations, of which the
first appears to come from the book of Malachi, with the words,
'as it is written in Isaiah', in place of the Textus Receptus reading, 'and it is written in the prophets'. But variants of even this
degree of importance are not many, and as we work through
the list we very soon find the importance of the factor of text
entirely overshadowed by the far greater importance of the
factor of interpretation. To put the matter concretely. We
could take two good modern translations of the Gospels (say
RSV and NEB) and regard the one as the standard and the other
as a variant text, and draw up a critical apparatus accordingly.
The result would be one mass of variants, identical sentences
being rarities. The differences would be many, many times
greater than the differences between the two most dissimilar
manuscripts that could be discovered among all the 5,000
known Greek manuscripts.

The contracting area of uncertainty

More than a century ago Gaussen described in vivid terms the
immense labour that had been expended by textual critics. He
recalled how the young Bengel at the beginning of the
eighteenth century had been perplexed by his inability to prove
the integrity of the New Testament text, and had plunged himself into laborious researches, only to emerge with 'pious wonder and gratitude at the preservation of that text'. Gaussen
comments : 'This immense toil has ended in a result wonderful
by its insignificance, and (shall I say) imposing by its nullity.'[8]
The toil has continued with undiminished vigour, and little by
little the area of doubt has continued to contract, and Gaussen's
comment is now truer than ever. His point has been expressed
from a different angle in our day by E. R. Goodenough : 'The
field of lower criticism ... was never so systematically cultivated as now. Yet ... I doubt if the course of civilization will
be appreciably changed by the production of the absolutely
ideal New Testament text, or indeed would be deeply affected
by the discovery of the complete set of New Testament autographs. I should imagine that if we had Paul's letter to the
Romans in its original form the problem of what he meant to

[8] L. Gaussen, *Theopneustia* (Glasgow, 1861), pp. 167f.

say in it would be just about what it is now when we read it in Nestle's text. And the question of the relevance for modern man of whatever Paul may have said would certainly be exactly what it is.'[9]

Ample evidence, not absolute proof

There is, then, no absolute proof that our Canon is precisely the true Canon and no absolute proof that any one word of the text is precisely as God gave it. But the quest for absolute proofs, whether historical or theological, is based on a misunderstanding of the nature of history, theology and the human mind. History is at best an approximation to truth based upon an incomplete induction of facts. Theology is a fallible human attempt to co-ordinate the data of revelation. The human intellect, even when renewed by the Holy Spirit, cannot know absolute certainty. In his inmost being the Christian believer has an absolute assurance (that is, an assurance which comes from God's direct witness within him), that he has heard the voice of God and that he is a child of God. But when he puts his beliefs into his own words the absoluteness of the truth of his statements vanishes. His every word lies open to the scrutiny of the probing philosopher, who may ask for definitions and amplifications, and who will soon prove to him that he does not know precisely what he does believe. But a conviction that is not absolute is not necessarily unreal. Conviction based on adequate evidence can be dynamic. There is good evidence that the Old Testament Canon was closed in Christ's day, and that he accredits all the thirty-nine books of the Old Testament to us. But the evidence for the canonicity of Ecclesiastes lacks the overwhelming force of that for books frequently quoted by Christ. Similarly in the New Testament the evidence for 2 Peter is weaker than for the Gospels. Yet, in spite of this less solid fringe at the edges of the Canon, we can see God's care for the well-being of the church, in that the evidence of canonicity is strongest where it is most needed. The fiercest attacks of scepticism have been on the Old Testament, but it is the Old Testament which has the direct attestation of our Lord. And within

[9] 'The Inspiration of N.T. Research', *Journal of Biblical Literature*, 71 (1952), p. 1.

the Old Testament the books most attacked are either those best attested (*e.g.* Pentateuch, Isaiah, Daniel, Jonah) or those least important from the point of revelation (*e.g.* Ecclesiastes, Canticles, Esther). Even these apparently unimportant books no-one will be inclined lightly to discard when they have seen them put to such valuable use as J. S. Wright has put Ecclesiastes, or W. Vischer has put the Book of Esther.[1]

The value of the uncertainty fringe

An uncertainty fringe of text or canon may be a positive blessing, if it forces us to focus our attention upon the central truths of revelation. The guidance of revelation is sufficient if clear on vital matters, even if not entirely clear on less important matters. Augustine taught his readers to work outwards, from the universally acknowledged scriptures to works of less authority. 'The most intelligent investigator of Sacred Scriptures will be the man who has in the first place read them all ... he may have some grasp ... at least with respect to those which are called canonical Scriptures. For, fortified by the belief of truth, he will read the others more securely ... He will keep to this method in canonical Scriptures, therefore preferring those which are accepted by all Catholic Churches to those which some do not accept.'[2] If this course is followed, and the Bible is treated as one whole, quite serious mistakes may do little harm. Even if the Apocrypha is admitted to the fringe it will be a long time before it does serious harm, provided weight is not placed on isolated texts that lack corroboration in the undoubted Scriptures. To omit the Epistle of James is to deprive oneself of a great delight, but it would not deprive one of any doctrine not taught clearly elsewhere in the Bible. Those who work from the centre outwards proceed safely, and they experience the joy of seeing more and more pieces that were once doubtful taking their place in the mosaic.

In the case of the text there is a similar fringe of uncertainty.

---

[1] *Evangelical Quarterly*, 'The Interpretation of Ecclesiastes', 18 (1946), p. 18; 'The Book of Esther', 11 (1939), p. 3.
[2] *De Doctrina Christiana* ii. 8 (Fathers of the Church, Vol. 2, New York, 1947, 69).

It has been said that, since there is no need for a guaranteed inerrancy now, there is no reason to suppose that inerrancy was ever given. (The so-called 'lost Princeton Bible' evoked great mirth.) But the distinction between the Scripture as it was originally given and the Scripture as it is now is not mere pedantry. We must hold, on the one hand, to the absolute truth of direct divine utterance. God does not approximately speak the truth. Human expositions of what God has said, on the other hand, do approximate to truth, and one can speak meaningfully of different degrees of approximation. If the term 'essential infallibility' is applied to a divine utterance, it has no precise meaning. It is like a medicine that is known to be adulterated, but adulterated to an unknown degree. When, however, 'essential infallibility' is referred to Scriptures once inerrant but now slightly corrupt, the meaning can, within limits, be precise. We know to a close approximation the nature of the tiny textual adulterations. The bottle is, as it were, plainly labelled : 'This mixture is guaranteed to contain less than 0.01% of impurities.' And our Lord himself (in the case of the Old Testament) has set us an example by taking his own medicine. A man's last will and testament is not invalidated by superficial scribal errors; no more are the divine testaments in the Bible.

It was evidently God's purpose to give to us a Book of Truth, rich in its diversity of concrete, personal experience and rich in its variety of forms of instruction, to be studied minutely and yet comprehensively. Could anything be better calculated to encourage the careful study of Scripture down to its smallest details than the doctrine of inspiration? And could anything be better calculated to discourage us from resting our ultimate trust in details than the textual uncertainty fringe? In searching for the truth the slight element of uncertainty encourages us to compare scripture with scripture and to look always for the convergent testimony of the Bible as a whole. If God had altogether preserved the Bible from the ordinary corruptions of manuscript transmission this purpose would actually have been served less well. Had the very autographs been preserved, they might well have become objects of idolatry. In any case, what reason have we to think that we should be better equipped for good works if all the loose ends of our theology could be neatly tied?

So then, starting with belief in the incarnation and a very general belief in the historical truth of the Gospels, we have found ourselves apparently compelled to accept our Lord's view of Scripture. According to his teaching God so guided the authors that the words they wrote were his words. We have seen that this applies not only to the Old Testament, but also in principle to the New. We have seen reason to believe that God guided the church in its recognition of the inspired books and that he preserved its text, so that down the centuries it might remain unimpaired as the vehicle of revelation.

We can adapt our conclusion concerning Jesus and the Old Testament and say :

To Christ the Bible is true, authoritative, inspired.
To him the God of the Bible is the living God,
    and the teaching of the Bible is the teaching of the
    living God.
To him, what Scripture says, God says.

INDEX OF
BIBLICAL
REFERENCES

INDEX OF
REFERENCES TO THE
APOCRYPHA AND
OTHER WRITINGS

AUTHOR
INDEX

SUBJECT
INDEX